ISLĀMIC

CW00545391

Islāmic Psychology: The Basics is a jargon-free and accessible introduction that explores psychology from an Islāmic perspective and provides a foundation-level overview of the fundamental principles and practices of Islāmic psychology. The book introduces concepts, models, approaches, themes, and theories you need to know to study the mind, soul, and behaviour based on Islāmic scripture.

Offering an overview of Islāmic psychology and what Islāmic psychologists do, chapters address key topics, including the history of the evolution of the science of the soul and the psychology of human behaviour and experiences. Rassool examines the concepts of the *Fitrah*, the *Nafs* (Self), the *Aql* (Intellect), the *Rūḥ* (Soul), the *Qalb* (Heart) as well as the concept of Islāmic healing and spiritual interventions. Other themes include the Qur'an and psychology, models and approaches in Islāmic psychology, interpreting Islāmic psychology for modern times, and the contemporary scope of the practice of Islāmic psychology.

Because it outlines the challenges of and solutions for the development of Islāmic psychology and potential future trends, and it includes features to aid learning, this is the ideal introductory book for students in Psychology, Islāmic Psychology, and Islāmic Studies as well as professionals, including counsellors, therapists, and anyone interested in psychology from an Islāmic perspective.

Dr. G. Hussein Rassool is a Professor of Islāmic Psychology and Consultant at the Riphah Institute of Clinical and Professional Psychology/Centre for Islāmic Psychology; Director of Studies, Department of Islāmic Psychology, Psychotherapy and Counselling, Al Balagh Academy; and Chair of Al Balagh Institute of Islāmic Psychology Research.

The Basics

The Basics is a highly successful series of accessible guidebooks which provide an overview of the fundamental principles of a subject area in a jargon-free and undaunting format.

Intended for students approaching a subject for the first time, the books both introduce the essentials of a subject and provide an ideal springboard for further study. With over 50 titles spanning subjects from artificial intelligence (AI) to women's studies, *The Basics* are an ideal starting point for students seeking to understand a subject area.

Each text comes with recommendations for further study and gradually introduces the complexities and nuances within a subject.

FOLKLORE
Simon J. Bronner

FORENSIC PSYCHOLOGY
Sandie Taylor

GERONTOLOGY
Jenny R. Sasser and Harry R. Moody

GENDER (second edition)
Hilary Lips

HUMAN THINKING
S. Ian Robertson

JAPAN
Christopher P. Hood

ISLĀMIC PSYCHOLOGY

THE BASICS

G. Hussein Rassool

LONDON AND NEW YORK

Cover image: Getty Images

First published 2023
by Routledge
4 Park Square, Milton Park, Abingdon, Oxon OX14 4RN

and by Routledge
605 Third Avenue, New York, NY 10158

Routledge is an imprint of the Taylor & Francis Group, an informa business

British Library Cataloguing-in-Publication Data
A catalogue record for this book is available from the British Library

ISBN: 978-1-032-32124-0 (hbk)
ISBN: 978-1-032-32123-3 (pbk)
ISBN: 978-1-003-31295-6 (ebk)

DOI: 10.4324/9781003312956

Typeset in Bembo
by MPS Limited, Dehradun

Dedicated to Idrees Khattab ibn Adam Ibn Hussein Ibn Hassim Ibn Sahaduth Ibn Rosool Ibn Olee Al Mauritiusy, Isra Oya, Asiyah Maryam, Adam Ali Hussein, Nabila Akhrif, Nusaybah Burke, Musa Burke, Reshad Hassan, Yasmin Soraya, BeeBee Mariam, Bibi Safian, Hassim, Dr. Najmul Hussein, and Mohammed Ali.

Abu Hurayrah reported the Prophet Muhammad (ﷺ) as saying: *"If anyone pursues a path in search of knowledge, Allāh will thereby make easy for him a path to paradise; and he who is made slow by his actions will not be speeded by his genealogy."*

(Sunan Abu Dawud)

CONTENTS

PREFACE

Islāmic Psychology: The Basics is the perfect companion for those wishing to develop their understanding of the basic principles of Islāmic psychology, the mesmerising science of the soul, and human behaviours. The book will introduce concepts, models, approaches, themes, and theories you need to know to understand the study of mind, soul, and behaviours from an Islāmic perspective.

The book offers an overview of what Islāmic psychology is and what Islāmic psychologists do. Chapters are dedicated to topics that attempt to address some themes in Islāmic psychology, such as focusing on Islāmic monotheism as the foundation of Islāmic psychology, examining a brief history of the evolution of the science of the soul, exploring the relationship between the Qur'an and Sunnah and the psychology of human behaviour and experiences, and considering the inner world of a human being. The book examines the concepts of the *Fitrah*, nature and nurture, the *Nafs* (Self), the *Aql* (Intellect), the *Rūḥ* (Soul), the *Qalb* (Heart), and Ibn al-Qayyim's types of hearts. It also features the Islāmic model of healing, religious coping in an Islāmic context, and spiritual therapeutic interventions. The author also outlines research methodologies for the study of Islāmic psychology.

The book features reflective questions designed to stimulate critical thinking. It contains further reading in each chapter, providing an excellent framework for broader exploration of the themes. This is a perfect easy-to-understand foundation text for students studying this exciting field for the first time. It is also a perfect primer for teachers, healthcare professionals, psychologists, psychotherapists, and anyone interested in the human soul and behaviours from an Islāmic perspective.

Professor Dr. G. Hussein Rassool is Professor of Islāmic Psychology and Consultant for the Centre for Islāmic Psychology, Riphah International University, Pakistan. He is a Fellow of the International Association of Islāmic Psychology (FIAIP) and the Royal Society of Public Health (FRSPH), a Member of the International Association of Muslim Psychologists, and Chair of the Al Balkhi's Islāmic Psychology Education and Research. His research interests include psychosocial and spiritual problems in relation to mental health, psychosocial and spiritual interventions, indigenous psychology, Islāmic counselling and psychotherapy, and Islāmic ethics in psychology. Professor Dr. G. Hussein Rassool is one of the leading academics of Islāmic psychology and psychotherapy, and a pioneer in Islāmic psychology education.

ACKNOWLEDGEMENTS

All Praise is due to Allāh and may the peace and blessings of Allāh be upon our Prophet Muhammad (ﷺ), his family, and his companions.

I would like to thank Eleanor Taylor and other supporting staff at Routledge for their valuable and constructive suggestions during the development of the proposal and during the process of writing. It is with immense gratitude that I acknowledge the support and help from Professor Dr Anis Ahmad, Vice Chancellor and Mr Umer Farooq, Regional Director, Riphah International University for the creation and development of the Centre for Islāmic Psychology (CIP), Riphah Institute of Clinical and Professional Psychology.

I am thankful to my beloved parents, who taught me the value of education. I owe my gratitude to Mariam, Idrees Khattab Ibn Adam Ali Hussein Ibn Hussein Ibn Hassim Ibn Sahaduth Ibn Rosool Al Mauritiusy, Adam Ali Hussein, Reshad Hasan, Yasmin Soraya, Isra Oya and Asiyah Maryam, Nabila Akhrif, Nusaybah Burke, Musa Burke, Dr. Najmul Hussein, and Mohammed Ali for their unconditional love and for providing unending inspiration.

I would like to acknowledge the contributions of my teachers, who enabled me, through my own reflective practices, to understand authentic Islām and, from their guidance, to follow the right path of the creed of *Ahlus-Sunnah wa'l-Jama'ah*. Finally, whatever benefits and correctness you find within this book are out of the Grace of Allāh, Alone, and whatever mistakes you find are mine alone. I pray to Allāh to forgive me for any unintentional shortcomings regarding the contents of this book and to make this humble effort helpful and fruitful to any interested parties.

> *Whatever of good befalls you, it is from Allāh; and whatever of ill befalls you, it is from yourself.*
>
> (An-Nisā' (The Women) 4:79)

Praise be to Allāh, we seek His help and His forgiveness. We seek refuge with Allāh from the evil of our own souls and from our bad deeds. Whomsoever Allāh guides will never be led astray, and whomsoever Allāh leaves astray, no one can guide. I bear witness that there is no god but Allāh, and I bear witness that Muhammad is His slave and Messenger.

(Sunan al-Nasa'i: Kitaab al-Jumu'ah,
Baab kayfiyyah al-khutbah)

- *Fear Allāh as He should be feared and die not except in a state of Islam (as Muslims) with complete submission to Allāh* (Ali-'Imran 3:102).[1]
- *O mankind! Be dutiful to your Lord, Who created you from a single person, and from him He created his wife, and from them both He created many men and women, and fear Allāh through Whom you demand your mutual (rights), and (do not cut the relations of) the wombs (kinship) Surely, Allāh is Ever an All-Watcher over you)* (Al-Nisā' 4:1).
- *O you who believe! Keep your duty to Allāh and fear Him and speak (always) the truth)* (Al-Ahzāb 33:70).
- *What comes to you of good is from Allāh, but what comes to you of evil, [O man], is from yourself* (An-Nisā 4:79).

The essence of this book is based on the following notions:

- The fundamental of Islām as a religion is based on the Oneness or Unicity of God.
- The source of knowledge is based on the Qur'ān and Hadith (*Ahl as-Sunnah wa'l-Jamā'ah*).
- Empirical knowledge from sense perception is also a source of knowledge through the work of classical and contemporary Islāmic scholars and modern research.

- Islām takes a holistic approach to health. Physical, psychological, social, emotional, and spiritual health cannot be separated.
- Muslims have a different worldview or perception of illness and health behaviour.
- There is a wide consensus amongst Muslim scholars that psychiatric or psychological disorders are legitimate medical conditions that are distinct from illnesses of a supernatural nature.
- Muslims believe that cures come solely from Allāh (God), but seeking treatment for psychological and spiritual health does not conflict with seeking help from Allāh.

It is a sign of respect that Muslims utter or repeat the words "Peace and Blessing Be Upon Him" after hearing (or writing) the name of Prophet Muhammad (ﷺ).

ISLĀMIC MONOTHEISM AS THE FOUNDATION OF ISLĀMIC PSYCHOLOGY

INTRODUCTION

Most students would probably not associate psychological knowledge with the Qur'ân and *Sunnah*. The science of the self or soul was examined in the Islāmic literature long before the term 'psychology' was introduced in modern literature. The label *Psychologia* (or psychology) was first used by Marko Marulić in his book, *Psichiologia de ratione animae humanae*, in the late 15th century or early 16th century (Krstic, 1964). In the *Physical Dictionary* (1694), which was in the English language, Blankaart refers to psychology as "treats of the Soul" (Colman, 2015). Islāmic psychology (*Ilm ul Nafs*), at its core, is rooted in the Qur'ân and *Sunnah*. The essence of Islāmic psychology is examining human behaviours and experiences from a holistic dimension (physical, psychological, social, and spiritual) based of an Islāmic worldview. The application of Islāmic psychology in clinical practice is based on Islāmic healing and spiritual interventions. This aim of the chapter is to examine Islāmic monotheism as the foundation of Islāmic psychology.

ISLĀMIC MONOTHEISM AS THE FOUNDATION OF ISLĀMIC PSYCHOLOGY

The concept of monotheism (known as *Tawhîd* in Arabic) is the single most important concept in Islām, and it is the foundation of Islāmic psychology. The concept of *Tawhîd* comes from the verb *Wahad*, which literally means "making one" or "asserting oneness" (Cowan, 1976, p. 1055). *Tawhîd* also refers "to the nature of that God – that he

DOI: 10.4324/9781003312956-1

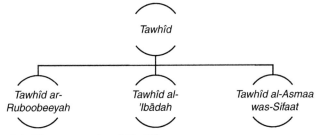

Figure 1.1 Three categories of *Tawḥîd*

is a unity, not composed, not made up of parts, but simple and un-compounded." (Britannica, n.d.). That is the unicity or oneness of God. It is the doctrine of the unity of God that everything in Islām is built upon. No act of worship or ritual, inwardly or outwardly, has any meaning or value if this concept is in any way compromised. Three themes preponderate in Islāmic monotheism (see Figure 1.1).

The Oneness of God in His Lordship is known as *Tawḥîd ar-Ruboobeeyah*; the Devotion of All Worship to God Alone is known as *Tawḥîd al-'Ibādah*; and the Oneness of God in His Names and Attributes is known as *Tawḥîd al-Asmaa was-Sifaat*. The Oneness of God in His Lordship means that Allāh has complete mastery over the universe in every way, and He alone, without partners, caused all things to exist when there was nothing. According to Philips (2005), "since God is the only real power in existence, it is He who gave all things the power to move and to change. Nothing happens in creation except what He allows to happen." (pp. 22–23). No one shares in His dominion, and Allāh is the Creator of the universe, He is One, and He has no partner.

The maintenance of the unity of Allāh's worship (Devotion of all worship to God alone) is the most important aspect of *Tawḥîd*. All forms of worship must be directed only to Allāh because He alone can grant benefit to humankind as a result of His worship. In devotion and supplications, there is no need for any form of intercessor or inter-mediary between man and God. Allāh placed emphasis on the im-portance of directing worship to Him alone by pointing out the essence and purpose of man's creation and the message brought by all the prophets. This is echoed in the following verses of the Qur'ān:

وَمَا خَلَقْتُ ٱلْجِنَّ وَٱلْإِنسَ إِلَّا لِيَعْبُدُونِ

- *I did not create the Jinn and Mankind except for My worship.*
(Az-Zariyat 51:56, interpretation of the meaning)

وَلَقَدْ بَعَثْنَا فِى كُلِّ أُمَّةٍ رَّسُولاً أَنِ ٱعْبُدُواْ ٱللَّهَ

- *And we certainly sent into every nation a messenger [saying], "Worship Allāh. And avoid false objects of worship (false Gods)."*
(An-Nahl, 16:36, interpretation of the meaning)

Philips (2005) suggested that the "confirmation of *Tawhīd al-'Ibādah* conversely necessitates the denial of all forms of intercession or association of partners with Allāh" (p. 36). That is the worshiping of Allāh alone without partners, and the greatest possible sin is to worship anyone other than Allāh. The oneness of Allāh in His names and attributes implies that God does not share in the attributes of created beings. In addition, they do not share in any of His names and attributes or give Him any new names or attributes. Allāh's attributes are all attributes of perfection and completeness. It has been suggested that

[i]t is a form of polytheism to ascribe to [Allāh] attributes of created things. It is likewise a form of polytheism to ascribe to created things attributes that belong to God alone. Anyone who believes that another being is, for instance, All-Knowledgeable or All-Powerful has committed the sin of polytheism, which is the greatest of all sins in Islām.

(www.islamreligion.com)

ARTICLES OF FAITH IN ISLĀM

In order to claim that psychology from an Islāmic perspective is considered to be Islāmic, it must meet all the criteria of the six axioms of the articles of faith (*Imān*) known as *Arkān al-īmān*. As Iakhin (2022) pointed out, no psychology can claim to be Islāmic if any of the foundations of the articles of faith are ignored. Figure 1.2 presents the Articles of Faith.

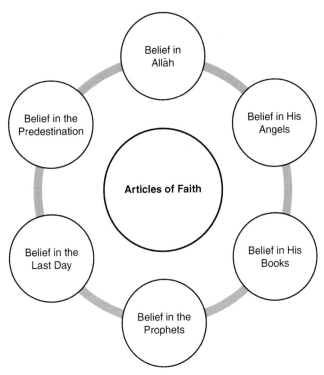

Figure 1.2 Articles of Faith

- Belief in one God (*Tawhîd*): This means having absolute faith in the oneness of God, that He is Unique in His Names and Attributes, and He is to whom worship is due.
- Belief in His Angels (*Malaikah*): Angels are honourable slaves of Allāh; they obey Him and execute His Commands.
- Belief in His Books (*Kutub*): The known Divine Scriptures are: The Torah revealed to Prophet Moses (Musa), The Psalm revealed to Prophet David (Dawud), and The Gospel revealed to Prophet Jesus ('Eesa). These books have been abrogated by the last of Allāh's Books, the Qur'ān.
- Belief in the Prophets (*Nubuwwah*). Prophet Muhammad (ﷺ) being the last of the Prophets and Messengers. All Prophets and Messengers were human beings with no Divine qualities, and they had no access to the unseen world.

- Belief in the Last Day and the Afterlife (*Akhirah*): All Muslims believe that this life is made of trials and tribulations. Both the Last Day and the Afterlife are important dimensions in the Islāmic worldview. The belief is that, after death, there is the continued existence of the soul and a transformed physical existence. All humankind will be divided between those destined to Paradise or Hell.
- Belief in Predestination (*Al Qadr*): This article of faith means believing that Allāh has created everything and has predestined everything that will happen, both in the universe and in the lives of individuals, as part of the divine masterplan.

SOURCES AND INTEGRATION OF KNOWLEDGE

The sources of knowledge in Islām are from the Qur'ān and *Sunnah* (*'Ilm naqli*) as well as from rational knowledge based on human intellect (*Akl*), observation, and empirical evidence (*'Ilm 'aqli*). This systematic integration of the sources and means of knowledge into a synthesised approach is known as epistemological [relating to theory of knowledge] integration (*al-takamul al-ma'arifi*). The foundation of knowledge is the Qur'ān, which

> is viewed as the springhead of all knowledge and all sciences, not because it contains the knowledge itself but, rather, because it inspires the Muslim to develop a distinctive vision of the unity among the various spheres of knowledge. The notion of this unity arises out of an awareness of the unity of the Divine and its applications to the various spheres of human knowledge.
>
> (Malkawi, 2014, p. 20)

In addition to the sources of knowledge from the Qur'ān, there is also the *Hādīth*. A *Hādīth* refers to the actions, statements, or tacit approvals of Prophet Muhammad (ﷺ). From the *Hādīth* we learn about the *Sunnah*, which are the practices of the Messenger of Allāh (ﷺ). It is divine revelation from Allāh and the *Sunnah* of Prophet Muhammad (ﷺ) that become the primary and most fundamental sources of knowledge. Utz (2011) suggested that

It is only through revelation that we can comprehend the true nature of the soul and the unseen world and ascertain the methods for purifying the soul and developing it to its fullest potential. Allāh is the only One with authentic and complete knowledge of the unseen world, so we turn only to Him for this understanding. Human beings, especially Muslims, must not speculate or guess in relation to this domain.

(pp. 39–40)

Knowledge is also gained from sense perception and rationalism (logical reasoning), and these sources should not be neglected. Giving priority to revelation does not debase science, knowledge from empiricism, intuition, and reason. However, scientific evidence would be judged and evaluated according to the criteria of Divine revelation. Rassool (2021a) suggested that Muslim psychologists should attempt to put Islāmic ethical considerations before rationality and empirical evidence, and these should become secondary to the primary sources. However, there is absolutely no contradiction between transmitted, divine knowledge from the Qur'ān and *Sunnah* and rational, empirical knowledge, as both approaches are from the same source, that is, God, The Almighty. Enquiring or probing is permissible in Islam so as to arrive at the truth (Leaman, 2006, p. 571). This is reflected in the following verse:

وَإِذْ قَالَ إِبْرَٰهِيمُ رَبِّ أَرِنِى كَيْفَ تُحْىِ ٱلْمَوْتَىٰ ۖ قَالَ أَوَلَمْ تُؤْمِن ۖ قَالَ بَلَىٰ وَلَٰكِن لِّيَطْمَئِنَّ قَلْبِى ۖ قَالَ فَخُذْ أَرْبَعَةً مِّنَ ٱلطَّيْرِ فَصُرْهُنَّ إِلَيْكَ ثُمَّ ٱجْعَلْ عَلَىٰ كُلِّ جَبَلٍ مِّنْهُنَّ جُزْءًا ثُمَّ ٱدْعُهُنَّ يَأْتِينَكَ سَعْيًا ۚ وَٱعْلَمْ أَنَّ ٱللَّهَ عَزِيزٌ حَكِيمٌ

- *And [mention] when Abraham said, "My Lord, show me how You give life to the dead." [Allāh] said, "Have you not believed?" He said, "Yes, but [I ask] only that my heart may be satisfied." [Allāh] said, "Take four birds and commit them to yourself. Then [after slaughtering them] put on each hill a portion of them; then call them — they will come [flying] to you in haste. And know that Allāh is Exalted in Might and Wise."*

(Al-Baqarah 2:260, interpretation of the meaning)

From the verse shown above, it has been suggested that it is evident that Allāh entertained the query [from Prophet Abraham] (Leaman, 2006, p. 572). Malkawi (2014) suggested that the classical Muslim scholars, despite their different school of thought, agreed that

> knowledge should be interconnected, complementary, and orga-nically linked to the knowledge of God. In the view of these scholars, the fact that all sciences originate from a single divine source is the foundation for the ultimate integration and unity of knowledge.
>
> (p. 12)

Malkawi (2014) also maintained that the Islāmic principle of divine oneness, i.e., *Tawḥîd*, is the foundation in both the unity of knowledge and epistemological integration (p. 6). This constitutes a frame of reference and foundation for a monotheistic Islāmic psy-chology.

ISLĀMIC WORLDVIEW: ELEMENT AND CHARACTER

Islāmic psychology is established on an Islāmic worldview (*Tasawur or Ru'yah al-Islām li al-Wujud*), which is based on the Qur'ān and *Sunnah* and the Qur'ānic civilization (Nursi, 2011, p. 745–746). Akhmetova (2021) defined worldview as "A collection of positions, attitudes, values, stories, and expectations about the world around us, which inform our every thought and action." This means that worldview is a set of parameters that include a wide range of fun-damental matters, including a philosophy, themes, values, emotions, ethics, language, culture, and religion. It a subjective way of thinking, having a vision about, and interacting with our world. The definitions of Islāmic worldview are presented in Box 1.1.

Islāmic worldview, based principally on a system of values and principles derived from the Qur'ān, is identical to Qur'ānic worldview. An Islāmic worldview is related to both the seen world and the unseen world. The characteristics of an Islāmic worldview are presented in Box 1.2. Based on the characteristics, an Islāmic worldview is basically an ethical and monotheistic worldview, which stems from the fundamental belief of only One God, and the

---

Box 1.1

- Syed Naquib Al-Attas (1995): Islāmic worldview is a "vision of reality and truth" that appears before our consciousness (all aspects of life) about an existence (*wujud*) and its ontological aspects. Or, it is a "metaphysical survey of the visible as well as the invisible worlds including the perspective of life as a whole" (p. 2).
- Sayyid Qutb (1983): Worldview in the perspective of Islam is called "*al-Tashawwur al-Islami*," which is a "vision that brings a Muslim closer to all the essence of the world, life, and others" (p. 5).
- Kamal M. Hassan (1994): "The Islamic Worldview is basically a theistic and ethical worldview which contrasts sharply with the secularist or atheistic alternatives. This worldview emanates from the fundamental belief that life and existence came into being as a result of the will, desire and design of the One and Only Creator. The Islamic conception of God has therefore to precede any discussions on the nature of the universe and man's relation to it" (Quotation 12).
- Fathi Hasan Malkawi (2014): An Islāmic worldview is "an expression of the overall belief-based conceptualisation embodied in Islamic doctrine" (p. 22).

Only relation to it needs to include the Islāmic conception of God (Hassan, 1994).

This is in contrast with the worldview of secularists or atheists, where the conception of God is non-existent. That is Al-Attas's (1995) rationale for coining Islāmic worldview as *Ru'yat al-Islām li'lwujûd*. The Islāmic worldview based on the Tawhîdic paradigm covers all aspects of life for its adherents. It is

> based on three fundamental principles which are: *Tawhîd* (Theism), *Khilâfah* (Vicegerency), and *'Adâlah* (Justice). These principles not only frame the Islāmic worldview, but they also constitute the fountainhead of the objectives (*Maqasid*) and the strategy of Man's life in this world.
>
> (Abdullah & Nadvi, 2011, p. 271)

Box 1.2   Characteristics of Islāmic worldview

- Derived from God (*Rabbaniy*).
- *Shari'ah* axis of the Revelation of Allāh.
- Comprehensive aspects of God, man, the universe, and the Hereafter.
- Balanced in understanding the divine values and aspects of humanity.
- Positive in realising a good relationship between God, humans, the universe, and the Hereafter.
- Recognises the reality of God and the divine nature behind the reality of existence.
- Monotheism is a source of belief about the existence of Allah that is understood from His Revelations to the Messenger of Allah.
- Based of *Tawhīdic* paradigm.

Source: Adapted from Taqiyuddin (2020).

In addition to the *Tawhīdic* dimension, there is also an ethical (moral – *akhlāq*) dimension to the Islāmic worldview. The ethical dimension is comprehensive and focuses on a number of fundamental elements, including respect for humankind, social justice, equality in society, inclusivity in human relations, moral courage to speak the truth, tolerance for plurality and differences, affirmation of moral restraint and forgiveness in times of provocation, an emphasis on disciplined and prudent living; a commitment to providing charity for those in need, respect for human life, the use of reason and intellect, accountability of one's action; and the primacy of justice (*adl*) for every human being and his social environment (Alwee, 2005). The ethical aspect of the Islāmic worldview is reflected in the following verse. Allāh says:

لَّيۡسَ ٱلۡبِرَّ أَن تُوَلُّواْ وُجُوهَكُمۡ قِبَلَ ٱلۡمَشۡرِقِ وَٱلۡمَغۡرِبِ وَلَٰكِنَّ ٱلۡبِرَّ مَنۡ ءَامَنَ بِٱللَّهِ وَٱلۡيَوۡمِ ٱلۡءَاخِرِ وَٱلۡمَلَٰٓئِكَةِ وَٱلۡكِتَٰبِ وَٱلنَّبِيِّۧنَ وَءَاتَى ٱلۡمَالَ عَلَىٰ حُبِّهِۦ ذَوِى ٱلۡقُرۡبَىٰ وَٱلۡيَتَٰمَىٰ وَٱلۡمَسَٰكِينَ وَٱبۡنَ ٱلسَّبِيلِ وَٱلسَّآئِلِينَ وَفِى ٱلرِّقَابِ وَأَقَامَ ٱلصَّلَوٰةَ وَءَاتَى ٱلزَّكَوٰةَ وَٱلۡمُوفُونَ بِعَهۡدِهِمۡ إِذَا عَٰهَدُواْۖ وَٱلصَّٰبِرِينَ فِى ٱلۡبَأۡسَآءِ وَٱلضَّرَّآءِ وَحِينَ ٱلۡبَأۡسِۗ أُوْلَٰٓئِكَ ٱلَّذِينَ صَدَقُواْۖ وَأُوْلَٰٓئِكَ هُمُ ٱلۡمُتَّقُونَ

- *Righteousness is not in turning your faces towards the east or the west. Rather, the righteous are those who believe in Allāh, the Last Day, the angels, the Books, and the prophets; who give charity out of their cherished wealth to relatives, orphans, the poor, "needy" travellers, beggars, and for freeing captives; who establish prayer, pay alms-tax, and keep the pledges they make; and who are patient in times of suffering, adversity, and in "the heat of" battle. It is they who are true "in faith", and it is they who are mindful "of Allāh".*

(Al–Baqarah 2:177, interpretation of the meaning)

These fundamental elements of ethical and moral values act as integrating principles, as they render the standards of behaviours and values into a coherent order as a unified system forming the Islāmic worldview. This is how Muslims view the realities of the world and interact with the world through the lens of an Islāmic worldview. It is important to note that the Islāmic worldview includes both the Islāmic epistemological system and Islāmic methodology.

THE QUR'ĀN, *SUNNAH*, AND ISLĀMIC PSYCHOLOGY

إِنَّا أَنزَلْنَا عَلَيْكَ ٱلْكِتَـٰبَ لِلنَّاسِ بِٱلْحَقِّ ۖ فَمَنِ ٱهْتَدَىٰ فَلِنَفْسِهِ ۖ وَمَن ضَلَّ فَإِنَّمَا يَضِلُّ عَلَيْهَا ۖ وَمَآ أَنتَ عَلَيْهِم بِوَكِيلٍ

- *Indeed, We sent down to you the Book for the people in truth. So, whoever is guided – it is for [the benefit of] his soul; and whoever goes astray only goes astray to its detriment. And you are not a manager over them.*

(Az–Zumar 39:41, interpretation of the meaning)

The Qur'ān is not an encyclopedia of psychology, but it is a spiritual, social, psychological, and economic guide in the understanding of human behaviours and experiences. It is a guidance for the whole mankind: Muslims and non-Muslims. Rassool (2021a) suggested that the

message of the Qur'ān has reference to individual self-care, relationships, family, marriage, social welfare, embryological and developmental stages, emotional behaviours, prosocial behaviours, spiritual and ethical intelligence, personality, need for learning and knowledge, and many other holistic facets of human behaviours and experiences. In addition, there are proscribed behaviours including suicide, sexual perversions, gambling, alcohol and drug misuse, crime, and racial discrimination.

(pp. 8–9)

The Qur'ān teaches us that Man is a part of the Universe created by Allāh, which has endowed each person with a soul and a body, and He is the Guardian, Sustainer, and Maintainer of both the body and soul of a person as well as the entire universe. This is reflected in the following verses of the Qur'ān:

ٱللَّهُ خَٰلِقُ كُلِّ شَىْءٍ ۖ وَهُوَ عَلَىٰ كُلِّ شَىْءٍ وَكِيلٌ

- *Allāh is the Creator of all things, and He is the Maintainer of everything.*

(Az–Zumar, 39:62, interpretation of the meaning)

وَٱللَّهُ أَخْرَجَكُم مِّنۢ بُطُونِ أُمَّهَٰتِكُمْ لَا تَعْلَمُونَ شَيْـًٔا وَجَعَلَ لَكُمُ ٱلسَّمْعَ وَٱلْأَبْصَٰرَ وَٱلْأَفْـِٔدَةَ ۙ لَعَلَّكُمْ تَشْكُرُونَ

- *And Allāh. brought you out of the wombs of your mothers while you knew nothing, and gave you hearing, sight, and heart so perhaps you would be thankful.*

(An-Nahl, 16:78, interpretation of the meaning)

According to the exegesis of Ibn Kathir (2000),

Among the favours Allāh has granted people are hearing, sight and the heart. Then Allāh mentions His blessings to His servants in that He brought them from their mothers' wombs not knowing a thing, then He gives them hearing to recognise voices, sight to see visible things and hearts – meaning reason – whose seat, according to the correct view, is the heart, although it was also said that its seat is the brain. With his reason, a person can distinguish between what is harmful and what is beneficial. These abilities and senses develop gradually in man. The more he grows, the more his hearing, vision, and reason increase, until they reach their peak. Allāh has created these faculties in man to enable him to worship his Lord, so he uses all these organs, abilities, and strengths to obey his Master.

That is, Allāh governs, provides sustenance, bestows life and takes it away, and manages the affairs of every creation without any assistance. According to Al-Faruqi (1980),

> Everything that happens in the world does so by His command, and by His action. From the movement of the protons and electrons in an atom to that of galaxies, from the growth and development of amoeba to the psychic processes of man every event happens by His knowledge, His design, His efficiency, and does so in fulfillment of His purpose. The world in which the Muslim lives is truly an enchanted world. Every object beheld is viewed as something created by God, designed by God, sustained at every moment of its existence by God. Every motion or change within or without the self is viewed and felt as something affected by God.
>
> (p. 12)

From the Qur'ānic teachings, we discover that at the core we are both physical and spiritual beings who are in need of sustaining a connection with our Creator, Allāh. The psychological language of the Qur'ān depicts all kinds of human behaviours and psychological experiences. Utz (2011) suggested that

> Our thoughts, emotions, will, and behaviour must focus on attaining the pleasure of Allāh. The key to sound mental health and well-being from the Islamic perspective is submission to Allāh, the Exalted, the Almighty and His commandments, and to subsequently purifying the soul.
>
> (p. 25)

Humans strive to maintain that spiritual connection with their Creator in order to obtain inner serenity, peace, and a sense of happiness.

Ideas about Divine decree or destiny (*qad.ā' wa'l-qadar*) and free will (*ikhtiyār*) are generally absent from modern psychology but are nonetheless considered central to Islāmic psychology. "The Qur'ān appears to support simultaneously both God's omnipotence and human free will, with an emphasis on human beings' personal responsibility for their own actions" (De Cillis, 2018). The belief in predestination is *Qadr*. This means that everything, good and bad, happens by the Will and Divine decree. Allāh, by His Will, already knows everything that will happen, and nothing happens unless it is according to Allāh's will. Allāh has decreed the conditions, sustenance, requirements, lifespan, and destiny of all creatures according to His prior knowledge, decree, and wisdom. Allāh says in the Qur'ān:

$$ إِنَّا كُلَّ شَيْءٍ خَلَقْنَاهُ بِقَدَرٍ $$

- *Indeed, We have created everything, perfectly preordained.*
  (Al-Qamar, 54:49, interpretation of the meaning)

In a *Hadīth*, it was narrated that 'Ali said:

The Messenger of Allāh (ﷺ) said: "No slave truly believes until he believes in four things: in Allāh alone with no partner; that I am the Messenger of Allāh in the resurrection after death; and in the Divine Decree (*Qadar*)."

(Ibn Majah (a))

According to the creed of *Ahlus Sunnah Wal Jamā'ah*, "belief in the divine will and decree cannot be perfect without four components, which are called the pillars of belief in the divine will and decree. This belief cannot be complete without all four, because they are interconnected" (Al-Athari, 2003, p. 115). The four components of divine will and decree are: knowledge, writing, divine will, and creation (see Al-Athari, 2003). Failure to believe in one of the components would make belief in the divine decree incomplete. However, this does not mean that the choices people make are not free choices. Instead, it means that Allāh knows what people will chose to do. The belief in free will is essential in Islam because life is a test of trials and tribulations. In this context, humans have free will to make decisions based on informed choices in regard to their beliefs and deeds. This is resonated in the following verses in the Qur'an. Allāh says:

لَا إِكْرَاهَ فِى ٱلدِّينِ ۖ قَد تَّبَيَّنَ ٱلرُّشْدُ مِنَ ٱلْغَىِّ ۚ فَمَن يَكْفُرْ بِٱلطَّـٰغُوتِ وَيُؤْمِنۢ بِٱللَّهِ فَقَدِ ٱسْتَمْسَكَ بِٱلْعُرْوَةِ ٱلْوُثْقَىٰ لَا ٱنفِصَامَ لَهَا ۗ وَٱللَّهُ سَمِيعٌ عَلِيمٌ

- *There shall be no compulsion in [acceptance of] the religion. The right course has become distinct from the wrong. So, whoever disbelieves in false objects of worship and believes in Allāh has grasped the most trustworthy handhold with no break in it. And Allāh is Hearing and Knowing.*

(Al-Baqarah 2:256, interpretation of the meaning)

إِنَّا هَدَيْنَـٰهُ ٱلسَّبِيلَ إِمَّا شَاكِرًا وَإِمَّا كَفُورًا

- *Indeed, We guided him to the way, be he grateful or be he ungrateful.*

(Al-Insān 76:3, interpretation of the meaning)

This means that an individual is free from compulsion, and he has the freedom of choice to believe and do righteous deeds or disbelieve and do bad or evil deeds. The ability of man to use his intellect (ability to think and reflect) makes him become responsible for his behaviours and deeds. This is necessary for accountability. Several verses in the Qur'an indicate that humans are free from compulsion but not free from causation. This is illustrated in the following verse of the Qur'an:

بَلْ طَبَعَ ٱللَّهُ عَلَيْهَا بِكُفْرِهِمْ فَلَا يُؤْمِنُونَ إِلَّا قَلِيلًا

- *Rather Allāh has sealed them because of their disbelief, so they believe not, except for a few.*

(An-Nisa, 4:155, interpretation of the meaning)

This verse suggests that Allāh has set a seal upon their hearts because of their disbelief. This is causation because of their disbelief and not compulsion. The causality of the seal from Allāh is their own disbelief. This is resonated in the following verses in the Qur'an. Allāh says:

وَقُلِ ٱلْحَقُّ مِن رَّبِّكُمْ فَمَن شَآءَ فَلْيُؤْمِن وَمَن شَآءَ فَلْيَكْفُرْ

- *And say, "This is the truth from your Lord. Whoever wills let them believe, and whoever wills let them disbelieve."*
  (Al-Kahf 18:29, interpretation of the meaning)

This means that if man start believing, of which they have free will to choose, the seal will be removed from their heart. However, man should not use predestination as an excuse for their sins or errors or to avoid responsibilities. Utz (2011) argues:

> It is unacceptable to use *Qadr* as an excuse for committing sins or failing to perform obligatory deeds. This would imply that the laws of Allāh are meaningless and that the judgment, rewards and punishments should not happen or are unjust. This is obviously not true of the mercy and justice of Allāh.
>
> (p. 92)

Iakhin (2022) suggests that there are some psychological consequences as a result of the belief in divine will, predestination, and free will:

> If one has the right understanding and application, such an attitude to the reality can become of paramount importance for the psychological state and development of a person. After all, knowing that only Allāh has the ability to bring good or evil to a person can free him from a significant mass of negative experiences and their consequences that are associated with the ongoing events of their lives, whatever they concern (work, family life, accidents, etc.). At the same time, the sincere and stronger the conviction in this [Belief in the Divine decree], the more balanced and harmonious the psychological state will be.

Thus, it involves adhering to the belief in the divine decree and man's freedom to choose to nurture a harmonious relationship between Allāh and His creation.

KNOWLEDGE IN ISLĀM

An important element of the belief in the divine decree is the eternal knowledge of Allāh. The divine knowledge of the Qur'ān is an infinite nature of knowledge. Allāh says in the Qur'ān:

قُل لَّوْ كَانَ ٱلْبَحْرُ مِدَادًا لِّكَلِمَٰتِ رَبِّى لَنَفِدَ ٱلْبَحْرُ قَبْلَ أَن تَنفَدَ كَلِمَٰتُ رَبِّى وَلَوْ جِئْنَا بِمِثْلِهِ مَدَدًا

- *Say, "If the sea were ink for [writing] the words of my Lord, the sea would be exhausted before the words of my Lord were exhausted, even if We brought the like of it as a supplement."*

(Al-Kahf 18:109, interpretation of the meaning)

This means, according to Ibn Kathir (2000),

> Say, O Muhammad, if the water of the sea were ink for a pen to write down the words, wisdom, and signs of Allāh, the sea would run dry before it all could be written down. (even if We brought like it) means, another sea, then another, and so on, additional seas to be used for writing. The Words of Allāh would still never run out.

Allāh mentions that nothing has been neglected in this Register (Qur'ān) and that the knowledge about all things is with Allāh. According to the Islamic perspective, the primary source of knowledge and authority in Islam is divine knowledge from the Qur'ān and guidance from the Traditions (*Sunnah*) of Prophet Muhammed (ﷺ). Allāh, the Almighty, has the knowledge of everything and knows us better than we know ourselves. Allāh says in the Qur'ān:

وَعِندَهُۥ مَفَاتِحُ ٱلْغَيْبِ لَا يَعْلَمُهَآ إِلَّا هُوَ ۚ وَيَعْلَمُ مَا فِى ٱلْبَرِّ وَٱلْبَحْرِ ۚ وَمَا تَسْقُطُ مِن وَرَقَةٍ إِلَّا يَعْلَمُهَا وَلَا حَبَّةٍ فِى ظُلُمَٰتِ ٱلْأَرْضِ وَلَا رَطْبٍ وَلَا يَابِسٍ إِلَّا فِى كِتَٰبٍ مُّبِينٍ

- *And with Him are the keys of the unseen; none knows them except Him. And He knows what is on the land and in the sea. Not a leaf falls but that He knows it. And no grain is there within the darkness of the earth and no moist or dry [thing] but that it is [written] in a clear record.*

(Al-An'am 6:59, interpretation of the meaning)

وَلَقَدْ خَلَقْنَا ٱلْإِنْسَانَ وَنَعْلَمُ مَا تُوَسْوِسُ بِهِۦ نَفْسُهُۥ ۖ وَنَحْنُ أَقْرَبُ إِلَيْهِ مِنْ حَبْلِ ٱلْوَرِيدِ

- *And We have already created man and know what his soul whispers to him, and We are closer to him than [his] jugular vein.*

(Qaf 50:16, interpretation of the meaning)

So, Allāh knows what is in our heart and soul. According to Ibn Kathir (2000), the above verse (Qaf 50:16) means that "Allāh the Exalted affirms His absolute dominance over mankind, being their Creator and the Knower of everything about them. Allāh the Exalted has complete knowledge of all thoughts that cross the mind of man, be they good or evil." In fact, mankind has been asked repeatedly in the Qur'ān to contemplate and reflect over the working of nature, paying attention to the signs that they can find within themselves or in the universe and find out the truths. The following two verses illustrate the contemplation and reflection of the universe. Allāh says in the Qur'ān:

قُلِ ٱنظُرُوا۟ مَاذَا فِى ٱلسَّمَـٰوَٰتِ وَٱلْأَرْضِ ۚ وَمَا تُغْنِى ٱلْآيَـٰتُ وَٱلنُّذُرُ عَن قَوْمٍ لَّا يُؤْمِنُونَ

- *Say, "Observe what is in the heavens and earth." But of no avail will be signs or warners to a people who do not believe.*

(Yunus 10:101, interpretation of the meaning)

سَنُرِيهِمْ ءَايَـٰتِنَا فِى ٱلْآفَاقِ وَفِىٓ أَنفُسِهِمْ حَتَّىٰ يَتَبَيَّنَ لَهُمْ أَنَّهُ ٱلْحَقُّ ۗ أَوَلَمْ يَكْفِ بِرَبِّكَ أَنَّهُۥ عَلَىٰ كُلِّ شَىْءٍ شَهِيدٌ

- *We will show them Our signs in the horizons and within themselves until it becomes clear to them that it is the truth. But is it not sufficient concerning your Lord that He is, over all things, a Witness?*

(Fussilat 41:53, interpretation of the meaning)

It is important to note that

the Qur'ān was revealed "to the heart" of the Prophet Muhammad (ﷺ) by [Angel] Gabriel (Al-Baqarah 2:97). From the chapter of Ash-Shu'arâ (26:193–194) we read that it was transmitted by the faithful spirit (*Rūḥ*) "upon your heart", thus cementing the links between the heart (*Qalb*) of humanity and the spirit (*Rūḥ*). The psychology of the Qur'ān takes seriously the idea that we are in between the material and the spiritual.

(Leaman, 2006, p. 441)

Revelation is the foundation upon which all knowledge is built, being perfect and complete.

PARADIGM OF ISLĀMIC PSYCHOLOGY

Box 1.3   A *paradigm* is defined "as a group of presumptions, outlooks, ideas, morals, processes, and methods which constitute a typically approved theoretical framework within, or a typical understanding of, a discipline."

Source: N. (2013), *Psychology Dictionary*.

A paradigm is a collection of beliefs, concepts, assumptions, and worldviews that create ways of thinking and methods of study for a particular discipline. It provides a framework in which a discipline may be made operational. The paradigm of Islāmic psychology, similar to other academic and theoretical disciplines, must be built on certain principles. These principles permeate all topics that pertain to the knowledge and methodology of Islāmic psychology. These principles include:

- Belief in monotheism or *Tawhîd*;
- Belief in Allāh as the Only Creator and Sustainer of everything, including man, and the only One who is worthy of worship;
- Belief in the six axioms of the articles of faith (*Imān*) known as *Arkān al-īmān*;

- Belief in Divine Revelation as a source of knowledge about Allāh, the hidden world, about the nature, meaning, and purpose of life;
- Belief in the religious characteristics – connection with belief in the supernatural and invisible world;
- Adoption of Prophet Muhammad (ﷺ) as a role model with an outstanding character (*khuluqyl 'adhiym*) and following his *Sunnah*;
- Belief in the metaphysical component of the self: *Qalb* (heart), *Rûh* (soul), *Nafs* (desire-nature or behavioural inclination), and *'Aql* (intellect, reason), each term signifying a spiritual entity;
- Belief in the fundamentals of Islāmic anthropology and the concept of *fitrah*;
- Belief in the Covenant with Allāh;
- Belief that Man is part of the Universe created by Allāh and part of the Cosmos ruled by Allāh;
- Belief in knowledge integration and integrated research as a methodology in Islāmic psychology; and
- Belief in the holistic dimension of Islāmic psychology: biological, social, psychological, and spiritual.

The above principles define the paradigm of Islāmic psychology. Islāmic psychology explores the working of the mind, body, and soul that drives behaviours and experiences from an Islāmic perspective. Islāmic psychology finds it roots in the Qur'ānic worldview and civilizations and Prophetic example as embodied by our Prophet Muhammad (ﷺ) as the best of the creations of Allāh. He is a source of guidance for all mankind and brings people from darkness to light through his teaching and behaviours. His statements and behaviours constitute a model for Muslims and non-Muslims to follow. There is also the understanding of the *fitrah* as the natural, pristine state of human nature that expresses an innate predisposition to monotheism, faith in Allāh, and the soul's connection to Allāh. True happiness and spiritual health are attained by bringing human beings back in touch with the *fitrah* (This will be covered in another chapter).

In the paradigm of Islāmic psychology another notion intricately connected with the concept of *fitrah* is an individual's covenant with

Allāh, which has an important psychological component. Allāh says in the Qur'ān:

وَٱذۡكُرُوا۟ نِعۡمَةَ ٱللَّهِ عَلَيۡكُمۡ وَمِيثَٰقَهُ ٱلَّذِى وَاثَقَكُم بِهِۦۤ إِذۡ قُلۡتُمۡ سَمِعۡنَا وَأَطَعۡنَا ۖ وَٱتَّقُوا۟ ٱللَّهَ ۚ إِنَّ ٱللَّهَ عَلِيمٌۢ بِذَاتِ ٱلصُّدُورِ

يَٰٓأَيُّهَا ٱلَّذِينَ ءَامَنُوا۟ كُونُوا۟ قَوَّٰمِينَ لِلَّهِ شُهَدَآءَ بِٱلۡقِسۡطِ ۖ وَلَا يَجۡرِمَنَّكُمۡ شَنَـَٔانُ قَوۡمٍ عَلَىٰٓ أَلَّا تَعۡدِلُوا۟ ۚ ٱعۡدِلُوا۟ هُوَ أَقۡرَبُ لِلتَّقۡوَىٰ ۖ وَٱتَّقُوا۟ ٱللَّهَ ۚ إِنَّ ٱللَّهَ خَبِيرٌۢ بِمَا تَعۡمَلُونَ

وَعَدَ ٱللَّهُ ٱلَّذِينَ ءَامَنُوا۟ وَعَمِلُوا۟ ٱلصَّٰلِحَٰتِ ۙ لَهُم مَّغۡفِرَةٌ وَأَجۡرٌ عَظِيمٌ

وَٱلَّذِينَ كَفَرُوا۟ وَكَذَّبُوا۟ بِـَٔايَٰتِنَآ أُو۟لَٰٓئِكَ أَصۡحَٰبُ ٱلۡجَحِيمِ

- *And remember the favour of Allāh upon you and His covenant with which He bound you when you said, "We hear and we obey"; and fear Allāh. Indeed, Allāh is Knowing of that within the breasts. O you who have believed, be persistently standing firm for Allāh, witnesses in justice, and do not let the hatred of a people prevent you from being just. Be just; that is nearer to righteousness. And fear Allāh; indeed, Allāh is [fully] Aware of what you do. Allāh has promised those who believe and do righteous deeds [that] for them there is forgiveness and great reward. But those who disbelieve and deny Our signs – those are the companions of Hellfire.*

  (Al-Ma'idah 5: 7–10, interpretation of the meaning)

The Qur'ān describes mankind who make a covenant with Allāh as having the following characteristics, including bearing witness that Allāh is their Master and submission to Him, the remembrance of Allāh's favour, worshiping Him only, being righteous (having *Taqwa*), being obedient only to Him, adhering to the principles of justice (*adl*) and fairness (*qist*), undertaking righteous deeds, reward in the Hereafter if he completes his duties, and a severe punishment if he breaks his oath. What is of upmost importance for the Islāmic worldview is the very fact of witnessing that in the soul of every person lies the knowledge of the One Lord – Allāh. The real purpose of such a covenant is that mankind will have no excuse on the Day of Judgment as they testify the existence of Allāh as their Lord and not direct any form of worship to others besides Him or without any intermediaries (see Al A'raf 7:172–174). The covenant is fulfilled by sincerely believing in *Tawhîd*, preserving this primordial pure human nature, and putting the principles and practices of Islāmic beliefs into practice. It is also important to note that humans have a dual role, simultaneously a slave (*'abd*) of Allāh and His vicegerent (*Khalifah*) on earth. That is, they have total submission to Allāh and obey totally His Commandments. Allah says in the Qur'ān:

وَمَا خَلَقْتُ ٱلْجِنَّ وَٱلْإِنسَ إِلَّا لِيَعْبُدُونِ

- *And I did not create the jinn and mankind except to worship Me.* (Adh-Dhāriyāt 51:56, interpretation of the meaning)

The paradigm of Islāmic psychology has a completely different approach and methodology in the study of human behaviours and experiences. The methodology of study is not limited to the sphere of knowledge gained from sense perception and rationalism (logical reasoning). It also deals with the supernatural phenomena of the invisible world, which cannot be measured or evaluated using the means of empiricism, intuition, and reason. This knowledge is more extensive than the visible world and is based upon divine revelation. There is interaction between the visible and invisible world. Belief involves the metaphysical components of the self: *Qalb* (heart), *Rûh* (soul), *Nafs* (desire–nature or behavioural inclination), and *'Aql* (intellect, reason). Each of these terms signifies a spiritual entity, and they are the key components of the influence and study of Islāmic psychology.

CONCLUSION

The psychological language of the Qur'ān depicts all kinds of human behaviours and psychological experiences. Utz (2011) suggested that

> Our thoughts, emotions, will, and behaviour must focus on attaining the pleasure of Allah. The key to sound mental health and well-being from the Islamic perspective is submission to Allah, the Exalted, the Almighty and His commandments, and to subsequently purifying the soul.
>
> (p. 25)

Islāmic worldview is basically an ethical and monotheistic world-view stems from the fundamental belief of *Tawhîd*. Islāmic psychology is a discipline that focuses on understanding the nature and structures of the self from an Islāmic perspective: the *Fiṭrah* (primordial disposition), *Nafs* (self), *Qalb* (heart), *Rûh* (soul/spirit), *'Aql* (intellect), and *ihsas* (emotional expressions). Islāmic psychology is underpinned by an Islāmic epistemological, ontological, and meta-physical worldview and is based on the religion of monotheism according to the Creed of *Ahlus-Sunnah Wal-Jama'ah*.

FURTHER READINGS

Al-Athari, 'Abd-Allah Ibn 'Abd al Hameed. (2003). *Islamic Beliefs: A Brief Introduction to the 'Aqeedah of Ahl Assunah wal-Jama'ah*. Riyadh: International Islamic Publishing House.

Badri, M.B. (1979). *The Dilemma of Muslim Psychologists*. London: MWH London.

Rassool, G. Hussein. (2021a). *Islamic Psychology: Human Behaviour and Experience from an Islamic Perspective*. Oxford: Routledge, Chapter 1.

Utz, A. (2011). *Psychology from an Islamic Perspective*. Riyadh: International Islamic Publishing House.

2

EVOLUTION OF THE SCIENCE OF THE SOUL
Historical perspective

INTRODUCTION

The Golden Age of Islām, the classical period between the 8th and 14th centuries, was an era of progress in academic, artistic, cultural, medical, philosophical, scientific and economic disciplines. This Islāmic Renaissance period started with the reign of the Abbasid Caliph Harun al-Rashid (c. 786–809 CE) and ended with the collapse of the Abbasid Caliphate following the Mongol invasions and the sack of Baghdad in 1258 CE. This was a truly remarkable period in human history that saw the inauguration of the House of Wisdom (*Bait-al-Hikmah*) in Baghdad, which was a public academy, intellectual centre, and library. In the House of Wisdom the scholars, who were multidisciplinary and had diverse religious affiliations, were mandated to gather and translate all of the world's classical knowledge from Greek to Syriac to Arabic and Persian and later into Turkish, Hebrew, and Latin.

What is remarkable, in the annals of history, are the accomplishments made by Islāmic scholars, philosophers, physicians, and theologians in diverse disciplines. The birth and evolution of *ʿIlm al-Nafs* or "knowledge of the soul" was mooted during this period. Thus, many of these classical scholars were driven by the Islāmic theological sources in addition to intuitive, rational, observational, and experimental sources in their quest for the study of the soul and for their contributions to psychology. They developed theories and various therapeutic techniques, including psychotherapy and a form

DOI: 10.4324/9781003312956-2

of cognitive behaviour therapy; and they promoted humane treatment for the mentally ill centuries before the introduction of 'humane' therapeutic treatment in the West. The modern "teaching hospital" and psychiatric ward were invented, and public health in the Islāmic world reached an astonishing height.

An understanding of the origins and historical contributions of the study of Islāmic psychology provides an orientation for where Islāmic psychology came from, its present status quo, and where it is going. The evolution or the resurgence of Islāmic psychology in the 21st century has been due to several factors, and Rassool (2019) has coined this renewal as the "Dodo Bird" revival. The aim of the chapter is to examine the contributions made by philosophers, physicians, and theologians in the evolution of science of the soul.

CONTEXT, SIGNIFICANT EVENTS, AND DEVELOPMENTS

During the Abbasid dynasty, Islāmic civilization reached new heights of creativity and entered a new age of expansion in architecture, fine arts, literature, philosophy, mathematics, sciences, medicine, and many other sciences. The principles and ideals of Islām were practiced. Tolerance, equality, and respect for the contributions of ethnic and religious minorities were a feature of the Caliphate. It was during this period that the inductive experimental method emerged. Al-Kindī (801–873 CE) and Jābir ibn Hayyān (d. 816 CE) started to put a greater emphasis on the use of experiment as a source of knowledge. Ibn al-Haytham combined observations, experiments, and rational arguments to support his theory of vision.

Muslim scholarship developed under the umbrella of philosophy, which embraced almost all areas of human enquiry. Philosophy (*falsafa*) in the Islāmic Renaissance period was elaborated as a "systematic investigation of problems connected with society, life, nature, and sciences in a global religious vision" (Renima et al., 2016, p. 31). Under the Abbasid dynasty there were two main approaches in intellectual discourses: *Kalam* (Examination of Islāmic theological questions using the logic and reflections) and *Falsafa* (Interpretations of Aristotelianism and Neoplatonism philosophies into Arabic). There was also the school of *Mu'tazilism*, which is viewed as the rationalist school of Islāmic theology. The *Mu'tazilites'* basic premise is that the injunctions of God are accessible to rational thought and inquiry. One of the most contentious questions in Islāmic theology is the notion by the *Mu'tazilites* that the Qur'ān, albeit the word of God, was created rather than uncreated. The *Ash'arite* philosophico-religious school of thought was developed as a response to the *Mu'tazilites* as an attempt not only to purge Islām of all non-Islāmic elements, which had quietly crept into it, but also to harmonise the religious consciousness with the religious thought of Islām. One way the Abbasid dynasty was able to spread written knowledge so quickly was the improvements on printing technology they had obtained from the Chinese. What are the factors that facilitated the emergence and the decline of the Islāmic Renaissance period? Box 2.1 and Box 2.2 respectively present the factors for the emergence and the decline of the Islāmic Golden Age.

Box 2.1 Factors for the emergence of the Islāmic Renaissance period

- The importance of acquiring knowledge, which played a vital role in influencing the Muslim search for knowledge.
- Assimilation of the scientific knowledge of diverse civilisation.
- The emergence of a political system.
- Economic development and trade.
- Language and education (Arabic was the functioning Lingua Franca of the period).
- Socio-political factors.
- The quest for knowledge.
- Practice of the principles and ideals of Islām.
- Tolerance, equality, and respect for the contributions of ethnic and religious minorities.
- The Islāmic State heavily patronised scholarship.
- The emergence of sciences and 'Islāmic psychology' as a result of Muslim religious motivation.
- New technology (paper and printing).

Box 2.2   Factors for the decline of the Islāmic Renaissance period

- Mongol invasion.
- Muslims veered away from the teachings of Islām.
- Infighting among the Muslim rulers.
- Wars took their toll on the Islāmic people.
- A majority of Ulema (religious jurists and scholars) came to the view that the Islāmic civilisation had reached its peak and all the interpretations (*Ijtihad*) needed had been accomplished.
- The anti-rationalist school was established: *Ash'arite* philosophico-religious school of thought.
- The Ottoman conquest of the Arabic-speaking Middle East.
- Colonisation of Muslim lands by non-Muslims.
- Religious knowledge took precedence over scientific knowledge.
- Economic and political factors.

The proposition that the decline of the Islāmic Renaissance period was due to the lack of rationalism and creative thinking has been refuted by Al-Hassan (1996). He argues that science was always kept separate from religious argument, and it was economic and political factors that made a significant contribution to the decline of Islāmic civilisation. Another point of contention is the period of the Islāmic Renaissance period. Al-Hassan (1996) extended the period from the 14th century to the 16th century, noting that scientific activity continued to flourish up until then. Others extended it to the 17th century. El-Rouayheb (2006) maintained that Muslim scholars produced works based on the rational-scientific paradigm during the 17th century.

THE PHILOSOPHERS' PERSPECTIVE

The philosophers who contributed to Islāmic psychology include Al-Kindī, Ibn Miskawayh, Ibn Rushd, and Al-Fārābi.

Abu-Yusuf Ya'qub ibn Ishâq ibn as-Sabbah ibn 'Omran ibn Ismâ'îl al-Kindī, known as al-Kindī, the "Philosopher of the Arabs", was born about 801 CE in Kufa, Iraq, and his theological orientation was from the school of *Mutazilite*. He was a polymath: philosopher, physician, pharmacist, psychologist, ophthalmologist, physicist, mathematician, geographer, astronomer, and chemist. He was also concerned with music, logogriphs, the manufacturing of swords, and even the art of cookery. Despite his synthesis, adaptation, and promotion of Greek and Hellenistic speculative philosophies, he held firm views on the nature and value of divine revelation as a source of knowledge. Al-Kindī's books related to psychology include: *Risalah Fī al-ʿAql*, an analysis of the nature and divisions of the intellect written in the Aristotelian tradition; *Māhiyyat al-Nawm wa al-Ruʾyah*, a treatise on dreams and visions; *Fī al-Qawl fī-al Nafs al-Mukhtasar min Kitab Aristii wa Flatun wa saʾir al-Falasifah (Discourse on the Soul)*; *Kalām fī al-Nafs Mukhtasar Wajiz (Discourse on the Soul)*, written in the Neoplatonic tradition; and *Al-Ḥīlah li Dafʿ al-Aḥzān (The Strategy for Repelling Sorrow)*. Al-Kindī addressed the disease of epilepsy and physiological reasons for the causes of epilepsy [called *Sarʾ* the falling-sickness]. He proposed several theories on perception, sleeping and dreams, and emotional processes (Awaad et al., 2019) and identified the therapeutic value of music. In his "The Strategy to Repelling Sorrows," Al-Kindī described sorrow as "a spiritual (*nafsani*) grief caused by loss of loved ones or personal belongings or by failure in obtaining what one lusts after," and he then added: "If causes of pain are discernible, the cures can be found" (Tahir, 2009). He also suggested the use of cognitive strategies in the treatment of depression (Awaad et al., 2020). He was the first to use the method of experiment in psychology, which led to his discovery that sensation is proportionate to the stimulus.

Ibn Miskawayh (d. 1030 CE), or Abu Ali Ahmad b. Muhammad b. Yaʾkub Ibn Miskawayh, was born in Rey, Persia (now Iran). He was a philosopher (attracted to Aristotle and Plato), theologian, physician, and historian, and his influence on Islāmic philosophy is primarily in the area of ethics. He made no attempt to reconcile philosophy and religion. He was the author of the first major Islāmic work on philosophical ethics, titled *The Refinement of Character (Tahdhīb al-Akhlāq)*, which focused on practical ethics, conduct, and refinement of character. Ibn Miskawayh's books related to psychology include: *al-Saʿādah fī Falsafit al-Akhlāq (Happiness from the Perspective of Ethical Philosophy)*, *Tahdhīb al-Akhlāq (Refinement of Ethics)*, *al-Fawz alAṣghar (The Minor Victory)*, *al-Saʿādah (Happiness)*, *Risālah fī al-Lazzāt wa al-Ālām (A Treatise on Pleasures and Pains)*, *Risālah fī Jawhar al-Nafs (On the Essence of the Soul)*, *Ajwibah wa*

As'ilah fī al-Nafs wa al-ʿAql (*On the Soul and Mind: Questions and Answers on the Soul*), and *Ṭahārat al-Nafs* (*Purity of the Soul*). Ibn Miskawayh introduced what is now known as "self-reinforcement" and response cost (Haque, 2004). His work on moral and positive psychology laid the foundation for many theories surrounding altering behaviours, attitudes, and manners in gradual, concrete steps (Awaad et al., 2019). Ibn Miskawayh's book on Tahdhīb *al-Akhlāq* (*Refinement of Ethics*) is related to positive psychology and how to reach supreme happiness. To realise happiness and its virtues some internal and some external conditions have to be met. According to Ibn Miskawayh, the internal conditions include health and temperament, the external conditions are to overcome weaknesses, and having the psychological conditions to achieve happiness centres on the human's will and his ability to raise his inclinations (Jamal al-Din, 1994). Ibn Miskawayh also discussed the need for self-awareness and for methods of treating the illnesses of the soul. He said that "a Muslim, who feels guilty about doing something pleasurable to his *Al-nafs al-ammārah*, should learn to punish himself by psychological, physical, or spiritual ways such as paying money to the poor, fasting, etc." (Haque, 2004, p. 365).

Ibn Rushd (d. 1198 CE), or Abuʾal Walid Ibn Rushd (known in the West as Averroes), was born in Cordova, Spain, and has been acknowledged as one of the greatest thinkers and scientists of history. He excelled in philosophy and jurisprudence and was nicknamed "the jurisprudent philosopher" (Famous Scientists, 2020). He integrated Aristotelian philosophy with Islāmic discourse. For Ibn Rushd, there is no incongruity between religion and philosophy when both are properly grasped. He wrote on logic, Aristotelian and Islāmic philosophy, Islāmic theology, the Maliki school of Islāmic jurisprudence, psychology, political theory, the theory of Andalusian classical music, geography, mathematics, as well as the medieval sciences of medicine, astronomy, physics, and celestial mechanics. Ibn Rushd was a defender of Aristotelian philosophy against Ashʾari theologians led by Al-Ghazālī. Ibn Rushd was criticised by many Muslim scholars for his book *Tuhafut al-Tuhafut*, which was written in response to Al-Ghazālī's work and had a significant influence on European thought in modern philosophy and experimental science.

Ibn Rushd's books on psychology and philosophy include: *al-Nafs* (*The Soul*); *alʿAql wa al-Maʿqūl* (*The Mind and the Rational*); *Talkbis*

Kitab al-Nafs (Aristotle on the Soul); and *Tahāfut at Tahāfut (Incoherence of the Incoherence)*, his polemical response to Al-Ghazālī's *Tahāfut al-Falāsifah (Incoherence of the Philosophers)*. His discourse on psychology is fully discussed in his *Talkbis Kitab al-Nafs (Aristotle on the Soul)*. Ibn Rushd divided the soul into five faculties: the nutritive, the sensitive, the imaginative, the appetitive, and the rational (Fakhry, 2001). He argued there are three different types of intellect: receiving intellect, producing intellect, and the produced intellect (Norager, 1998). In his discussions of cognition, he argued that both sensation (perception) and imagination must be used to perceive objectively (Haque, 2004).

In his educational philosophy, the learning and knowledge acquisition strategies suggested by Ibn Rushd include reflection (*i'tibār*), examination (*faḥṣ*), deduction and discovery (*istinbāṭ*), demonstrative study (*naẓarburhānī*), intellectual reasoning (*Qiyās 'aqlī*), comparison and analogy (*tamthīl*), allegorical interpretation (*Ta'wīl*), dialectical reasoning (*Aqāwīljadalīya*), demonstrative reasoning (*Aqāwīlburhānīya)*, and rhetorical reasoning (*Aqāwīlkhiṭābīya*) (Günther, 2012, p. 9). Ibn Rushd argues that we know from our everyday experience that there exists health and illness, and religious texts contain important information as to how we should behave (Leaman, 1998).

Al-Fārābī (d. 951 CE), or Abū Naṣr Muḥammad ibn Muḥammad Al Fārābī (known in the West as Alpharabius), was a philosopher, jurist, scientist, cosmologist, mathematician, and music scholar. He made contributions to physics, logic, music, political philosophy, and social and educational psychology. In Arabic philosophical tradition, he is known with the honorific "the Second Master" (*al-Mou'allim al-Thani*) after Aristotle. Al-Fārābī's most influential work shaped social psychology, especially his well-known treatise *Ārā' Ahl al-Madīnah al-Fāḍilah (Opinions of the People of the Righteous City)*, where he described several principles of social psychology using invented exemplars (Soueif & Ahmed, 2001). His psychological and philosophical treatises include *Taḥṣīl al-Sa'ādah (Attaining Happiness)*, *Kitāb al-Tanbīh 'alā Sabīl al-Sa'ādah (A Guide to the Path of Happiness)*, *Risālah fī al-'Aql (Epistle on the Intellect)*, *'Uyūn al-Masā'il (The Depth of Matters)*, *al-Siyāsāh al-Madaniyyah (Civil Policies)*, *Fuṣūṣ al-Ḥikmah (The Cloves of Wisdom)*, *al-Da'āwī al-Qalbiyyah (Internal Claims)*, and *Kitāb iḥṣā'al-'ulūm (On the Introduction of Knowledge)*. Al-Fārābī suggested that the perfect human being (*al insan al kamil*) has both theoretical virtue (intellectual knowledge) and practical moral virtues (moral behaviour).

According to Al-Fārābī, perfection is achieved by an individual with the help of other people (social relationship and network) (Norager, 1998). Al-Fārābī specifies that a person's innate psychological dispositions drive them to maintain social cohesion (Haque, 2004). At the heart of Al-Fārābī's political philosophy is the concept of happiness, in which people cooperate to gain contentment (Tiliouine, 2014), as well as having social cohesion in small and large groups (Soueif & Ahmed, 2001). Al-Fārābī wrote on dreams and explained the distinction between dream interpretation and the nature and triggers of dreams. His writings on the therapeutic effect of music on the soul later influenced modern mental health and treatment (Haque, 1998).

THE PHYSICIANS' PERSPECTIVE

The important Islāmic figures in medicine are Abū Bakr Muḥammad ibn Zakariya al-Rāzī, Abū Zayd Aḥmad ibn Sahl al-Balkhī, and Abū Alī al-Ḥusayn ibn Sīnā. The House of Abbasids supported research developments, especially medical research. Knowledge of the medical sciences and techniques were part of the medical curriculum throughout the world until about a century ago (Nasr, 1975). Box 2.3 presents the context and development of health services in the treatment of people with health and spiritual problems.

Box 2.3   The context and development of health services

- The Caliph Harun al-Rashid established the first hospital in Baghdad, and by the 9th century there were several other hospitals in Cairo, Makkah, and Medina as well as mobile medical units for rural areas.
- Hospitals known as Bimaristans (Persian for "hospital") were built throughout the Islāmic state.
- These Bimaristans treated males and females, had outpatient facilities, and offered services for the poor. The medical treatment was free, supported by waqf (endowments) and government patronage (Sonn & Williamsburg, 2004, p. 52).
- The Islāmic state had a pioneering approach concerning mental health and psychiatry.

- The first psychiatric hospitals were founded in Baghdad (c. 705 CE, during the kingship of the caliph El Waleed ibn Abdel Malek), Cairo (c. 800 CE), and Damascus (c. 1270 CE).
- Many of the hospitals house libraries, classrooms, and central courtyards with pools, and the patients were benevolently treated using baths, drugs, music, and activities. In contrast, the first psychiatric asylum in the Western Europe, the Bethlem Hospital in Bishopsgate, London, was founded in the 13th century (Forshaw & Rollin, 1990).
- The physicians produced rich, authoritative, multivolume medical books. It has been suggested that they adopted Hippocratic organic psychiatry (biological psychiatry), but they also applied psychosocial therapeutic methods (Dubovsky, 1983).
- The authority of the great physicians of the Islāmic Renaissance period has influenced the art and science of medicine as well as medical ethics for many centuries, even to this day.
- Their ideas about the conduct of physicians and the doctor-patient relationship are discussed as potential role models for physicians of today (Lakhtakia, 2014).

Al-Rāzī (d. 925 CE), or Abū Bakr Muḥammad ibn Zakariya al-Rāzī (known as Rhazes in the West), was one of the greatest Islāmic physicians and perhaps second only to Ibn Sina. He was born in Rey (Iran). Al-Rāzī was appointed Director of the first Royal Hospital at Rey and had a similar position in Baghdad. He originated a treatment for kidney and bladder stones, clarified the nature of various infectious diseases, established research on smallpox and measles, was the first to announce the use of alcohol for medical purposes, used mercurial ointments, used opium for anaesthesia, made accurate and controlled nutrition intake part of his treatment package (Afridi, 2013), and used honey as a simple drug (Katouzian-Safadi & Bonmatin, 2003). He developed instruments used in apothecaries (pharmacies), such as mortars and pestles, flasks, spatulas, beakers, and glass vessels (Amr & Tbakhi, 2007). The fame of Al-Rāzī as one of the greatest Muslim physicians is mainly due to the case records and histories written in his books (Amr & Tbakhi, 2007), which established qualifications and ethical standards for the practice of medicine (Modanlou, 2008). The May 1970 *Bulletin of the World Health Organization* pays tribute to

Al-Rāzī by stating, "His writings on smallpox and measles show originality and accuracy, and his essay on infectious diseases was the first scientific treatise on the subject" (cited in Modanlou, 2008, p. 675). Al-Rāzī's selected books include *Kitāb al-Ḥāwī fī al-Ṭibb* (*The Comprehensive Book of Medicine*), a 23-volume tome in which he described many mental illnesses, their symptoms, and their cures (Husayn & Al-ʿUqbi, 1977; Tibi, 2006), and *Kitab Man la Yahdurûhu Al-Tabib* (*Book of Who is not Attended by a Physician or A medical Advisor for the General Public*), which is equivalent to a modern health-education booklet on services and treatment interventions. *Kitab Man la Yahdurûhu Al-Tabib* is dedicated to the poor, the traveller, and the ordinary citizen, who could consult or refer to it to treat common ailments when a doctor was not available (Amr & Tbakhi, 2007). In *Kitab al-Ṭibb al-Rūhānī* (*Book of Spiritual Medicine*), Al-Rāzī focuses on the soul (or psyche, mind) and its remedy, spiritually, morally, and psychologically (Najātī, 1993).

Al-Rāzī was a pioneer in the treatment of mental illnesses. As the director of the hospital in Baghdad, he established special wards for the treatment of the mentally ill and treated his patients with respect, care, and empathy (Daghestani, 1997, p. 1602). He emphasised the importance of the client–practitioner relationship (Farooqi, 2006) and provided psychiatric aftercare as part of his discharge planning (Daghestani, 1997). Al-Rāzī describes memory problems, disturbed thinking, mood disorders (including both melancholic and manic symptoms), and anxiety (Mohamed, 2012). He differentiated between the exposure of intrinsic positive reinforcement and extrinsic positive reinforcement when learning new behaviours (Al-Rāzī, 1978).

Abū Zayd Al-Balkhī (d. 934 CE) was born in Shamistiyan in Balkh, Khorasan (present-day Afghanistan). He was a polymath: a geographer, mathematician, physician, psychologist and scientist. Al-Balkhī introduced concepts of mental health and "mental hygiene" related to spiritual health and was the first to successfully discuss diseases related to both the body and the soul. He used the term *Al-Tibb al-Rûhani* to describe spiritual and psychological health, and he used the term *Tibb al-Qalb* to describe mental medicine. He criticised many doctors for placing too much emphasis on physical illnesses and neglecting the psychological or mental illnesses of patients (Awaad et al., 2019). Al-Balkhī believed in the interaction of body and mind and the interaction between physical and psychological disorders, which resulted in psychosomatic disorders (Mohamed, 2012). Al-Balkhī's book on psychology is

Masalih al-Abdan wa al-Anfus (*Sustenance for Body and Soul*). In this book, Al-Balkhī argued that "since man's construction is from both his soul and his body, therefore, human existence cannot be healthy without the *ishtibak* (interweaving or entangling) of soul and body" (Al-Balkhī, cited in Deuraseh & Abu Talib, 2005, p. 76). Throughout his book, Al-Balkhī offers "do it yourself" cognitive and spiritual therapies (Awaad & Ali, 2015). Box 2.4 provides an overview of aspects of mental health problems and therapeutic interventions from Al-Balkhī. Al-Balkhī's description of obsessional disorders in his manuscript, *Masalih al-Abdan wa al-Anfus*, reflects the description and criteria of obsessive compulsive disorder (OCD) found in modern diagnostic manuals of psychiatry, such as the *Diagnostic and Statistical Manual of Mental Disorders, Fifth Edition* (DSM-5) (American Psychiatric Association, 2013).

Box 2.4   Overview of Al-Balkhī

- Systematically distinguished between psychosis and neurosis.
- Categorised neuroses into four emotional disorders: (1) anxiety and fear, (2) aggression and anger, (3) depression and sadness, and (4) obsessions (Haque, 1998, 2004).
- Categorised depression into sadness, normal depression, reactive depression, and endogenous depression (Haddad, 1991).
- Described, classified, and distinguished the illnesses now known as obsessive compulsive disorder (OCD) and phobias (Awaad & Ali 2015).
- Suggested that psychological symptoms of anxiety, anger, and sadness are common among 'normal' people, most of which are learned behaviour and are a reaction to emotional stress (Awaad et al., 2019).
- Pioneered psychotherapy, psychophysiology, and psychosomatic medicine and was the father of modern cognitive behaviour therapy (CBT) (Badri, 2013; Awaad et al., 2019).
- For the treatment of a phobia, suggested a technique he called *riyāḍat al-nafs* (psyche-training) (Al-Balkhī, Misri, & Al-Hayyat, 2005; Awaad & Ali, 2016).
- Promoted the preventive approach, which encouraged individuals to keep positive 'cognition sets' to use in times of trials and tribulations (stress), and which is compared to contemporary rational cognitive therapy (Badri, 2013).

Al-Balkhī observes that "obsessive whispers are among the most intrusive psychological symptoms that linger deep within the core of the human being, triggering echoing thoughts that cage the person within themselves" (Al-Balkhī, 2005, p. 127). He developed techniques of reciprocal approaches (cognitive behaviour therapy), which Joseph Wolpe (1968) later introduced as the idea of "reciprocal inhibition".

Ibn Sīnā (d. 1037 CE), or Abu Ali al-Husayn Ibn Abdullah Ibn Sīnā, was born at Afsana near Bukhara (now in present-day Uzbekistan). Ibn Sīnā was one of the most celebrated physicians, astronomers, thinkers, and writers in the Renaissance Age of the Islāmic Empire. Ibn Sīnā memorised the entire Qur'ān by the age of ten and became a knowledgeable physician at the age of 16. He introduced new methods of treatment by the age of 18. Ibn Sīnā is considered a father of modern medicine, a pioneer of neuropsychiatry, and first recognised 'physiological psychology' for the treatment of illness involving emotions. Ibn Sīnā produced a number of books on medicine and psychology: *Al-Qanun fi't-Tibb* (*The Canon of Medicine*), an encyclopaedia of medicine; *Maqala fi'l-nafs* (*Compendium on the Soul*); *Kitab al-shifa* (*The Book of Healing*) on philosophy and existence, the mind-body relationship, sensation, and perception (Haque, 2004); *Kitab al-najat* (*The Book of Deliverance*); and *AndarDanesh-e Rag* (*On the Science of the Pulse*), which contains nine chapters on the science of the pulse and is the

> most detailed clinical description on the characteristics of the pulse that had been ever written. The pulse section consists of techniques for feeling the pulse. In this book he explained the certain types of arrhythmias such as atrial fibrillation, premature and dropped beats, and more than fifty different pulses.
>
> (Roudgari, 2018)

The Canon of Medicine (*al-Qanun fi'l-Tibb*) was taught as a medical textbook in the Islāmic world and Europe, for example, at the University of Montpellier, France (1650). The five-volume book still plays an important role in Unani medicine [Perso-Arabic traditional medicine] (Rahman, 2003). According to Ibn Sīnā,

> Ordinary human mind is like a mirror upon which a succession of ideas reflects from the active intellect. Before the acquisition of

knowledge that emanates from the active intellect the mirror was rusty but when we think, the mirror is polished and it remains to direct it to the sun (active intellect) so that it could readily reflect light.
(Cited in Haque, 2004, pp. 365–366)

Box 2.5 provides an overview of Ibn Sīnā's psychopathology and therapeutic interventions.

Box 2.5   Overview of Ibn Sīnā

- First described numerous neuropsychiatric conditions, including insomnia, mania, hallucinations, nightmares, dementia, epilepsy, stroke, paralysis, vertigo, melancholia, and tremors (Abbasi et al., 2007).
- Called melancholia (depression) a type of mood disorder in which the person may become suspicious and develop certain types of phobias (Majeed & Jabir, 2017).
- Identified a condition that seems like schizophrenia and was defined as *Junun Mufrit* (severe madness) with symptoms including agitation, sleep disturbance, giving inappropriate answers to questions, and occasional inability to speak (Majeed & Jabir, 2017, p. 70).
- Strategy in assessing his patient was to identify the source of the client's emotional conflict, sometimes using crude bio-feedback techniques (Awaad & Ali, 2016; Farooqi, 2006).
- Therapeutic interventions included meditation, self-awareness, dialogue, reflection, imagery, and conditioning to treat mental illnesses (Farooqi, 2006).
- Pioneered psychophysiology and psychosomatic medicine, developing a system for associating changes in the pulse rate with inner feelings. This idea anticipated the word-association test attributed to Carl Jung (Syed, 2002; Mohamed 2012).
- Used both relaxation methods and a form of systematic desensitisation (hierarchy of anxiety-inducing words) with pulse-checking to identify anxiety provoking words. The techniques were used in the treatment of a prince suffering from anorexia nervosa (Haque, 2004; Awaad & Ali, 2015).

THE THEOLOGIANS' PERSPECTIVE

The Islāmic Renaissance period produced some luminaries of Islāmic theology. Many of the Islāmic theologians were instrumental in the development of the nature of Islāmic psychology because the discipline of *Ilm an Nafs* was linked to Islāmic theology and the religiosity of the soul. Awaad et al. (2020) suggest that "Muslim theologians contributed to the development of an 'Islāmic psychology' through their work in three fields: (1) Islāmic creed, (2) Islāmic law, and (3) Islāmic spirituality" (p. 74). There are many polymath scholars and theologians who made significant contributions to Islāmic sciences, and they directly and indirectly enabled the development of Islāmic psychology. It is not within the scope of this chapter to include all of them, however influential Islāmic scholars and theologians include Al-Ghazālī, Ibn Taymīyyah al-Ḥarrānī, Ibn Qayyim al Jawziyyah, Al-Raghib Ar-Rāghib al-Aṣbahānī Jamāl al-Dīn Abū al-Faraj 'Abd al-Raḥmān Ibn al-Jawzī, Ibn Khaldūn al-Ḥaḍramī and Ibn Rajab al-Hanbali. The next sections will address the contributions of three theologians: Al-Ghazālī, Ibn Taymīyyah, and Ibn Qayyim Al Jawziyyah.

Al-Ghazālī (d. 1111 CE), or Abu Ḥāmid Muḥammad al-Ghazālī, was born 1058 CE at Tûs, Greater Khorasan, Seljuq Empire. Al-Ghazālī was one of the most prominent and influential philosophers, theologians, jurists, and mystics of Sunni Islām. In 1091 Nizâm al-Mulk appointed Al-Ghazālī to the prestigious Nizâmiyya Madrasa in Baghdad. After performing the pilgrimage in 1096, Al-Ghazālī returned via Damascus and Baghdad to his hometown Tûs, where he founded a small private school and a Sufi convent (*khânqâh*) (Griffel, 2009). He was active at a time when Sunni theology had just entered a period of intense challenges from Shiite Ismâ'îlite theology and the Arabic tradition of Aristotelian philosophy (*falsafa*). For Al-Ghazālī

> the purpose of society is to apply the *Sharī'ah*, and the goal of man is to achieve happiness close to God. Therefore, the aim of education is to cultivate man so that he abides by the teachings of religion and is hence assured of salvation and happiness in the eternal life hereafter.
>
> (Nofal, 1993, p. 524)

His religious work, *Tahāfut al-Falāsifa* (*Incoherence of the Philosophers*), favours Muslim faith over philosophy and was extremely influential in turning medieval Muslim thought away from Aristotelianism, philosophical debate, and theological speculation. Al-Ghazālī

> reinstated the "principle of fear" in religious thinking and emphasised the role of the Creator as the centre around which human life revolves, and an agent intervening directly and continuously in the course of human affairs (once the "principle of love" had gained supremacy among the Sufis).
>
> (Nofal, 1993, p. 531)

In *Iḥyā 'Ulūm al-Dīn*, Al-Ghazālī outlines six steps for self-purification:

- "*Mushāraṭah* (self-contract with goals)
- *Murāqabah* (self-monitoring)
- *Muḥāsabah* (self-examination; holding oneself accountable)
- *Mujāhadah* (self-penalisation; implementing, consequences for breaking the self-contract [lapse and relapse])
- *Mu'āqabah* (self-struggle; working diligently to overcome sinful inclinations)
- *Mu'ātabah* (self-admonition; regretting breaking and recommitting to upholding the contract)."

(Keshavarzi & Haque, 2013, p. 242)

Box 2.6 provides on overview of Al-Ghazālī's psychology.

Box 2.6 Overview of Al-Ghazālī

- Advocated introspection and self-analysis to understand the psyche and psychological issues.
- Described a concept of the self expressed by four terms in Arabic [as conceived by the Qur'ān]: (1) *Qalb* (heart), (2) *Rûh* (soul), (3) *Nafs* (desire-nature), and (4) *'Aql* (intellect, reason). Each of these terms signifies a spiritual entity.
- Preferred to use the term *Qalb* for the self in his work. One is essentially required to know this *Qalb* in order to discover ultimate reality (Amer, 2015).

- Believed that our focus should shift from "treating diseases of the body, such diseases compromise an already fleeting life. More attention should be directed to treating diseases of the heart [psyche], which has an infinite lifetime" (Al-Ghazālī, 2005, p. 929).
- Believed in the use of therapeutic interventions, including negative reinforcement, modelling, labelling, and shaping (Farooqi, 2006).
- Discussed the spiritual diseases of the heart, including arrogance, miserliness, ignorance, envy, and lust (Haque, 2004) and encouraged purification of the soul (*Tazkiyat al-nafs*) (including its cognitions and behavioural inclinations) to cure these diseases (Awaad et al., 2020).

Ibn Taymīyyah (d. 1328 CE), or Taqī al-Dīn Abū al-ʿAbbās Aḥmad bin ʿAbd al-Ḥalīm al-Ḥarrānī, was born Harran, Sultanate of Rum, and died on 26 September 1328, in Damascus, Sham (now Syria). Ibn Taymīyyah was a Sunni Muslim scholar, *Muhaddith*, theologian, judge, jurisconsult, and logician. He has been acknowledged by some as the *Mujaddid* [one who reforms in society and gives a new spirit to Islām when it is in danger] of the 7th century in the Islāmic calendar (Ansar, 2019). A member of the Hanbali school, he is considered to be one of the leading scholars of the *Ahlus Sunnah wal Jamāʾah* and has been accepted as Sheikh-ul-Islām by all major Sunni schools. During his time, Islāmic philosophers and theologians had introduced various innovations within the Islāmic creed. Ibn Taymīyyah rebutted all the innovations that were prevalent during this period, including the veneration of saints and visitation to their tomb-shrines, which made him unpopular with many scholars and rulers of the time, who ordered him to be imprisoned several times (Laoust, 2012). Ibn Taymīyyah maintains that the Qurʾān and the Sunnah are not only the sources of Islāmic law, they are also the sources of Islāmic faith and belief (Ansar, 2019).

His criticism of "*Ash'ari kalam*, Greek logic and philosophy, monistic Sufism, Shi'i doctrines, and Christian faith have proved great obstacles to appreciating his contribution" (Ansar, 2019, xvii). He was critical of the Aristotelian and Neoplatonist philosophers, including Al-Fārābī, Al-Kindī, and Ibn Sīnā for "breaking away from the fundamentals of Islām in their pursuit of knowledge, saying that they were dressing up Greek thought in Islāmic clothing"

(Awaad et al., 2020, p. 76). It is through divine revelation, not rationality and emotions, that we can examine the world in order to acquire ultimate truths (An-Najār, 2004). Ibn Taymīyyah authored more than five hundred manuscripts and short treatises on various branches of the Islāmic sciences, three of which are related to psychology (Awaad et al., 2020). It is reported that Ibn Taymīyyah was a prolific writer, he wrote about 40 pages in one sitting, and he produced a complete volume of work in one day. Ibn Taymīyyah's books include *'ilm al-sulūk*, a chapter on the diseases and treatments of the heart, that was published in *Majmū'al-Fatāwā*, his encyclopaedic fatwa collection. *Risālah fī al-'Aql wa al-Rūḥ* was a treatise on the soul and intellect, and *al-'Ubūdiyyah* is on obedience. Box 2.7 presents Ibn Taymīyyah's psychology.

Box 2.7   Overview of Ibn Taymīyyah

- Discussed moral emotion and the merit of an empathetic sadness (Awaad et al., 2020).
- Examined the relationship between cognitive and affective states and the influence of emotional nuances in the rational thinking process (Awaad et al., 2020).
- Highlighted constructive and unproductive sadness, urging people to use constructive sadness for a purpose. This is illustrated in the following quote:

> As for sadness that does not bring about a benefit nor displace a harm, there is no benefit in it, and God does not command that which has no benefit ... However, some forms of sadness are divinely rewarded ... including sorrow over the calamities of the Muslims in general.
>
> (Ibn Taymīyyah, 2004, pp. 13–14)

- Expounded his understanding of psychological disease by arguing that just as the body of an individual suffers from a disease by losing its capacity to conceive, as in the form of losing eyesight or the ability to hear or in the form of hallucinating about something that does not exist in reality, the heart suffers from a similar form of imbalance.

> • *Tawhīd* purifies the heart from all that is sought to worship other than Allāh and this obedience protects the heart from falling victim to the traps of *Shayṭān* and one's own desires.
> • A believer can diagnose the disease that is afflicted to the heart and does not delay its treatment. There are certain diseases that affect a believer's will (i.e., *irādah*), while others affect his conception (*taṣawwur*) (Ibn Taymīyyah, 1402, p. 4).

Ibn Taymīyyah expounds his understanding of psychological diseases in his treatise *Amrāḍ al-Qulūb wa Shifā'uhā* (*Diseases of the Hearts and their Cure*), which was published along with another epistle, *al-Tuḥfah al-'Irāqīyah fī al-A'māl al-Qalbīyah* (*The Iraqi Gift on the Actions of the Heart*). He maintains that the matter of life and death of the heart is far more important than the life and death of the body. Consequently, having a hard heart is a clear sign of a misguidance and deviation. A heart only acquires its life from the oneness of Allāh and by responding to His call through obedience. It is important to note that Taymīyyah does not differentiate between the soul (*rūh*) and the self (*nafs*).

Ibn Al-Qayyim (d. 1350 CE), or Abu 'Abd Allāh Shams al-Dīn Abū 'Abd Allāh Muḥammad ibn Abī Bakr ibn Ayyub ibn Sa'd ibn Harz ibn Makki Zayn al-Din al-Zur'ī al-Dimashqī al-Hanbali, is more reverentially known as Imam Ibn al-Qayyim in Sunni tradition. Ibn al-Qayyim received extensive training in the traditional fields of Islāmic scholarship including: *Aqeedah* (Islāmic creed), *Fiqh* (Islāmic jurisprudence), *Tafsir* (Qur'ān exegesis), *Ilm al Kalam* (Islāmic theology), and Arabic grammar. His other famous students include Al-Hafidh Abul Faraj ibn Rajab, the Hanbali legal scholar; Al Hafidh Ismail ibn Kathir, a Shafi'i traditionalist and historian; and Al Hafidh Muhammad bin Abdul Hadi. Ibn Rajab (b) stated that Ibn al-Qayyim

> was extremely (*ilá al-ghayah al-quswá*) dedicated to divine devotion ('*ibadah*), spending the night in prayer (*tahajjud*) as well as prolonging ritual prayer, and he invoked the name of God (*ta'Allāha*), was eager to recall him (*lahija bi-al-dhikr*), articulated affection, repentance, and petitions of forgiveness and longing

directed to God (*shaffafa bi-al-mahabbah, wa-al-inabah wa-al-istighfar, wa-al-iftiqar ilá Allāh*), and expressed that he could be broken by him (*wa-al-inkisar lahu*) and that he is cast into his hands (*wa-al-itrah bayna yadayhi*), [all] while entering or leaving prayer ('*alá 'atabat 'ubudiya-tihi*) – to which I never witnessed anything comparable therein [the prayer] (*lam ushahid mithlahu fidhalik*).

(p. xiii)

Ibn al-Qayyim's books include *Tahthib Sunan Abi Dawud* (*Emendation of Sunan Abu Dawud*); *Al-Kalam al-Tayyib wa-al-'Amal al-Salih* (*The Essence of Good Words and Deeds*); commentaries on the book of Shaikh Abdullah al-Ansari, *Manazil-u Sa'ireen* (*Stations of the Seekers*); and *Zad al-Ma'ad* (*Provisions of the Hereafter*), from which his book on the Medicine of the Prophet (ﷺ) is extracted. Box 2.8 presents Ibn Al-Qayyim's psychology.

Box 2.8   Overview of Ibn Al-Qayyim

- One of the flag bearers of Islāmic psychology, though mainstream Islāmic psychologists today do not recognise him as one of the forerunners of the field.
- Highlighted the importance of meditation, reflection, and intro-spection in the pursuit of happiness (Awad et al., 2020).
- Identified three categories of pleasure: (1) necessity for survival, including food, shelter, and procreation; (2) advancing in social and professional circumstances to attain a position of power or authority; and (3) living a life of virtue and dedication to God (Abdul-Rahman, 2017).
- Offered a description of the different types and process of thinking, now known as metacognition, the study of how people think (Metcalfe & Shimamura, 1994).
- Types of thinking include: *Tafakkur* (thinking), *Tadhakkur* (remem-bering), *I'tibaar* (realising), and *Tadabbur* (deliberating) (Ibn al-Qayyim Al-Jawziyyah, 2011; Abdul-Rahman, 2017).
- Developed a stage-theory of cognition and behaviour: "An individual first has an involuntary thought. If the individual chooses to deliberate over this thought, it becomes an emotional motivation to act. If the individual continues to feed the emotional inclination, it will turn into a firm decision to act, and

then into an action, and then finally into a habit." (Abdul-Rahman, 2017; Badri, 2000, Cited by Awaad et al., 2020, p. 77).

- Proposed a number of spiritual interventions for curing psycho-spiritual diseases, which include faith in Allāh, worship, *Dhikr*, patience, supplication, and others.
- Proposed a model for cognitive restructuring that is based on the *Tawakkul* (reliance and trust) in Allāh for those who are suffering from deprivation or loss.

Ibn al-Qayyim wrote more than sixty books in various areas of Islām and compiled a large number of studies. Ibn al-Qayyim indicates that there are positive and negative kinds of pleasure seeking. Illegitimate pleasure is pleasure that results in pain, whereas legitimate pleasure is in the worship of God (Abdul-Rahman, 2017). While discussing the diseases of the heart, he maintains that there is not a diseases or sickness, whether it relates to one's heart or his body, that an observer who is gifted by Allāh with a sound understanding cannot find a cure for in the revelation (*Wahy*, i.e., Qur'ān and Sunnah). Ibn al-Qayyim went on to discuss the issue of satanic whispering or "*Waswâs al Qahri*", and he favoured the use of cognitive or conscious interventions to treat this disorder. That is, the individual has to resist the illegitimate pleasure, which will enable their resilience (*firasah*) to overcome these negative pleasures and will eventually bring the individual closer to God (Abdul-Rahman, 2017). It is stated,

The domain of satanic whispering in the unconscious can be tempered through conscious interventions. It is possible that through breaking free of distractions and attaining knowledge and consciousness of God a person can transform the entire dynamic of the unconscious. This struggle between the individual and Satan is a key dimension of the unconscious and the conscious that Ibn al-Qayyim also speaks about.

(Abdul-Rahman, 2017)

Ibn al-Qayyim advocated for the importance of mental health as

the second category of diseases of the heart are based on emotional states such as anxiety, sadness, depression, and anger.

This type of disease can be treated naturally by treating the cause or with medicine that goes against the cause ... and this is because the heart is harmed by what harms the body and vice versa.

(Ibn al-Qayyim, 2011, p. 26)

CONCLUSION

This is an overview of the contributions of theologians, philosophers, and physicians to the evolution and development of Islāmic psychology through the classical Golden Age. In the 20th and 21st centuries there are many scholars, thinkers, and clinicians who may or may not be directly related to the field of Islāmic psychology but who have made significant contributions to the integration of knowledge, including Allama Muhammad Iqbal, Sayyid Abul A'la Maududi, Syed Muhammad Al Naquib Bin Ali Al-Attas, Isma'il Raji Al-Faruqi, Anis Ahmad, and many others. Contemporary academics and clinicians who have made significant contributions to the revival of Islāmic psychology include Malik Badri, Amber Haque, Aisha Utz, Rasjid Skinner, Akhbar Husain, Rania Awaad, Muhammad Tahir Khalily, Suleyman Derin, Hamid Rafiei Honar, Saleh bin Ibrahim Al-Sanie, Ola Pavlova, Bagus Riyono, Hanan Dover, and G. Hussein Rassool. It is evident that the history of Islāmic psychology has been greatly influenced by many other Islāmic scholars, who have further established a foundation for contemporary Islāmic academics and clinicians. The biggest challenge is to keep Islāmic psychology within the paradigm of *Ahlus-Sunnah wa'l-Jamā'ah*, and beyond the realm of esoteric Sufism.

FURTHER READING

Haque, A. (2004). Psychology from Islamic Perspective: Contributions of Early Muslim Scholars and Challenges to Contemporary Muslim Psychologists. *Journal of Religion and Health*, 43(4), 357–377.

Rassool, G. Hussein, & Luqman, M.M. (2022). *Foundation of Islāmic Psychology: From Classical Scholars to Contemporary Thinkers*. Oxford: Routledge.

3

WHAT IS ISLĀMIC PSYCHOLOGY?

Box 3.1 Reflective practices

- What are the stages in the evolution of the definitions of psychology?
- What are the limitations of secular psychology?
- Why was the study of the soul abandoned in contemporary psychology?
- What is Islāmic psychology? Formulate your own definition of Islāmic psychology.

INTRODUCTION

Contemporary psychology has been promoted on a global scale, and its dominance has remained unchallenged in most clinical and academic institutions in the developing world, especially in Muslim-majority countries. Psychological knowledge has been increasingly criticised for Orientalist and Eurocentric perspectives and biases due to colonisation and globalisation (Rassool, 2022), though most psychologists generally adopt a generalist view that human behaviours and experiences are to some extent universal. What is certain, however, is that psychology and applied psychology can no longer be dissociated from the cultural and religious contexts that frame the lives of indigenous communities. However, Muslim psychologists, who have been educated in Western universities or even in their own countries, have been

DOI: 10.4324/9781003312956-3

acculturated as Muslim Freuds within a 'psycho-secular bubble' and as blind followers of the 'Master's Voice'.

The 1979 publication of Malik Badri's magnum opus, *The Dilemma of Muslim Psychologists*, acted as a beacon in the development of contemporary Islāmic psychology. This groundbreaking study was a warning to Muslim psychologists of the inherent dangers of blindly copying Western, non-Islāmic ideas and practices. I call this a form of "psychological *Taqleed*," which is imitating psychological theories and approaches and their applications in clinical practice with Muslim clients. Badri (1979) used the prophetic epitaph "in the Lizard's Hole" to describe the status quo of the activity of Muslim psychologists.

It was narrated from Abu Hurairah that the Messenger of Allāh (ﷺ) said: "You will most certainly follow the ways of those who came before you, arm's length by arm's length, forearm's length by forearm's length, hand span by hand span, until even if they entered a hole of a mastigure (lizard) you will enter it too." They said: "O Messenger of Allāh, (do you mean) the Jews and the Christians?" He said: "Who else?"

(Ibn Majah (b))

In this chapter, the aims are to examine the concept of Islāmic psychology, the evolution in the development of psychology, and the different approaches to Islāmic psychology.

CONTEXT OF DEVELOPMENT OF ISLĀMIC PSYCHOLOGY

The Islāmic awakening (*aṣ-Ṣaḥwah l- 'Islāmiyyah*) motivated by a desire to return to the fundamentals of Islāmic teaching and practices based on the Qur'ān and *Sunnah* and the work of Islāmic scholars has been in existence for a few decades (Rassool, 2021a). The emergence, current conceptualisations, and status of Islāmic psychology should be viewed in their broader context, namely, the Islamisation of Knowledge (IOK) movement (Rassool, 2021a). According to Ragab (1999), Islamisation refers to the "integration of Islāmic revealed knowledge and the human sciences" (p. 29). The Islamisation of Knowledge movement gained momentum in the 1970s with the "rise of the plight of the Muslim Ummah [due to colonisation], the secularisation of the educational system in Muslim majority countries, the global re-awakening of

Islāmic consciousness, and the concern of Muslim scholars towards the adoption of Western-oriented values and life-styles by Muslims" (Rassool, 2021a, p. 4). At the same time there was the "incompatibility of a reductionist, scientific naturalist and secular traditions in contemporary psychology. Academic institutions including the International Islāmic University of Malaysia, and the emerging publications from the International Institute of Islāmic Thought paved the way to "Islamise" the social sciences, including the discipline of psychology.

The evolution and development of 21st-century Islāmic psychology has been enabled by both individual scholars and organisations. The International Association of Muslim Psychologists (IAMP), located in Indonesia, was founded in 2006 by the late Professor Dr. Malik Badri. IAMP's mission is to promote a body of knowledge based on scientific investigations through human endeavours grounded in Islāmic teaching. There are other organisations that have been involved in the Islāmic psychology movement and have contributed, directly and indirectly, to the development of Islāmic psychology, including the Society for Advancement of Muslim Psychology (Pakistan); the Indian Council on Islāmic Perspective in Psychology (India); the Khalil Centre (US); the Islāmic Psychology Professional Association (UK); the Centre for Islāmic Psychology/Riphah Institute of Clinical and Professional psychology, Riphah International University (Pakistan); ISRA Academy- Charles Sturt University (Australia) and the International Association of Islāmic Psychology.

PSYCHOLOGY: DEFINITION AND CONTEXT

Etymologically, 'psychology' means the science of the soul, that is, 'psyche' means "breath, spirit, soul" and 'logia' means "study of" or "research" (Etymonline, 2020). With the advent of the separation of science and religion and the emergence of the Western scientific paradigm, the study of the soul became redundant as a discipline in psychology. From a historical viewpoint, there are several stages in the definition and study of psychology (Figure 3.1). The definitions of psychology from the literature vary from the scientific study of human behaviour and experience to the study of the human mind, its functions, and behaviour to the study of consciousness and unconsciousness. As a science, psychology attempts to study various phenomena in the areas of

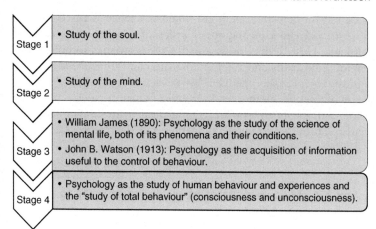

Figure 3.1 Stages in the study of psychology

biological or evolutionary processes, cognitive processes, emotional processes, behavioural processes, developmental processes, psychosomatic processes, organisational behaviours, health behaviours, and illnesses as well as how behaviours can be modified or changed. These subdisciplines are objects of psychological investigation through research and the use of the scientific method, which entails observation, experiment, cause and effect, comparison, generalisation, and the robust analysis of data. The main goals of psychology are to describe, explain, predict, and change human behaviours and mental processes.

It is important to provide a context for the abandonment of the study of the soul in contemporary psychology. From a historical perspective, the study of the soul held a prominent place in discussions related to psychology before the separation of science and religion and the emergence of Western scientific paradigm. The formal separation of science and religion resulted, in part, from the secularisation of Western contemporary societies. This alienation of religion within the paradigm of 'soulless' psychology means that "religious ideas, practice, and organizations lose their influence in the face of scientific and other knowledge" (McLeish, 1995, p. 668). The emphasis on the secularisation of modern psychology is based on the premise that religion is based upon faith, which cannot be evaluated by objective methods, whereas science is based on empiricism and experimentation in order to establish facts that are verifiable. Despite the uneasy coexistence between psychology and religion, spirituality and religion still matter and are embedded in the worldviews of many people. However, psychologists deny the reality of the unconscious, and a significant majority deny the reality of the soul. Zarabozo (2002) highlighted the main weaknesses of the secular approaches to psychology (Box 3.2).

Box 3.2   Main weaknesses of secular approaches to psychology

- Humans are viewed as independent of their Creator and Lord.
- Theories are based upon human intellect alone, while discounting revelation from the Creator.
- Knowledge and research focus only on the tangible aspects of humans, ignoring the spiritual and unseen elements.
- Behaviours are generally seen to be determined solely by drives, reflexes, conditioning, and social influences.

Source: Zaraboso, 2002, p. 49.

WHAT IS ISLĀMIC PSYCHOLOGY?

Islāmic psychology or *'ilm al-nafs* is concerned with the science of the *Nafs* ('self', 'soul', or 'psyche') based on an Islāmic perspective. Muslim classical scholars have used various terms to describe the concept of Islāmic psychology and psychotherapy, including *Tibb al-nufus, Ilaj al-nafs, al-Tibb al-rûhaniy, Tahdhib al-nufus, Tathir al-nufus, Tazkiyat al-nafs, Tasfiyat al-nufus,* and *Mudawat al-nufus* (Sham, 2015). Various terms used by scholars are presented below (Box 3.3) Though the focus of Islāmic psychology is on the science of the soul, it is more integrated within the holistic paradigm in the understanding of human nature and behaviour in the physical, social , psychological and spiritual dimensions.

Box 3.3   Terms for Islāmic psychology

- Miskawayh in *Tahdhib al-akhlaq*: *Tib al-nufus, Atibba' al-nufus*, or c *Ilaj al-nafs*.
- Abu Bakar al-Razi in *al-Tibb al-ruhani*: *al-Tibb al-ruhani*.
- Ibn Bajjah in *Ibn Bajjah's Psychology*: *'Ilm al-nafs*.
- Ibn al-Qayyim al-Jawziyya in *Risalat fi amrad al-qulub*: *Ilaj al-nafs*.
- Shaykh ibn Ata Allâh 'Sakandari in *Taj Al-Arus Al-Hawi Li Tahdhib Al-Nufus*: *Tahdhib al-nufus*.
- Muhammad c Uthman Najati in *'A1-Hadith al-Nabawi wa ilm al-Nafs'*: *Ilaj al-nafs*.

A review of the literature suggests that various themes have been used to explain the concept of Islāmic psychology. Table 3.1 presents a summary of the themes of Islāmic psychology from the literature.

Table 3.1 Summary of the themes of Islāmic psychology

Approach	Themes
Fitrah	*Rûh, Qalb, 'Aql, Nafs, Ihsas, Irada*.
Sufism (*Tasawwuf*)	Inner [*batin*] dimension and outer [*dhahir*] dimension.
Action	*Tawhîd, Taqwa, Tawba, Jihad al-Nafs*.
Rida	Reliance and attachment to God
Islāmic Personality Theory	Completely surrender and submit and obey the laws of God.
Spiritual diseases of the heart	Manifestation of God in nature. Behavioural patterns of all living. Islāmic paradigm.
Sufism (*Tasawwuf*)	Islāmic concepts or spiritual therapies: *Dhikr, Ruqya*, etc. Psychotherapy.
Tazkiyat al-nafs	Synonymous with the works of Al-Kindī, Al-Razi, Al-Balkhī, Al-Ghazālī.
Qur'ānic psychology	Soul, mental processes, and behaviour: principles of psychology and Islāmic sciences.

(Continued)

Table 3.1 Cont.

Approach	Themes
Muslim mental health	Teaching from the Holy Qur'ān, *Hādīth*, and *Sunnah*. Human psyche. Healthy mental state.
Western psychology and Islāmic theology	Theo-ethics, socio-ethics, and psycho-ethics.
Islāmic psychotherapy and counselling	Psychology about Muslims, by Muslims or for Muslims.
Islāmically integrated psychotherapy	Equate to Western conceptions (such as Freud's psychosexual development).

Table 3.1 demonstrates that themes regarding the concept of Islāmic psychology are diverse. In reality, there are bound to be multiple themes and definitions of Islāmic psychology based on the schools of thought, orientations, and worldviews of the author(s). In some cases, no attempt is made to define Islāmic psychology; rather, author(s) offer a description of some of its features, which could easily be labelled as "old wine in a new bottle". The definitions of Islāmic psychology are not a homogeneous academic entity. Let us examine a few definitions of Islāmic psychology from Kaplick & Skinner (2017), Alizi (2017), the International Association of Islamic Psychology (2018), and Keshavarzi et al. (2021) (Box 3.4).

Box 3.4   Definitions of Islāmic psychology

- Kaplick & Skinner (2017): Islam and psychology is "the inter-disciplinary field that explores human nature in relation to Islāmic sources and which uses this knowledge to bring human beings into their best possible state, physically, spiritually, cognitively, and emotionally" (p. 199).
- Alizi (2017): "The scientific study of manifestation of the soul in the form of behaviour and mental process."
- International Association of Islamic Psychology (2018): "Psychology, as it is generally practiced, only represents a part of the whole. Often the soul is not taken into account. Islamic psychology is a holistic approach that endeavours to better understand the nature of the self and the soul and the connection of the soul to the Divine. It

conceptualises the human being with a focus on the heart as the centre of the person more so than the mind and is grounded in the teachings of the Qur'an, Prophetic teachings, and the knowledge of the soul from the Islamic tradition. Islamic psychology embraces modern psychology, traditional spirituality, metaphysics and ontology."

- Keshavarzi et al. (2021): "The empirical, rational, and revelatory study of human cognition (*'Aql*), emotions (*Ihsas*), behavioural inclinations (*Nafs*), and spirit (*Rūḥ*)."

One of comprehensive definitions of Islāmic psychology is from the International Association of Islamic Psychology (2018), which explains what is lacking with contemporary psychology but does not define it. It provides some elements of Islāmic psychology based on Al-Ghazālī's concept of the soul. Though this is a comprehensive definition, the main concern is its fuzziness in contents and approach. The definition focuses on a one-size-fits-all paradigm and reads more like the principles of Islāmic psychology rather than an operational definition. Alizi's (2017) definition has the dual components of the use of scientific methodologies (Qur'ānic sciences and scientific method) and the inclusion of the soul. According to Alizi, the "definition will make Muslim psychologists use soul as the general framework in interpreting psychological data (behaviour and mental processes) instead of the limited approach of biological, psychodynamic, behavioural, humanistic, and cognitive perspectives in psychology." Kaplick and Skinner (2017) did not define Islāmic psychology, rather they defined Islām and psychology, which refers to the broader movement that relates Islam to psychology. This is a holistic definition of Islam and psychology that involves all the dimensions of human nature using knowledge from Islāmic sources. However, there is some deficit in the sources of knowledge in this definition. Does this mean that knowledge from other sources, such as empirical evidence, will not be entertained? The definition of Islāmic psychology of Keshavarzi et al. (2021) uses knowledge from different sources, including empirical, rational, and divine sources, to study the multidimensional nature of human behaviours and experiences. This definition is based on the use of Al-Ghazālī's conceptualisation of the human self. Though, it would be interesting to observe how this definition can be applied to the study of diverse clinical psycho-pathologies. Although any definition of Islāmic psychology is bound to be controversial, even among Islāmic psychologists, the following definition comes as close to encapsulating the essence of Islāmic psychology as is possible in a few words (Box 3.5).

> **Box 3.5**   Islāmic psychology has been defined as "the study of the soul, mental processes, and behaviour according to the principles of psychology and Islāmic sciences" (Rassool et al., 2020a).

The definition infers that aspects of the soul as well as cognitive, affective, and behavioural processes are studied within an evidence-based paradigm that is compatible with Islāmic beliefs and practices as well as Islāmic sciences. This dual discipline examines the understanding the nature of human behaviour and experiences involving all the dimensions of human nature from an Islāmic perspective. If we analyse the above definition, we can see an element of the study of the science of the soul. The author has now revised the definition of Islāmic psychology (Box 3.6), which is the definition that will be used in the context of this book.

> **Box 3.6**   Islāmic psychology is the study of the science of the soul, mental processes, and behaviour according to the principles of empirical psychology, rationality, and divine revelation from the Qurʾān and *Sunnah*.

Ibn Sina provides an explanation of the soul (Box 3.7). The soul is the essence of a human being, and it is a part of the physical body but not an image of the physical body. In Islāmic psychology it is the 'soul' that drives the behavioural, cognitive, emotional, physical, and spiritual dimensions. Utz (2011) suggested that the "essence of man is spiritual and metaphysical. And since the soul true nature is spiritual, the soul requires a spiritual connection to its source, the Creator" (p. 35). As the body itself can be affected by different psychosomatic disorders (body and mind), the human soul also suffers from the same ailments and symptoms as the body. In this context, diseases are related to spiritual matters, while secular psychologists often deny their effects on healing and curing. In addition, the human soul can also suffer from ailments that result, for example, from paranormal phenomena, including evil eye, possession syndrome (*Jinn*), and black magic (*Sihr*). In Islāmic psychology the *Fitrah* is an important concept in understanding human nature. The essence of the *Fitrah* is a natural predisposition to submit to the One God and the covenant of monotheism, which is embedded on each soul whether the person is Muslim or not.

Box 3.7   Ibn Sina defines the soul as the "primary perfection as it completes the race to become an actually existing kind" (Cited in Afesh, n.d.). Ibn Sina asserts that we infer the existence of the soul from the fact that we observe bodies that perform certain acts with some degree of will. These acts are exemplified in taking nourishment, growing, reproducing, moving, and perceiving. Since these acts do not belong to the nature of bodies, for this nature is devoid of will, they must belong to a principle they have other than bodies. This principle is what is called 'soul'.

The study of mental processes and behaviour involves the understanding of the cognitive, behavioural (normal and abnormal), emotional, and biological predispositions that influence the behaviour of people. This understanding depends on the best available research evidence, clinical expertise, and the individual characteristics of the client. This is known as evidence-based practice and is one source of knowledge. In contrast with contemporary scholarship in psychology, Islāmic psychology acknowledges that one of the most important sources of knowledge regarding human nature and behaviours is divine revelation. One of the weaknesses of the scientific method is its limited focus "on the physical world and almost complete disregard for spiritual aspects of the human being" (Utz, 2011, p. 36).

In effect, in an Islāmic epistemology (intellectual discourse that concerns the theory of knowledge in Islam and justifications) the

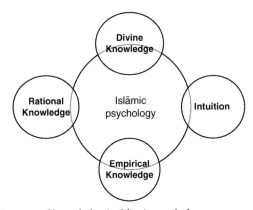

Figure 3.2 Sources of knowledge in Islāmic psychology

sources of knowledge are derived from divine revelation, intuition (process of knowledge acquisition through direct knowledge without reasoning or inferring), empirical evidence (acquisition of knowledge through experience), and the rational process (acquisition of knowledge through reasoning). Islāmic psychology uses all four sources of knowledge in the study of human behaviours and experiences: empirical evidence, rationality, intuition, and divine revelation. Figure 3.2 presents the sources of knowledge in Islāmic psychology.

In the paradigm of Islāmic psychology, it is the revelation from the Creator (the Qur'ān) that becomes the primary and most fundamental source of knowledge and understanding. This gives the Qur'ān precedence in dictating the main source of knowledge. The other form of knowledge is from the *Sunnah* of the Prophet Muhammad (ﷺ), which is the verbally transmitted record of the teachings, deeds and sayings, and silent permissions (or disapprovals) of the Messenger of Allāh (ﷺ), as well as the companions (*Sahaba*). The Islāmic sciences (*Ulūm al-dīn*) are a set of traditionally defined religious sciences, which include the study of Islāmic jurisprudence (*Fiqh*), prophetic traditions (*Hādīth*), interpretation of the Qur'ān (*Tafsīr*), rules for the proper recitation of the Qur'ān (*Tajwīd*) and the various ways in which the Qur'ān can be recited (*Qirā'ā*), and the biography of Prophet Muhammad (ﷺ) (*Seerah*). Within the paradigm of Islāmic psychology, to explain human behaviours there are the inherent dimensions of the nature of man and the inborn tendency to the unicity of God (*Fitrah*); the nature of the self with the multifaceted constellation of relationships between the heart (*Qalb*), soul (*Rûh*), desire-nature or behavioural inclination (*Nafs*), and intellect or reason (*'Aql*); and additional aspects of the unseen world.

DIFFERENCE BETWEEN PSYCHOLOGY AND ISLĀMIC PSYCHOLOGY

The differences between secular, mainstream psychology and Islāmic psychology are presented in Table 3.2. They contrast in terms of the basis of religious relationship; the sources of knowledge; what causes illness and maintains sound mental health; the responses to illness; and their values, growth, and development. In addition, the focus, purpose, and process of psychology are compared.

Table 3.2 Differences between psychology and Islāmic psychology

Factors	Psychology (Mainstream)	Islāmic psychology
Orientation	Judeo-Christian	Islāmic
Religious relationship	Oppositional Secular	Integrated
Sources of knowledge	Man-made theories Empirical Parochial	Divine revelation: Qur'ān and *Sunnah*
What causes illness?	Bio-psychosocial factors	Bio-psychosocial factors + Spiritual factors
Sound mental health	No divine intervention	Submission to God Integration of material and spiritual life
Values	Materialistic Socio-moral value structure Value laden Value dependent	God consciousness Spiritual-Divine will Islāmic values and morality

(*Continued*)

Table 3.2 Cont.

Factors	Psychology (Mainstream)	Islãmic psychology
Growth and development	Psychosocial development	Spiritual and psychosocial development
Focus	Limited focus on the physical world	Physical and metaphysical world
	Disregard for spiritual aspects of human beings	Regard for spiritual aspects of human beings
		Seen and unseen worlds
Purpose	Promotes personal growth/self-understanding	Promotes the clear purpose and meaning of life
Process	Individual based	Mutual responsibility
	Individual focused	Social obligation
		Healthy altruism
		Community cohesion
Responses to illness	Psychological reactions	Spiritual reactions: patience and prayers, charity, and reading the Qur'ãn
Relationship between mind and body	Mind-body interaction	Mind-body-soul interaction
Personal development	Unlimited freedom	Bonded freedom

Source: Adapted from Rassool (2016).

KINDS OF ISLÃMIC PSYCHOLOGY

Since the 20th century many kinds of Islãmic psychology have been developed and are in existence. A diversity of labels have been ascribed to Islãmic psychology. Some academics and clinicians have misused the concept outside the conceptual paradigm of Islãmic psychology. Al-Karam (2018) suggested,

Most of the contemporary scholarship that has been somewhat indiscriminately characterised as Islãmic Psychology might better be referred to as "Islam and Psychology" partly due to the lack of an agreed upon definition or theoretical model, and partly because the work is coming from a broad array of disconnected disciplines including psychology, theology, Arabic literature, philosophy, history, and mental health to name a few.

(p. 97)

Some of the kinds of Islámic psychology are presented in Figure 3.3.

One important figure in the Indian subcontinent is Ashraf Ali Thanvi (1873–1943), an Indian Muslim scholar and Sufi mentor of the Hanafi school. He is referred to as the "Physician of the Muslims" [*Hakim al-ummat*] and can be regarded as "Hakim-Psychologist". His work discusses personality theory in relation to the different stages of the *Nafs*, causes and classification of disease, and treatment or therapies. He used various psychosocial and spiritual interventions in the treatment of psychological and spiritual disorders. His therapy is known as *Sulook*, and he divided his therapies into two kinds: reading therapy and communication therapy.

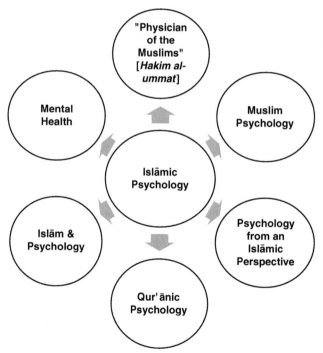

Figure 3.3 Kinds of Islámic psychology

Muslim psychology was developed in Pakistan in the late 1970s by Muhammad Ajmal and A.A. Rizvi. Rizvi later established the Society for Advancement of Muslim Psychology (SAMP) and the Institute of Muslim Psychology in Lahore, Pakistan. Muslim psychology is also taught as a module in the undergraduate psychology programme in a few universities in Pakistan. A Centre for Islāmic Psychology (Lahore Campus) was established in 2019 with the Riphah Institute of Clinical and Professional Psychology (RICPP), thus switching from Muslim Psychology to Islāmic Psychology. The first university-accredited course, a certificate course in Islāmic Psychology, was launched in September 2019 under the directorship of Professor Dr. G. Hussein Rassool (Saleem and Khalily, 2021). In 2022, the Centre for Islāmic Psychology launched the first university-accredited Advanced Diploma in Islāmic psychology and psychotherapy.

In India, there is the Indian Council on Islamic Perspective in Psychology (ICIPP) and the Centre for Study and Research (CSR), which promote and advance Islāmic perspectives in psychology. ICIPP and CSR provide a platform for students, academicians, researchers, and practitioners to discuss issues related to the nature, methods, and application of Islāmic psychology.

Lately, there is a new kind of psychology on the scene ascribed the label of Qur'ānic Psychology (Bakhtiar, 2019). The description of Bakhtiar's book states:

> Qur'ānic Psychology has a goal – to prepare us for our return to whence we came – to strengthen or return to our *fitrat* [*fitrah*] Allāh. As the monotheist we were created to be through engaging our moral intelligence (MI). We do this, according to Qur'ānic Psychology, by strengthening our *Nafs al-muṭma'innah* ('*aql*, reason, intellect, spirit) to dominate over our *Nafs al-ammārah* (affect-behaviour) through our reasoning, adhering to our mind (*sadr*), and *Nafs al-lawwāmah*, bringing awareness and consciousness to our *Nafs al-mulhamah* (*qalb*, "heart") of God-consciousness (*taqwa*) and the constant Presence of God in our lives.

What is of great interest and challenging is the identification of a fourth Qur'ānic aspect of the soul, the *Nafs al-mulhamah* (the inspired soul that fluctuates). Allāh knows best.

APPROACHES IN ISLĀMIC PSYCHOLOGY

A number of schools of thought have emerged in the midst of the knowledge gap in the conceptualisation of Islāmic psychology (Figure 3.4). Long (2014) described the two strands of forms of Islāmic psychology as having a theocentric-individualistic perspective. He suggested "that one approach is a critical revision of Western psychology – involving the exegesis of relevant passages from the Qur'ān or an elaboration of the classical Islāmic legacy" (p. 15). Kaplick and Skinner (2017) identified three broad approaches: the Islāmic filter approach, the comparison approach, and the Islāmic psychology approach.

Islāmic filter approach is the filtering of Western psychology through an Islāmic lens but operating within the paradigm of Western psychology. It may incorporate 'Indigenous' psychology. The comparison approach focuses on finding a common ground between Western psychological concepts and concepts from Islāmic sources, which may lead to duplicity in approach. The Islāmic psychology approach places emphasis on traditional Islāmic thought as the foundation of the discipline and is rooted in the Islāmic paradigm. Long's strands are similar

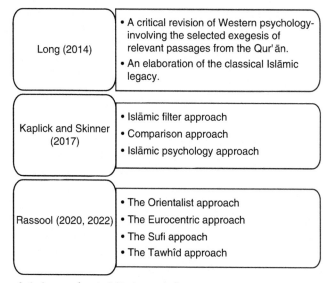

Long (2014)	• A critical revision of Western psychology-involving the selected exegesis of relevant passages from the Qur'ān. • An elaboration of the classical Islāmic legacy.
Kaplick and Skinner (2017)	• Islāmic filter approach • Comparison approach • Islāmic psychology approach
Rassool (2020, 2022)	• The Orientalist approach • The Eurocentric approach • The Sufi appoach • The Tawhîd approach

Figure 3.4 Approaches in Islāmic psychology

to the 'Filter and Islāmic psychology' approaches illustrated by Kaplick and Skinner (2017). Seedat (2020) commented,

> Both the comparison approach, attempting to demonstrate convergences, and the filter approach, aspiring to incorporate "Indigenous" Islāmic psychological practices into contemporary psychology, seem to be referenced primarily against Western psychological theory and thought. Whether and how knowledge from subaltern cultures may be transposed to dominant ones is highly contested.
>
> (p. 2)

In contrast, Rassool (2020) identified four schools of thought that emerged in the Islam and psychology movement. The four strands of Islāmic psychology are: the Orientalist approach, the Eurocentric approach, the Sufi approach, and the *Tawḥîd* paradigm approach. The Orientalist approach focuses on equating concepts in secular Western psychology with knowledge from Islāmic sources. A good example of this approach is the

> proposition that the Freudian seminal theory of the three structures of personality – namely the id, ego, and superego – are the same as the three spiritual ego states of the soul that are mentioned in the Noble Qur'ān. They claimed that the commanding soul *Nafs Ammārah* stands for the id, the soul *Nafs* is exemplified by the ego, and the tranquil soul *Nafs Muṭma'innah* stands for the superego. This undermined the richer and metaphysical nature of these Qur'ānic concepts.
>
> (Badri, 2021, p. xxi)

Instead of decolonising psychology, the Eurocentric approach, with minimalist Islāmic traditions embedded within its framework, is globalising Islāmic psychology.

The Sufi approach to Islāmic psychology places emphasis on the use of sources derived from the Qur'ān, *Sunnah*, and classical Islāmic scholars mixed with Sufi psychology, ideologies, and practices. Their conceptual and theoretical framework is rooted in the principles and teachings of Sufism, which are applied to contemporary psychology and psychotherapy. Sufi psychology is considered the science of the soul, and its application is the unification of oneness in the holistic dimension of one's being. Through this lens, this approach

> focuses on the health of the human soul or spiritual heart, with the purpose of changing the attributes of the heart and resultant social actions and relationships. This is because Sufis assume that human action is a manifestation of the state of the heart.
>
> (Şentürk, 2021, p. xviii)

The whole approach to Sufi tradition is reflected in the nature and scope of the therapist focused on the subject of *Tazkiyah* (Purification of the self) and *Tarbiyah* (Purification of the Heart). This is illustrated in the following statement:

> The TIIP [Traditional Islāmically Integrated therapist] is con-stantly engaged in this process of *Tarbiyah* both within themselves and in their relationship with either their own *Shaykh* or "righteous companion", as in al-Ghazālī's suggestion, so too do they employ this process as a central principle in their role as a therapist in working with each patient.
>
> (Khan et al. 2021, p. 58)

However, many scholars in the Creed ('*Aqeedah*) of *Ahlus-Sunnah Wal-Jamā'ah* "versed in Islāmic psychology believe that Sufism differs from the major branches of the Islāmic faith, such as jurisprudence or phi-losophy, because it stresses on *Ma'rifa* – a direct mode of knowing the world, the human soul, and God" (Abidi, 2021, p. 339). It was agreed upon by the Standing Committee (Islam Q&A, 2003a), who in their answer to a question about the ruling on Sufism said:

> Usually those that are called Sufis nowadays follow *bid'ahs* (innova-tions) that constitute *shirk*, as well as other kinds of *bid'ah*, such as when some of them say "*Madad ya sayyid* (Help, O Master)", and call upon the *Qutubs* ("holy men") and recite *dhikr* [a form of devotion] in unison using names which Allāh has not called Himself, like saying "*Huw, Huw* (He, He)" and "*Ah, Ah* (a contraction of the word 'Allāh')". Whoever reads their books will be aware of many of their innovations that constitute *shirk*, and other evils.
>
> (Islam Q&A, 2003a)

On the question of the Creed of the Sufi that stipulates that Allāh (Exalted be He) is Everywhere, His Eminence Shaykh Abdul-`Aziz ibn `Abdullah ibn Baz (n.d.) stated:

> The Sufi `Aqeedah (creed) which stipulates that Allāh (Exalted be He) is everywhere is a false one that contradicts the way of Ahl-ul-Sunnah wal-Jamā'ah (adherents to the Sunnah and the Muslim mainstream) among the Sahabah (Companions of the Prophet) and their followers, which is the true `Aqeedah. It entails believing that Allāh (Glorified be He) is established on His `Arsh (Allāh's Throne) above the heavens, and that He is above all His Creatures, according to His saying in the Qur'ān, The Most Gracious (Allāh) rose over (Istawâ) the (Mighty) Throne (in a manner that suits His Majesty). In Surah Taha [Qur'ān: 20], He (Glorified be He) also says in Surah Al-A`raf (Qur'ān: 7] Indeed, your Lord is Allāh, Who created the heavens and the earth in Six Days, and then He rose over (Istawâ) the Throne (really in a manner that suits His Majesty). This was mentioned in seven Ayahs (Qur'anic verses). He (Exalted be He) also says, Do you feel secure that He, Who is over the heaven (Allāh), will not cause the earth to sink with you, and then it should quake? Or do you feel secure that He, Who is over the heaven (Allāh), will not send against you a violent whirlwind? There are many Ayahs [verses] that stress this meaning. We recommend that you meditate on the Noble Qur'ān, as it includes light and guidance to all forms of goodness, according to Allāh's saying, Verily, this Qur'ān guides to that which is most just and right The Sunnah of the Messenger of Allāh (ﷺ) also guides us to all forms of goodness.

The final approach is the Tawhîd paradigm. This approach focuses on the monotheistic psychology of believing in Allāh Alone as God and Lord and attributing to Him Alone all the attributes of Lordship and Divinity. The Tawhîd paradigm approach subscribes to the articles of faith and Islāmic worldview, but its philosophy can be applied to psychological knowledge. According to the Tawhîdic paradigm approach, man's relationship and connection with Allāh revolve around the Oneness of God without partners. This relationship is based on the Qur'ān and Sunnah. The Qur'ān reminds us to not associate partners with God. These partners are not only idols but also considering someone else, like the Sufi Shaykhs and Saints, in the provision of good health, protection, and life. It is the remembrance of Allāh that give you *Shifa* (healing), sincerity, and happiness, not Sufi-oriented therapists. There is a set of beliefs and values within the *Tawhîd* paradigm approach that is disseminated in the principles of Islāmic psychology (see Chapter 1). The *Tawhîd* paradigm approach also guides the academic discipline and clinical application of Islāmic psychology in the integration of knowledge. That is acquired knowledge gained from the intuition, empirical evidence, rationality, and revealed knowledge from the Qur'ān and *Sunnah*. In a way, Islāmic psychology is a representation of the *Tawhîd* paradigm for knowledge integration. In Islāmic psychology all elements of knowledge in human nature, behaviours, and experiences are bound together and become integrated. The significant influence of the *Tawhîd* paradigm on Islāmic psychology is that it gives the latter unity and coherence through a dynamic relationship between man and His Creator. Islāmic psychology needs this *Tawhîd* framework for its identification and continued existence.

However, all approaches claim that they are in line with the traditions of *Ahl al-Sunnah wa'l-Jamaa'ah* for "those who adhere to the *Sunnah* and who unite upon it, not turning to anything else, whether that be in matters of belief (*'Aqeedah*) or matters of actions which are subject to *Shari* [*Shari'ah*] rulings" (Islam Q&A, 2001). It was narrated from 'Awf bin Malik that the Messenger of Allah (ﷺ) said:

> The Jews split into seventy-one sects, one of which will be in Paradise and seventy in Hell. The Christians split into seventy-two sects, seventy-one of which will be in Hell and one in Paradise. I swear by the One Whose Hand is the soul of Muhammad, my nation will split into seventy-three sects, one of which will be in Paradise and seventy-two in Hell. It was said: "O Messenger of Allah, who are they?" He said: "The main body."
>
> (Ibn Majah (c))

These indicated approaches are reflected in their conceptual framework and their clinical and educational practices.

NEW CONCEPT, NEW DANGER!

Despite all the labelling, ascribed and prescribed, there is a general consensus amongst academics and clinicians of the different schools of thought regarding the operational use of Islāmic psychology in the literature and clinical application. However, with new labelling there is new danger! Unfortunately, the concept of Islāmic psychology is now vulnerable to simplification, distortion, and false dichotomies when pounced on by lay and Muslim psychologists in the "Lizard's hole" with ideological and academic agendas. Fundamentally, anything related to medicine, psychiatry, psychopathology, and psychosocial issues is indicated under the umbrella of Islāmic psychology. There is what can be described as a 'potpourri' of psychology from Islāmic perspectives. In the literature and in academic Islāmic psychology, the emergence of bias or the favouring of information has become more apparent, which means that "confirmation bias causes people to give more weight to information that supports their beliefs, and less weight to information that contradicts them" (Effectiviology, 2022). Some academics and clinicians are being selective in the information they present in the general literature or at national and international conferences. Some are biased in promoting the works of certain authors; or they 'cherry pick' from those who share the same school of thought, approaches, or ideologies; or they focus only on evidence that supports their stance. This is happening with many students of Islāmic psychology, who blindly follow their 'Master's Voice'. I call this phenomenon "psychological *Taqleed*". Unfortunately, new conceptual and theoretical frameworks are being promoted on a global scale based on epistemological and ontological biases and inadequate methodology.

CONCLUSION

Islāmic psychology finds it roots in the Qur'ān and *Sunnah* and the Islāmic worldview, and it is regarded as a monotheistic psychology. At its core, Islāmic psychology focuses on the holistic dimension of the human being, and it examines and approaches human behaviours, motivations, emotions, spirituality, and healing through an Islāmic lens. Islāmic psychology centres on the concept of the inner-self, which is made up of four constructs: the heart (*Qalb*), the soul (*Rûh*), the self (*Nafs*), and the intellect (*'Aql*). Each part reflects a different aspect of the psyche, although they interact with each other in ways that overlap. With the *Fitrah*, they are the key components of the influence and study of Islāmic psychology. However, in order to have a valid and robust Islāmic psychology, it must meet all the criteria to be considered 'Islāmic'. That means it must adhere to authentic sources and proofs that are employed to understand human nature and behaviour from an Islāmic perspective based on the *Tawhîd* paradigm.

FURTHER READING

Rassool, G. Hussein. (2021d). Islamic Psychology: Context, Definitions, and Perspectives. In G. Hussein Rassool, *Islamic Psychology: Human Behaviour and Experience from an Islamic Perspective* (Chapter 1). Oxford: Routledge.

ROLE, COMPETENCE, AND SCOPE OF PRACTICE OF THE ISLĀMIC PSYCHOTHERAPIST

INTRODUCTION

Islāmic psychology is an emerging field. Its clinical applications are in demand due to the psychosocial and mental health issues encountered by the Muslim *Ummah* on a global scale. A number of socio-political occurrences both inside countries with large Muslim majorities and outside of them have triggered civil destabilisation and unrest, war, the displacement of people, ethnic cleansing, and refugees, resulting in generated a multiplicity of social and psychological problems. Major events and psychosocial issues affecting endogenous populations and Muslim migrants include Islamophobia, "gendered Islamophobia", hate rhetoric, discrimination, acculturative stress, trauma, post-traumatic stress disorders, microaggressions, chronic daily hassles, harassment, and many other psychosocial and psychiatric problems. Muslims with mental health problems are faced with a duality of discrimination as a result of their mental health problems and their Muslim identity. The failure to address problems faced by Muslims places high demands on medical and psychological healthcare services. These demands have not been matched by the service provision and delivery needed to meet the holistic needs of the Muslim clients. Despite increased progress in multicultural counselling and therapy, there is still a lack of therapeutic services that incorporate Islāmic worldview in their practice. Hence, there is growing demand for Muslim psychologists as well as growth in Islāmic psychology and psychotherapy. This chapter focuses on identifying the role of the Islāmic psychologist and psychotherapist as well as examining the process of entering the discipline, essential characteristics, competences, and the scope of practice.

ENTRY ROUTE INTO PSYCHOLOGY AND CLINICAL PSYCHOLOGY

There are several disciplines in psychology, and clinical psychology is one of the sub-disciplines. We can apply Islāmic principles in all fields of psychology, for example, in health psychology, counselling psychology, educational psychology, community psychology, social psychology, and other subdisciplines of psychological science. In fact, Muslim psychologists are required in all of the different branches of psychology. Many Muslim clients prefer to consult a Muslim psychologist because the therapeutic interventions will generally be in line with their Islāmic worldview. This section focuses on clinical psychology.

Once you have completed your basic degree in psychology, you can then choose the branch of psychology in which you wish to specialise. However, it is important to determine the requirements to become a licensed psychologist, because this differs from country to country. In some cases you will need to have completed a postgraduate degree relevant to clinical psychology, whilst in others you will need to complete a Doctorate to become a licensed psychologist. In addition, some countries require that after graduating in psychology you need to obtain experience working or volunteering in clinical-psychology settings, typically as an assistant psychologist. This route is the conventional route. Figure 4.1 presents the entry route to clinical psychology.

Figure 4.1 Entry route into clinical psychology

In some countries, like the United Kingdom, there is a fast-track route into clinical psychology where the BSc and MSc in psychology are integrated with the Doctorate in Clinical Psychology. The conventional route for entry into the study of psychology leads to a wide range of choices. If you do not have a degree in psychology, you can be eligible to undertake a conversion course in psychology. Though these courses are secular in approach, there may be an option to choose a theme in Islāmic psychology or psychotherapy for your dissertation, subject to the approval of your supervisor.

UNDERGRADUATE COURSE IN INTEGRATED ISLĀMIC PSYCHOLOGY

Currently, a limited number of universities on the global scale provide a direct route to undergraduate and postgraduate courses in integrated Islāmic psychology. Integrated Islāmic psychology, in this context, means evidence-based psychology with revealed knowledge from the Qur'ān and *Sunnah* as well as acquired knowledge from classical scholars and contemporary thinkers. Just a few universities will be mentioned here. One example is the Centre of Islāmic Psychology, Riphah Institute of Clinical and Professional Psychology (RICPP), Riphah International University, Pakistan. The RICPP provides a four-year BS Psychology programme and postgraduate courses in Clinical Psychology integrated with revealed knowledge. The basic goal is to integrate the scientific foundation of psychology with Islāmic sciences and ethics to support students as professionals and as Muslim citizens. At, Riphah International University, graduate students study in the postgraduate course in Clinical Psychology and then top up with the Advanced Diploma in Islāmic Psychology and Psychotherapy.

In Malaysia, the Abdulhamid Abusulayman Kulliyyah of Islāmic Revealed Knowledge and Human Sciences, International Islāmic University of Malaysia, offers an undergraduate degree in psychology integrating Islāmic revealed knowledge and human sciences. Its aims are to produce graduates who are knowledgeable about Islāmic and conventional perspectives on psychology in order to enable them to provide expertise and skills in serving the country and the *Ummah*. In Indonesia, over the years the Faculty of Psychology and Social

Cultural Sciences, Universitas Islām Indonesia, has become a pioneer in developing Islāmic psychology. The focus of the Bachelor of Psychology programme is to provide a strong vision pertaining to scientific development (learning, research, community service, and Islāmic mission) and commitment to values, especially in the development of Islāmic psychology. They may be other universities that offer these types of courses, but definitely not in Western universities. Some universities may offer, as part of their graduate programme in psychology, a module on Muslim psychology (Pakistan), Psychology in the Islāmic Tradition (Ibn Haldun University, Turkey), or Islāmic psychology. This approach to education had been called the "bolt-on" approach (Rassool, 2020b).

HOW TO BECOME AN ISLĀMIC PSYCHOTHERAPIST OR COUNSELLOR

There is no direct route to becoming an Islāmic psychotherapist or counsellor. Usually, you need to undertake training in a mainstream course in psychotherapy or counselling. Most employers and many clients look for practitioners with professional qualifications who are members of or accredited by a professional association. In the UK, there are no compulsory training courses or qualifications for therapists. However, the British Association for Counselling and Psychotherapy (BACP) and other professional associations set their own standards for training in counselling and psychotherapy. Students can choose to undertake a degree in counselling or psychotherapy that is accredited by either the BACP or by the UK Council for Psychotherapy (UKCP). Students on training courses are required to join a professional body as student members. There is also another independent route to training as a counselling psychologist, which is the Qualification in Counselling Psychology (QCoP).

BACP recommends a three-stage route to counselling or psychotherapy training, which can take three or four years: Stage 1 – Introduction to counselling; Stage 2 – Certificate in counselling skills, and Stage 3 – Core practitioner training (minimum level of a diploma in counselling or psychotherapy, but could be a bachelor's degree, master's degree, or doctorate). To become a BACP student member, you must be currently taking a course that meets the requirements for Stage 3. The course does not have to be BACP-accredited, but you will need to take the BACP Certificate of Proficiency before you can progress to become a registered member or be eligible for the BACP accreditation scheme. UKCP accredits training in psychotherapy. To become a UKCP-registered psychotherapist or psychotherapeutic counsellor, there is a need to complete accredited training, which typically takes between three and six years (part time). In addition, UKCP also requires approximately 450 hours of clinical practice, theory, and skills, and students must have therapy and supervision throughout.

The Institute of Islāmic Counselling and Well Being (UK) also provides a progression route into Islāmic Counselling with the provision of four qualifications of increasing advancement. It starts with the VRQ (Vocationally Related Qualification) Level 2 Certificate in Counselling Skills and continues with the Level 3 Certificate in Counselling Studies and the Islāmic Counselling Diploma in Therapeutic Counselling, the professional diploma. The Islāmic Counselling Level 5 qualification is intended to enable students to work in private practice. All are awarded by the Counselling and Psychotherapy Central Awarding Body (CPCAB).

UNIVERSITY-ACCREDITED COURSES IN ISLĀMIC PSYCHOLOGY AND PSYCHOTHERAPY

Currently, there are only two postgraduate-level, university-accredited courses being offered on Islāmic psychology and psychotherapy (Table 4.1). One is the Advanced Diploma in Islāmic Psychology and Psychotherapy at the Centre of Islāmic Psychology, Riphah Institute of Clinical and Professional Psychology (RICPP), Riphah International University, Pakistan. The aims of the course are to provide participants with in-depth knowledge of Islāmic psychology and ethics as well as the use of Islāmic psychotherapy or counselling with a strong research focus. It offers an opportunity to critically and creatively evaluate current approaches and practice issues in psychotherapy and counselling that are congruent with Islāmic ethics. The programme aims to equip participants to work as psychotherapists or counsellors while being cognisant of spiritual interventions and making independent clinical decisions in a variety of

Table 4.1 University-accredited courses in Islāmic psychology and psychotherapy

ADVANCED DIPLOMA IN ISLĀMIC PSYCHOLOGY & PSYCHOTHERAPY

CORE MODULES
- **MODULE 1: INTRODUCTION & CONTEXT OF ISLĀMIC PSYCHOLOGY AND PSYCHOTHERAPY**
  - Unit 1: Overview of Islāmic Psychology and Psychotherapy
  - Unit 2: History and Philosophy of Islāmic Psychology
  - Unit 3: Islāmic Ethics and Psychotherapy
  - Unit 4: Models and Approaches: Islāmic Psychotherapy and Counselling
- **MODULE 2: ADVANCED THEORY TO PRACTICE INTEGRATION THERAPIES CONGRUENT WITH ISLAMIC BELIEFS AND PRACTICES**
  - Unit 5: Psychodynamic Therapy
  - Unit 6: Humanistic Approach to Therapy
  - Unit 7: Cognitive-Behaviour Therapy
  - Unit 8: Solution-Focused Brief Therapy
  - Unit 9: Existentialist and Jungian Therapy
  - Unit 10: Marriage: Pre-Marital and Marital Therapy
- **MODULE 3: ISLĀMIC SCIENCES AND ETHICS**
  - Unit 11 : Islāmic Sciences and Ethics
- **MODULE 4: RESEARCH METHODS IN ISLĀMIC PSYCHOLOGY AND PSYCHOTHERAPY**
  - Unit 12: Islāmic Research Methods
- **MODULE 5: SPIRITUALITY AND SPIRITUAL INTERVENTIONS**
  - Unit 13: Spirituality: Use Of Qur'ān and *Hādīth* in Therapy
  - Unit 14: Spiritual Interventions from an Islāmic Perspective

ELECTIVE MODULES
- **MODULE 6: EDUCATIONAL DEVELOPMENT AND CLINICAL PLACEMENT**
  - Unit 15: Islāmic Psychology: Curriculum Development and Teaching
- **MODULE 7: CLINICAL PLACEMENT**
  - Unit 16: Clinical Placement

GRADUATE CERTIFICATE IN ISLĀMIC PSYCHOLOGY

- ISL401 Introduction to Islāmic Psychology
- ISL402 Islāmic Psychology: Human Behaviour and Experience
- ISL403 Applied Islāmic Psychology and Experience
- ISL470 Essentials of Islāmic Spirituality

settings based on an Islāmic perspective. The course duration is three semesters (based on the University's semester), and it is totally online. Admission requires a completed bachelor's degree in Psychology or Behavioural Sciences or an MA/MSc Degree in Psychology/Applied Psychology. Extra credit is given to those who have work experience in counselling, psychiatry, academia, or research. The course leads to the award of Riphah International University's Advanced Diploma in Islāmic Psychology and Psychotherapy.

Charles Sturt University, Australia, which has a compelling reputation in Islāmic education, established the Centre for Islamic Studies and Civilisation in partnership with the Islamic Sciences and Research Academy (ISRA Academy). Its Graduate Certificate in Islamic Psychology aims to examine the intersection of several disciplines – psychology of religion, spirituality, counselling, and Islam – and to explore the novel connections between them to formulate a holistic understanding of the psychology of the Muslim experience and mental health among Muslims. The ISRA Academy course runs for three semesters between February to November. The entry requirement is a completed Bachelor's degree (or AQF equivalent) in any discipline from a university or other tertiary education provider or, for those without a degree, no less than three years of work experience within the same industry as the course profile.

ROLE OF THE ISLĀMIC PSYCHOTHERAPIST OR COUNSELLOR

The focus of this section is to examine the role of the Islāmic psychotherapist or counsellor. Muslim psychologists working as clinicians or psychotherapists in statutory, non-statutory, or private settings have roles that, in many ways, are no different from other clinical psychologists. The clinical role of psychologists or psychotherapists as health providers is diverse, involving varying areas of care giving (primary, secondary, and tertiary care) and a variety of sub-specialties. There are some commonalities between the role of the mainstream psychotherapist and the role of the Islāmic psychotherapist. However, there are also significant differences. The most significant differences are the Islāmic understanding of the nature of human beings, the Islāmic worldview, and the incorporation of spirituality into the therapeutic process. In order to understand the role of the Islāmic psychotherapist or counsellor, it is important to understand the differences and commonalities between mainstream psychotherapy and Islāmic psychotherapy (Table 4.2).

Table 4.2 Differences between mainstream psychotherapy and Islāmic psychotherapy

	Psychotherapy (Mainstream)	*Islāmic psychotherapy*
Orientation	Judeo-Christian	Islāmic
Religious relationship	Oppositional Secular	Integrated
Sources of knowledge	Man-made theories Empirical Parochial	Divine revelation (Qur'ān) and *Sunnah*
What causes illness?	Bio-psychosocial factors	Bio-psychosocial factors + Spiritual factors
Sound mental health	No divine intervention	Submission to God Integration of material and spiritual life
Values	Materialistic Socio-moral value structure Value laden Value dependent	God consciousness Spiritual-Divine will Islāmic values and morality
Growth and development	Psychosocial development	Spiritual and psychosocial development
Focus	Limited focus on the physical world Disregard for spiritual aspects of human beings	Regard for spiritual aspects of human beings Seen and unseen worlds
Purpose	Promotes personal growth/self-understanding	Promotes the clear purpose and meaning of life
Process	Individual based Individual focused	Mutual responsibility Social obligation Healthy altruism
Responses to illness	Psychological reactions	Spiritual reactions: patience and prayers
Relationship between mind and body	Mind-body interaction	Mind-body-soul interaction

(*Continued*)

Table 4.2 Cont.

	Psychotherapy (Mainstream)	*Islāmic psychotherapy*
Personal development	Unlimited freedom	Bonded freedom
Intervention strategies	Based on Humanistic, cognitive-behavioural, and psychoanalytical interventions	Based on Humanistic, cognitive-behavioural, and spiritual interventions
Dream technique	Dream analysis (Freudian)	Use of Prophetic dream analysis
Undesired (negative) behaviour	Rationalisation	Therapy of repentance

Source: Adapted from Rassool (2016).

Contrasts between the two approaches are found in the relationship of religion, sources of knowledge, causes of illness, ways to maintain sound mental health, responses to illness, and their values, growth, and development. In addition, Table 4.2 compares each approach's focus, purpose, process, and intervention strategies. The Islāmic psychotherapist or counsellor has a multitude of roles, in addition to their conventional role (Table 4.3).

One important role of the Islāmic psychotherapist or counsellor is to understand the Islāmic worldview of the Muslim client. This has implications for the therapist, who should understand the client's interpersonal dynamics and individual, social, and community orientation, including familial, cultural, and religious factors, as well as have a vision of the world from an Islāmic lens. Ibrahim (1985) suggested that the concept of worldview, focusing on values, beliefs, and assumptions, is important in understanding the client's cultural perspectives. Understanding the worldview of the Muslim client enables the enhancement of rapport and the building of the therapeutic relationship. In addition, having a shared Islāmic worldview (therapist and client) increases clients' trust, leading to a positive therapeutic relationship (Ibrahim, 1999), enhanced trust, and hope, which brings about a solution (Frank and Frank, 1991).

Table 4.3 Role of the Islāmic psychotherapist or counsellor

Understand the Islāmic worldview of the Muslim client

Identify the spiritual dimension of aspects of illness behaviours

Enable the adoption of healthy and acceptable behaviours according to the *Shari'ah*

Enhance psychological and spiritual development

Practice enjoining what is right and forbidding what is wrong

Facilitate a return to the *Fitrah*, which may have been clouded

Instill that trials and tribulations are part of a Muslim's journey in this life

Instill hope

Give advice (*Nasseah*)

Develop intervention strategies for modifying deviant or distorted health beliefs

Promote self-care and self-management

Provide spiritual and psychosocial education

Challenge behaviours, if appropriate

Engage in clinical supervision/mentorship of others

Educate and train

Research

One role of the Islāmic psychotherapist or counsellor that is the antithesis of the role of a conventional psychotherapist is the giving of advice. In the mainstream view, giving advice is seen as a therapeutic error that can be counterproductive. However, recent evidence supports advice giving in psychotherapy that depends on the cultural and social context as well as on client and therapist variables (Duan et al., 2018). On the authority of Tameem ibn Aus ad-Daree, the Prophet (ﷺ) said, '"The *deen* (religion) is *Naseehah* (advice, sincerity).' We said, 'To whom?' He (ﷺ) said, 'To Allāh, His Book, His Messenger, and to the leaders of the Muslims and their common folk'" (Muslim (a)). Ibn Kathir (2000) (may Allāh have mercy on him) stated, "Sincerity towards the common folk of the Muslims means: guiding them to that which is in their best interests." In Islām, there is a general etiquette for giving sincere advice. Ibn Rajab (a) (may Allāh have mercy on him) said:

> With regard to giving sincere advice to the Muslims, [the one who wishes to do that] should love for them what he loves for himself, hate for them what he hates for himself, feel compassion for them, show mercy to their young ones, show respect to their elders, and share their grief and their joy, even if that is detrimental to his worldly interests, such as loving for prices to be dropped for them, even if that causes him to lose some profits on what he sells of trade goods. By the same token, he should hate everything that could cause them harm. He should love what is good for them and hope for harmony to exist among them and for them to continue enjoying the blessings of Allāh. He should pray that they always prevail against their enemies and that all harm be warded off from them. Abu 'Amr ibn as-Salaah said: Naseehah (sincerity, sincere advice) is a comprehensive word which means that the one who is sincere should want all kinds of good for the one to whom advice is offered and should try to achieve that for him.

Abu Hurayrah said, "I heard the Messenger of Allāh, (ﷺ) say, 'The rights a Muslim has over another Muslim are six' and then he mentioned that among them is 'When he asks him for advice, he should give him good counsel'" (Al-Adab Al-Mufrad (a)). Rassool (2016) suggested,

> Giving *Naseehah* involves guiding them towards that which will correct their affairs in both this life and the next. It involves

protecting them from harm, helping them in times of need, providing what is beneficial for them, encouraging them to do good, and forbidding them from evil with kindness and sincerity, and showing mercy towards them.

(p. 18)

In addition, it is also ordering them with *al-Ma'roof* (good), forbidding them from al-*Munkar* (evil) with kindness and sincerity, and showing mercy towards them. Rassool (2016) suggested that giving *Naseehah* (advice) is a community obligation (*Fard Kifayah*). That is, if a sufficient number of people perform it, then the obligation is lifted from the community as a whole, and it is obligatory according to the ability of the individual.

Allah, may He be exalted, says in the Qur'ān:

ٱدْعُ إِلَىٰ سَبِيلِ رَبِّكَ بِٱلْحِكْمَةِ وَٱلْمَوْعِظَةِ ٱلْحَسَنَةِ ۖ وَجَٰدِلْهُم بِٱلَّتِى هِىَ أَحْسَنُ ۚ

- *Invite to the way of your Lord with wisdom and good instruction and argue with them in a way that is best.*

(An-Nahl 16:125, interpretation of the meaning)

The giving of advice should be done on the basis of knowledge and clear proof. As-Sa'di (may Allah have mercy on him) said:

Wisdom dictates that giving advice to others should be done on the basis of knowledge, not ignorance, and that one should start with that which is more important, then that which is less important, and with that which is easy to explain and understand, and that which is more likely to be accepted. The advice should be given in a kind and gentle manner. If the person to whom the advice is given pays heed to this approach, which is based on wisdom, all well and good; otherwise, we should move on to exhorting him with good instruction, which means enjoining what is right and forbidding what is wrong, accompanied by mention of the reward from Allāh for doing good and the punishment for doing wrong.

(Sa'di, n.d., p. 452)

One neglected role of an effective therapist is the instillation of hope. The instillation of hope is an important part of psychotherapy and counselling, especially in existential psychotherapy. Yalom (2005) cites it as the first of eleven 'primary factors' in the therapeutic experience. The instillation of hope is also important in Islāmic psychotherapy and counselling. The instillation of hope offers a path back to a sense of possibility in our lives when almost all seems lost. For believers, it is asking God, the Almighty, to offer forgiveness, true blessings, and hope in trials and tribulations. Allāh informs us in the Qur'ān that with difficulty there is ease, and then He reaffirms this information (by repeating it).

فَإِنَّ مَعَ ٱلْعُسْرِ يُسْرًا

إِنَّ مَعَ ٱلْعُسْرِ يُسْرًا

- *For indeed, with hardship [will be] ease [i.e., relief]. Indeed, with hardship [will be] ease.*
  (Ash-Sharh 94:5–6, interpretation of the meaning)

Hope is an acknowledgment of the reality that things will get better and a time of ease will come. Hope and fear are components of the Islāmic spiritual model of motivation, and both fear and hope are beneficial to the heart (*Qalb*) in the purification of the soul (Rassool, 2021). Hope Therapy (Cheavens & Guter, 2018) is a therapeutic system in its own right, using narrative, solution-focused, and cognitive-behavioural techniques, and can be adapted for use in Islāmic psychotherapy and counselling. In addition, hope plays a leading role in the promotion of healthy behaviour, preventing diseases, and improving clients' quality of life. The Islāmic psychotherapist can contribute to the training and supervision of other staff in the practice of Islāmically modified psychosocial interventions and spiritual healing. They perform their clinical roles according to rigorous ethical principles and codes of conduct.

The role of the Traditional Islāmically Integrated Psychotherapy (TIIP) (Islāmic psychotherapist) practitioner has also been examined by Khan et al. (2021), who suggested,

It is important to understand that a TIIP therapist is not the first type of healer that al-Ghazālī mentions, i.e., a *Ṣūfī shaykh*. Nor is he/she solely a generic clinician who treats medical illnesses but is rather a combination of both domains.

(p. 41)

This means that the TIIP therapist serves a role that is an overlap between a clinician and a *Shaykh*, and the label they ascribed to this type of practitioner is *Rafiq/Khalil* (pp. 42–43). Khan et al. (2021) maintained that in the TIIP model, based on *Ṣūfī* traditions and ideologies,

therapeutic interventions reflect both Islāmic and clinical methods, but are delivered within an Islāmic worldview and are consistent with Islām's foundational principles of change. Modern behavioural research is integrated into the model inasmuch as it is consistent with these Islāmic principles.

(p. 49)

It is debatable how many clinicians would be able to reach the stage of *Rafiq/Khalil* practitioners, besides there is no available evidence to suggest the effectiveness of those pseudo *Shaykhs* in bringing real change to the Muslim clients.

CHARACTERISTICS OF AN ISLĀMIC PSYCHOTHERAPIST

وَجَـٰهِدُواْ فِى ٱللَّهِ حَقَّ جِهَادِهِۦ ۚ هُوَ ٱجْتَبَٮٰكُمْ وَمَا جَعَلَ عَلَيْكُمْ فِى ٱلدِّينِ مِنْ حَرَجٍ ۚ مِّلَّةَ أَبِيكُمْ إِبْرَٰهِيمَ ۚ هُوَ سَمَّٮٰكُمُ ٱلْمُسْلِمِينَ مِن قَبْلُ وَفِى هَـٰذَا لِيَكُونَ ٱلرَّسُولُ شَهِيدًا عَلَيْكُمْ وَتَكُونُواْ شُهَدَآءَ عَلَى ٱلنَّاسِ ۚ فَأَقِيمُواْ ٱلصَّلَوٰةَ وَءَاتُواْ ٱلزَّكَوٰةَ وَٱعْتَصِمُواْ بِٱللَّهِ هُوَ مَوْلَٮٰكُمْ ۖ فَنِعْمَ ٱلْمَوْلَىٰ وَنِعْمَ ٱلنَّصِيرُ

- *And strive for Allah with the striving due to Him. He has chosen you and has not placed upon you in the religion any difficulty. [It is] the religion of your father, Abraham. Allah named you "Muslims" before [in former scriptures] and in this [revelation] that the Messenger may be a witness over you and you may be witnesses over the people. So, establish prayer and give zakāh and hold fast to Allah. He is your protector; and excellent is the protector, and excellent is the helper.*

(Al-Haj 22:78, interpretation of the meaning)

The above verse is a direct appellation by Allāh to those who are believers in the religion of Islām and in the Qur'ān. This is also applicable to the Islāmic psychotherapist or counsellor. To be effective in psychotherapy or counselling, the Islāmic therapist needs to have certain characteristics. The underlying essence of good character and manners is to embody justice, righteousness, God-consciousness (*Taqwā*); to enjoin what is good and forbid what is wrong; to have love, kindness, and compassion; and to display the moral qualities exhibited by the Prophet Muhammad (ﷺ). In addition, the therapist should show the following generic characteristics: good psychological health, self-awareness, open mindedness, empathy, unconditional positive regard (with certain exception), genuineness and congruence, being non-judgmental, being judgemental when appropriate, tolerance for ambiguity, and cultural sensitivity and competence. However, those clinicians who have attained a high degree of proficiency and have accumulated experiences and wisdom are regarded as 'master' therapists. Skovholt and Jennings (2016) indicate several characteristics of an ideal master therapist (Box 4.1).

Box 4.1 Characteristics of an ideal 'master' therapist

- Is a voracious learner;
- Accumulates professional experiences;
- Values cognitive complexity and the ambiguity of the human condition;
- Is emotionally receptive, self-aware, reflective, non-defensive, and open to feedback;
- Possesses emotional wellbeing;
- Is aware of how their emotional health affects the quality of their work;
- Has enhanced interpersonal skills (listening, responding, and caring);
- Cultivates a working therapeutic alliance;
- Uses advanced therapeutic skills;
- Trusts that their patients have sufficient potential for positive change; and
- Has cultural competence.

Source: Adapted from Skovholt & Jennings, 2016, p. 13.

Some brief comments on the characteristics of the master therapist. Master therapists are practitioners who operate at the highest optimum level of therapy based on continuing professional development, skills development, and wisdom. It is assumed that the 'master' therapist is not bound by one particular school of psychology or set of assumptions but is inclined to operate in an integrated approach using tools and techniques that are tailor-made to meet the complex needs of their clients. Master therapists provide services within the boundaries of their competence, based on their education, training, supervised experience, consultation, study, personal and professional experiences.

Learners with an insatiable thirst for knowledge (voracious learner) is one of the significant key to developing a 'master' therapist. This type of learner will always manage to stay at the forefront of the psychology discipline and always open up to new learning. Islām has given great importance to the process of seeking knowledge. Allāh says in the Qur'ān:

اقْرَأْ بِاسْمِ رَبِّكَ ٱلَّذِى خَلَقَ

خَلَقَ ٱلْإِنسَـٰنَ مِنْ عَلَقٍ

اقْرَأْ وَرَبُّكَ ٱلْأَكْرَمُ

ٱلَّذِى عَلَّمَ بِٱلْقَلَمِ

عَلَّمَ ٱلْإِنسَـٰنَ مَا لَمْ يَعْلَمْ

- *Read in the name of your Lord Who created. He created man from a clot. Read and your Lord is the Most Honourable. Who taught by the pen. Taught man what he knew not.*
  (Al-'Alaq 96:1–5, interpretation of the meaning)

It is a religious duty upon Muslims to seek knowledge. Anas reported God's messenger (ﷺ). as saying, "The search for knowledge is an obligation laid on every Muslim" (*Mishkat al-Masabih*). However, it is important to seek authentic knowledge that is beneficial for the *Ummah* and humanity as a whole.

The acquisition of interpersonal relationships and caring skills is another characteristic of an effective master therapist. This is reflected in the statement by Ibrahim bin Al-Junaid, who stated that a "wise man said to his son: 'learn the art of listening as you learn the art of speaking. Listening well means maintaining eye contact, allowing the speaker to finish the speech, and restraining yourself from interrupting his speech'" (Cited in Bone, 2010). The Prophet (ﷺ) would listen attentively to anyone – his companions, wives, anyone on the streets, or the disbelievers. The master therapist also gives the person he is listening to the feeling that he or she is the most important person. It is stated that the Messenger of Allah (ﷺ) would

> turn his complete body towards the person making eye contact. His body language would reflect to the wants, feelings or thought being expressed. He would allow the person to complete his/her thoughts and would paraphrase to let the person know what he understood before responding to the communication.
>
> (Rahmaa Institute, n.d.)

The acquisition and maintenance of the relational skills of listening, responding, and caring indicate the role of empathy in this process. The Prophet (ﷺ) was fully conscious of the pivotal role empathy plays in developing astute and diligent human beings and was always keen to educate people from an early age on this important value (Rassool, 2016). In another verse of the Qur'ān, Allāh says:

$$لَقَدْ جَآءَكُمْ رَسُولٌ مِّنْ أَنفُسِكُمْ عَزِيزٌ عَلَيْهِ مَا عَنِتُّمْ حَرِيصٌ عَلَيْكُم بِٱلْمُؤْمِنِينَ رَءُوفٌ رَّحِيمٌ$$

- *There has certainly come to you a Messenger from among yourselves. Grievous to him is what you suffer; [he is] concerned over you and to the believers is kind and merciful.*
  (At-Tawbah 9:128, interpretation of the meaning)

This explanation is given by Ibn Kathir (2000) in his *Tafsir* (exegesis).

(He is eager for you), means that you gain guidance and acquire benefits in this life and the Hereafter, and He is kind and merciful. In addition, He is concerned by your suffering, anxious for your well-being, and gracious and merciful to the believers. There is an element of empathy in the behaviour of Messenger of Allah (ﷺ).

Empathy is the ability to put yourself in someone else's shoes and understand their emotions. In a *Hadīth*, the Prophet (ﷺ) wanted to try to have the believers understand one another and to understand what each other were feeling. Anas narrated that the Prophet (ﷺ) said: "None of you believes until he loves for his brother what he loves for himself" (Tirmidhi (b)). The significance of this *Hadīth* is that it stipulates one of the most important rules of behaviour in Islām. It underlines ways to develop love, kindness, compassion, and empathy.

One characteristic of an effective therapist that is neglected in the literature is the instillation of hope, which was examined in the previous section. The instillation of hope is an important part of therapeutic process. For master therapists, it is important that they trust that their clients have the potential to make positive change. The instilling of hope enables this process. Within the model of Khan et al. (2021), the TIIP practitioner's characteristics that should be present in such a facilitator of change are based on Al-Ghazālī's scheme. The characteristics include "(1) uprightness in character, (2) *Rifq* or companionship, and (3) scholarship, possessing strong foundational knowledge in the intricate process of facilitating change" (Al-Ghazālī, 2014, p. 257).

PROPOSED COMPETENCE OF THE ISLĀMIC PSYCHOTHERAPIST AND COUNSELLOR

Competence within the field of Islāmic psychology is an important area for development. It can be regarded as dynamic, multifaceted, and interconnected relationships that include knowledge, skills, attitudes, beliefs, and values based on an Islāmic paradigm. Competence is generally interpreted as a "measurable pattern of knowledge, skill, abilities, behaviours, and other characteristics that an individual needs to perform work roles or occupational functions successfully" (Rodriguez et al., 2002, p. 310). Competence in Islāmic psychology is a fluid process and is based on a continuum where different components of competency can be expanded. A proposed model for the development of competence for the Islāmic psychotherapist based on some of the domains of the Cube Model (Rodolfa et al., 2005) provides four specific domains in which any psychotherapist should retain competency during their career development (Figure 4.2).

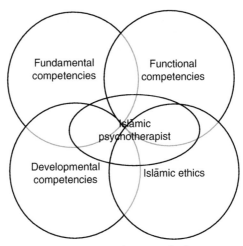

Figure 4.2 Model of competence in Islāmic psychotherapy

The component of ethics or Islāmic ethics is an area of competence not outlined by the diverse models of professional competence. The concept of ethical competence can be defined

> in terms of character strength, ethical awareness, moral judgement skills and willingness to do good. Virtuous professional [*sic*], experience of a professional, human communication, ethical knowledge and supporting surroundings in the organisation can be seen as prerequisites for ethical competence.
>
> (Kulju et al., 2016, p. 401)

The domains of competence include Islāmic ethics, fundamental competencies, functional competencies, and developmental competencies.

The first domain is composed of Islāmic ethics (*'Akhlaq*), which is derived from the Qur'ān and *Sunnah*. The Qur'ān reminds humankind of a number of basic moral and ethical values. Allāh mentions in the Qur'ān:

وَلْتَكُن مِّنكُمْ أُمَّةٌ يَدْعُونَ إِلَى ٱلْخَيْرِ وَيَأْمُرُونَ بِٱلْمَعْرُوفِ وَيَنْهَوْنَ عَنِ ٱلْمُنكَرِ ۚ وَأُوْلَٰئِكَ هُمُ ٱلْمُفْلِحُونَ

- *Let there be [arising] from you a nation inviting to [all that is] good,*
  enjoining what is right and forbidding what is wrong.
  (Ali-'Imran 3:104, interpretation of the meaning)

The directives in the Qur'ān primarily focus on the application of the universal ethical principles to personal and professional attitude and behaviours. It has been suggested that the

origin or the motivating factor in adherence to ethical principles under the Islāmic ethical philosophy is primarily the articles of faith of Islām. The practical application of ethical principles of the *Shari'ah* [Islāmic Law] with the basic universal ethical principles themselves, are a part of the basic code of ethical conduct in Islām.
(Understanding Islam, 2000)

This means that ethical behaviours, both personal and professional, are based on the *Shari'ah*, and any deviation from the ethical and moral principles is a practical negation of the elements of Islāmic faith. The aims of the *Shari'ah* are to protect five essentials (Box 4.2)

Box 4.2   The aims of the *Shari'ah* are to protect five essentials

- Protection of religion (*Deen*).
- Maintenance of life (*Nafs*).
- Protection of intellect ('*Aql*).
- Preservation of honour and progeny (*Nasl*).
- Protection of wealth (*Mal*).

According to Al Shatibi (Al-Raysuni, 2005), these five protections are necessities for the establishment of welfare in this world as well as in the world hereafter. Within this framework, Islāmic law covers both medicine and medical practices and include all the aspects of professionalism required to appropriately serve the individual, the family, and the community (El-Hazmi, 2002). This is also applicable to the Islāmic psychotherapist. Table 4.4 presents the domain of Islāmic ethics.

Table 4.4 Domain of Islāmic ethics

Type	Content
Knowledge-based competencies	The entry-level Islāmic psychotherapist will have knowledge of:
	• What is Islāmic ethics?
	• Islāmic bioethics
	• Professional codes of ethics and practice
	• Ethical principles
	• Islāmic code of medical and health ethics
	• Objectives of *Shari'ah* (Al-Raysuni, 2005)
	• Development of ethical behaviour
	• Ethical issues and dilemmas
	• Confidentiality
	• Informed consent
	• Conflicts arising from having multiple roles as an Islāmic psychotherapist
	• Role legitimacy
	• Self -development
	• Purification of the soul
Applied competencies	The entry-level Islāmic psychotherapist will be able to:
	• Observe guidelines and standards for Islāmic psychotherapy practice
	• Discuss the objectives of the *Shari'ah*
	• Apply the *Shari'ah* to personal and professional behaviours
	• Examine the professional codes of ethics and practice
	• Develop awareness of ethical issues and dilemmas in the psychotherapy relationship
	• Develop sound knowledge and understanding of the legal issues relevant to psychotherapy practice
	• Resolve ethical conflicts in relation to issues including autonomy, beneficence, privacy, informed consent, and confidentiality in the Islāmic context
	• Discuss the issues arising from having multiple roles as an Islāmic psychotherapist
	• Reflect values that are the underpinnings of Islāmic psychotherapy as a discipline in therapeutic interventions with patients

Table 4.4 Cont.

Type	Content
	• Appreciate and apply Islāmic values in the caring for and managing of patients • Embrace Islāmic values that will contribute to positive outcomes in work settings • Relay hope and optimism when working with people with mental health problems • Develop the capacity to reflect on and evaluate own values, priorities, etc.

The second domain is composed of fundamental competencies. These are the knowledge and values which underlie the function of the Islāmic psychotherapist. Basically, what fundamental knowledge does an Islāmic psychotherapist need to have to be able to function? There is the prerequisite of having a formal academic background in one of the following disciplines: psychology, clinical psychology, counselling psychology, or psychotherapy, which is accredited by a university or academic institution. In addition to knowledge of psychology, the therapist needs to have a sound background in Islāmic studies as well as formal training in Islāmic psychotherapy or counselling at an accredited university.

In this proposed domain, the curriculum contents of Islāmic studies would include the etiquette of seeking knowledge, sources of knowledge, fundamentals of Islamic belief/creed, principles of Islāmic law (*Usul al-Fiqh*), principles of *Hādīth* and *Hādīth* methodology, *Seerah*, and Qur'ān science. This is in contrast with TIIP, which requires their therapists (*Khalil/Rafiq*) to have

> Proficiency in Arabic; Prerequisite courses in Islāmic studies; Basic Islāmic law (*Mukhtaṣar al-Qudūrī* or its equivalent); Basic Islāmic theology (*Sharḥ al-'Aqīdah al-Ṭaḥāwiyyah* and *Bad' al-Amālī*); *Hadīth* studies (*Riyāḍ al-Ṣāliḥīn* and *Mishkāt al-Maṣābīḥ*); and Qur'ān studies (*Tarjumat al-Qur'ān* and *Tafsīr al-Jalālayn/al-Nasafī*) (the latter being taught for therapists specifically).
> (Khan et al., 2021, p. 52)

In fact, an Islāmic therapist may not need to be proficient in Arabic to attain a good comprehension of Islām or Islāmic psychotherapy. However, they should be able to recite the Qur'ān with adequate *Tajweed* (rules), which may come into use in the therapeutic process with clients. This could be supplemented by the use of *Tafsir* of the Qur'ān in English language. Table 4.5 presents the domain of the fundamental competencies.

Table 4.5 Domain of fundamental knowledge

Type	Content
Knowledge-based competencies	The entry-level Islāmic psychotherapist will have knowledge of:
	• Overview of Islāmic psychology and psychotherapy
	• History and philosophy of Islāmic psychology
	• Models and approaches of Islāmic psychotherapy and counselling
	• Psychodynamic therapy
	• Humanistic approach to therapy
	• Cognitive behaviour therapy
	• Solution-Focused Brief Therapy
	• Existentialist and Jungian therapy
	• Marriage: pre-marital and marital therapy
	• Narrative therapy
	• Islāmic sciences
	• Spirituality: Use of Qur'ān and *Hadīth* in therapy
	• Spiritual interventions from an Islāmic perspective
	• Religious coping strategy and spiritual interventions
	• Religious and spiritual coping
	• Types of coping strategies
	• Religious coping in an Islāmic context
	• Remembrance of Allāh
	• Prayer as a coping strategy
	• Making supplications
	• Healing from the Qur'ān

Table 4.5 Cont.

Type	Content
	• *Ruqyah* • Islāmic modified therapies
Applied competencies	The entry-level Islāmic psychotherapist will be able to: • Critically examine the concept of psychology and Islāmic psychology • Critically examine the concept of psychotherapy and Islāmic psychotherapy • Distinguish between the Western and Islāmic paradigms of psychology • Examine the role of the Islāmic psychotherapist • Examine the Islāmisation of psychology • Briefly trace the historical development of Islāmic psychology and psychotherapy • Discuss some of the models of Islāmic psychotherapy as well as their strengths and limitations • Discuss why psychoanalytic therapy is not congruent with Islāmic beliefs and practices • Discuss how congruent client-centred therapy is with Islāmic beliefs and practices • Discuss how congruent cognitive behaviour therapy is with Islāmic beliefs and practices • Discuss how congruent Solution-Focused Brief Therapy is with Islāmic beliefs and practices • Discuss how congruent Jungian therapy is with Islāmic beliefs and practices • Discuss how congruent narrative therapy is with Islāmic beliefs and practices • Discuss the principles of pre-marital and marital counselling from an Islāmic perspective • Discuss the various spiritual interventions that can be used during therapy • Discuss the fundamentals of Islāmic belief/creed • Examine the different authentic sources of knowledge in Islām

(Continued)

Table 4.5 Cont.

Type	Content
	• Differentiate between the reliable and non-reliable interpretations of the Qur'ān (*Tafsīr*) • Explain the basic features of the principles of *Tafsīr* • Examine the principles of Islāmic Law (*Usul al-Fiqh*) • Identify the methodology used in *Hadīth* • Examine the approaches used by Prophet Muhammad (ﷺ) in interpersonal relationships and communication

The third domain of the proposed model is functional competencies, which encompass the professional activities of the Islāmic psychotherapist. The competencies focus on therapeutic skills, assessment, therapeutic interventions, research, clinical supervision, and education and training. The practitioner should have embedded in their clinical and professional practice values, virtues, and morals grounded in the Islāmic tradition. The psychosocial interventions include evidenced-based interventions, Islāmically modified interventions (for example, Islāmically modified cognitive behaviour therapy), and spiritual interventions. In the case of spiritual interventions in this domain, there is *Ruqyah* (incantation), which is the practice of treating illnesses through Qur'ānic verses and invocations as prescribed by the Messenger of Allah (ﷺ), known as *Al Ruqyah al Shari'ah*. It is recommended that this should be performed by an *Imam* or *Raqi*. In relation to the research dimension of this domain, it is important to highlight that the requirements of Islāmic research are very similar to the requirements of *ijtihad*. Ijtihad "is a technical term of Islamic law that describes the process of making a legal decision by independent interpretation of the legal sources, the Qur'ān, and the Sunnah" (newworldencyclopedia.org, n.d.). Table 4.6 presents the domain of the functional competencies.

Table 4.6 Domain of functional competencies

Type	Content
Knowledge-based competencies	The entry-level Islāmic psychotherapist will have knowledge of:

- Islāmic etiquette in working with Muslim clients
- Therapeutic relationship and alliance
- Characteristics of the Islāmic psychotherapist
- Internal variables of the Islāmic psychotherapist
- Principles of assessment
- Integrated interdisciplinary assessment
- Use of religiosity instruments and other tools
- Theory and research guiding psychosocial interventions methods
- Therapeutic skills and interpersonal relationships
- Promotion of spiritual health
- Psychoeducation in mental health
- Psychiatric services and how to make referrals
- Research methodologies in social sciences
- The traditional methodology of the *Fuqaha'* (Jurists)
- Stages of research in Islāmic studies
- Integrated research methods in Islāmic psychology and psychotherapy
- Clinical supervision
- Models of clinical supervision
- Consultation and supervision
- Provision of consultation services to other professionals
- Management and leadership
- Islāmic psychology curriculum development and teaching
- Outcome-based learning outcomes
- Rasool's educational and conceptual framework for the integration of Islāmic ethics in the curriculum at all levels

(Continued)

Table 4.6 Cont.

Type	*Content*
Applied competencies	The entry-level Islāmic psychotherapist will be able to: • Apply Islāmic etiquette in working with Muslim patients • Discuss the ingredients in the development of an effective therapeutic relationship and alliance • Identify the characteristics of the Islāmic psychotherapist • Discuss the principles of assessment • Develop skills in integrated interdisciplinary assessment • Develop skills in the use of empirically supported religiosity instruments and other tools • Demonstrate the ability to access, evaluate, and utilise information to assist in assessment using emerging health technologies • Evaluate the theory and research guiding psychosocial intervention methods • Develop skills in communication and interpersonal relationships • Implement the promotion of spiritual health • Develop skills in the provision of psychoeducation in mental health • Utilise an evidence-based practice in the context of patient characteristics and worldview • Monitor and evaluate the process and outcomes of therapeutic interventions • Identify local mental health services and develop skills in how to make referrals • Assist with programme development, programme evaluation, and quality assurance efforts • Write research proposals • Conduct research on the outcomes of psychological treatments • Implement integrated research methods in Islāmic psychology and psychotherapy • Supervise students at all levels of training • Conduct peer supervision

Table 4.6 Cont.

Type	*Content*
	• Provide consultation in health and social-care settings
	• Provide training in Islāmic psychology and psychotherapy to mental health professionals and other disciplines
	• Provide effective leadership
	• Demonstrate the ability to integrate Islāmic psychology and ethics in the educational curriculum
	• Apply Rasool's educational and conceptual framework for the integration of Islāmic ethics in the curriculum at all levels
	• Promote meaningful, engaged learning for diverse students, regardless of their race, gender, ethnic heritage, or cultural background
	• Produce learning and teaching resources in Islāmic psychology
	• Reflect values that are the underpinnings of psychology as a discipline in therapeutic interventions with patients
	• Appreciate and apply Islāmic values in the caring and management of patients
	• Embrace Islāmic values that will contribute to positive outcomes in work settings
	• Relay hope and optimism when working with people with mental health problems
	• Develop the capacity to reflect on and evaluate own values, priorities, etc.

The fourth domain of the proposed model is a developmental perspective on competency known as continuing professional development. This set of competencies addresses the requirement to keep up to date on knowledge and address any knowledge gaps after the completion of training as a psychotherapist, because psychology knowledge is constantly growing and changing, which makes area of competency a lifelong goal. This is also a stage of professional development for those who pursue a higher degree, such as a Doctorate in Clinical Psychology or any other equivalent academic qualification. There is evidence to suggest that "interpersonal experiences in the personal life domain (early family life and adult personal life) and the professional life domain (interacting with clients, professional elders, and peers) are significant sources of influence for professional development" (Rønnestad & Skovholt, 2003, p. 5).

This domain is a self-directed process that incorporates self-reflection, reflective practices, undertaking clinical supervision, detoxification, and purification of the soul in the Islāmic traditions. These methods are also supplemented with professional continuing development courses in the field of Islāmic psychology and psychotherapy as well as keeping up-to-date by consulting peer-reviewed journals and books. Joining a self-help group, study circle, or professional association is also part of the process of continuous learning. Islāmic psychotherapists and counsellors have an ethical, personal, and professional responsibility to be cognisant of new knowledge from empirical research as well as to augment learning in Islamic studies. The purification of the soul (*Tazkiyah al-nafs*) is a continuing, ongoing process.

Table 4.7 Domain of developmental competencies

Type	Content
Knowledge-based competencies	The entry-level Islāmic psychotherapist will have knowledge of:
	• Islāmic studies
	• Evidence-based practice in psychology
	• Islāmic psychotherapy
	• Publishing
	• Virtues and morals in the Islāmic tradition
	• Purification of the soul (continuing)
Applied competencies	The entry-level Islāmic psychotherapist will be able to:
	• Increase knowledge of Islāmic studies
	• Increase knowledge of evidence-based practice in psychology

Table 4.7 Cont.

Type	Content
	• Undertake continuing professional development courses in Islāmic psychotherapy and counselling
	• Undertake continuing professional development courses in Islāmic-adapted interventions
	• Undertake a doctorate in Islāmic, clinical or counselling psychology
	• Read peer-reviewed journals
	• Read books on Islāmic psychology and psychotherapy
	• Write papers for peer-reviewed journals
	• Write book reviews for professional journals
	• Contribute a chapter to an edited collection or write a book on Islāmic psychology and psychotherapy based on clinical practice
	• Undertake research and evaluation of service provision and delivery
	• Reflect the values underpinning psychology as a discipline in therapeutic interventions with patients
	• Appreciate and apply Islāmic values in caring for and managing patients
	• Embrace Islāmic values that will contribute to positive outcomes in work settings
	• Relay hope and optimism when working with people with mental health problems
	• Develop the capacity to reflect on and evaluate own values, priorities, etc.

FOUR STAGES OF THE COMPETENCE MODEL

The competence model suggest that psychotherapists and counsellors progress through four stages when acquiring knowledge and developing therapeutic skills: unconscious incompetence, conscious incompetence, conscious competence, and unconscious competence (Figure 4.3). 'The Four Stages of Competence' was originally established by Gordon Training International in the 1970's. In the stage of unconscious incompetence, psychotherapists and counsellors are unaware of what they

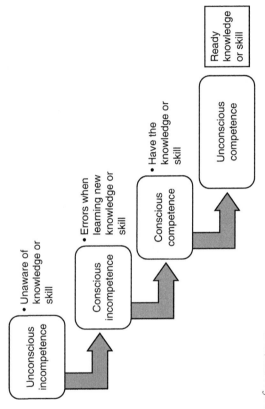

Figure 4.3 Four levels of competence

do not know, and they may not be able to identify their deficits in knowledge or skills in Islāmic psychology and psychotherapy. This the most vulnerable and risky stage for both the therapist and the client in the context of therapeutic interventions, as inappropriate relational interventions may be used, which may be harmful to clients. In the stage of conscious incompetence, psychotherapists and counsellors are able to identify the deficits in both knowledge and skills that result in error. In this context, in most cases, because they are conscious of incompetence, psychotherapists and counsellors may be able to recognise mistakes, redeem errors, or minimise their potential consequences. The stage of unconscious competence is a learning plateau. At this stage therapists are actively working on the development of newly acquired skills; however, more knowledge or skills refinement are needed to be fully competent on continuous basis. The final stage, unconscious competence, is when the novice has become the expert by mastering the knowledge and skills to the point that interventions become automatic and competence is well-established.

CONCLUSION

The above model and the taxonomy of the four domains in professional and clinical competence are not intended to be definitive. This is a preliminary attempt to formulate a model of competence for Islāmic psychotherapists. In future iterations of the competencies, it may be necessary to identify more explicitly the meaning of psychology knowledge based on the Islāmic tradition as well as the accompanying values and attitudes.

It should be noted that our goal was to provide an agenda for furthering the development and refinement of these competencies. For example, the Advanced Diploma in Islāmic Psychology and Psychotherapy at Riphah International University is based on the proposed model. It would be valuable to evaluate the model to assess whether the competencies summarised in the chapter are likely to be achieved by all students in this educational programme.

In sum, in order to produce the highest quality Islāmic psychotherapists and counsellors, it is important to have a synthesis of faith (*Iman*), knowledge (*Ilm*), good character (*Akhlaq*), and the qualities of the 'master' therapist.

THE *FITRAH*

The spiritual nature of human behaviour

INTRODUCTION

Fitra or *Fitrah* (Arabic: فطرة) is an important concept in Islāmic psychology because it is embedded in the human soul and it is an essential facet of human behaviour. In the *Encyclopaedia of Islam*, the Arabic word *Fiṭrah* is

> often translated as "original disposition," "natural constitution,"
> or "innate nature," … The related verb form *faṭara* occurs eight
> times in the Qurʾān, in the sense of "create" or "constitute"
> (Al-Anʾam 6:79, Al-Israʾ 17:51, and elsewhere) … [The word]
> *fāṭir* [appears] six times, to describe God as the "creator" of the
> heavens and the earth (Al-Anʾam 6:14, Yusuf 12:101, and
> elsewhere).
>
> (Hoover, 2016)

The Qurʾān makes it clear that we are all born with an innate sense of the truth and belief of God's existence, and we possess a certain intuitive knowledge of the moral good. The essence of the *Fitrah* is the natural spiritual nature of man and having a predisposition to submit to the One God. The *Fitrah* of human nature is to love God, truth, and beauty. The *Fitrah* embodies the notion that human beings are not endowed with a blank moral slate (tabula rasa) but are hardwired with an innate sense of morality and truth. This chapter examines the concept of *Fitrah*, its characteristics, its role, its alienation, and its relationship with human behaviour.

DOI: 10.4324/9781003312956-5

EXPLANATIONS AND DEFINITIONS OF *FITRAH*

This concept and explanation of *Fitrah* is derived from the Qur'ān; *Hadīth* literature; Islāmic jurisprudence; and classical, neo-classical, modern, and postmodern scholars. The explanations and concept of *Fitrah* is based on linguistic, religious, and pre-existential dimensions (Haque, n.d.). Accordingly,

> The linguistic meaning of *fitrah* refers to a person's *tabiya* or *mizaj*, which is the innate nature that exists in all human beings and is unalterable. In the religious dimension, *fitrah* is considered as a natural predisposition of a person to accept the Oneness of God (*Tawhîd*) or that a person is born with an innate faculty to know God. The pre-existential or metaphysical dimension refers to the notion that *fitrah* existed before the creation of humans, meaning that God created *fitrah* so humans could acknowledge Him as the One and Only God who has power over everything.
>
> (Haque, n.d., p. 2)

In contrast, Mohamed (1996) provides an explanation of *Fitrah* from a linguistic, religious, predestinarian, positive, neutral, and modern interpretation (pp. 35–83).

The Qur'ān uses the concept of *fitrah* in the following way:

فَأَقِمْ وَجْهَكَ لِلدِّينِ حَنِيفًا ۚ فِطْرَتَ ٱللَّهِ ٱلَّتِى فَطَرَ ٱلنَّاسَ عَلَيْهَا ۚ لَا تَبْدِيلَ لِخَلْقِ ٱللَّهِ ۚ ذَٰلِكَ ٱلدِّينُ ٱلْقَيِّمُ وَلَٰكِنَّ أَكْثَرَ ٱلنَّاسِ لَا يَعْلَمُونَ

- *So, direct your face toward the religion, inclining to truth. [Adhere to] the Fitrah of Allāh upon which He has created [all] people. No change should there be in the creation of Allāh. That is the correct religion, but most of the people do not know.*
  (Ar-Rum 30:30, interpretation of the meaning)

According to the exegesis of Ibn Kathir (2000), the above verse is the command to adhere to *Tawhîd*. Allāh says:

> so set your face and persevere in the religion which Allāh has prescribed for you, the worship of Allāh Alone, the religion of

Ibrahim, to which Allāh has guided you and which He has perfected for you with the utmost perfection. In this manner, you will also adhere to the sound *Fitrah* with which He created His creation. Allāh created His creation to recognise Him and know His *Tawhîd*, and that there is no God except Him.

It is worth noting that natural inclination towards the affirmation of *Tawhîd* is part of the *Fitrah*. *Tawhîd* is sometimes referred to as monotheism, meaning the belief in the Unicity or Oneness of Allāh, and He alone deserves to be worshipped. This covenant of monotheism is inscribed on every soul. Allāh mentions the covenant in the following verse:

وَإِذْ أَخَذَ رَبُّكَ مِنْ بَنِي آدَمَ مِنْ ظُهُورِهِمْ ذُرِّيَّتَهُمْ وَأَشْهَدَهُمْ عَلَى أَنْفُسِهِمْ أَلَسْتُ بِرَبِّكُمْ

قَالُوا بَلَى ۛ شَهِدْنَا ۚ أَنْ تَقُولُوا يَوْمَ الْقِيَامَةِ إِنَّا كُنَّا عَنْ هَذَا غَافِلِينَ

- *And (mention) when your Lord took from the children of Adam – from their loins – their descendants and made them testify of themselves, (saying to them): "Am I not your Lord?" They said: "Yes, we have testified." (This) lest you should say on the Day of Resurrection, "Indeed, we were of this unaware."*
(Al-Aʾraf 7:172, interpretation of the meaning)

The concept of *Tawhîd* is rooted in the metaphysical implications of *Fitrah*, and it is through the purification of the soul (*Tazkiyah-an Nafs*) that man can actualise his *Fitrah*. It has been suggested that it is the

[c]onscious verbal affirmation of the *Shahada* [Arabic term for the declaration of faith in One God (Allāh) and His messenger; this scared statement is: "There is no God but God (Allāh, i.e., there is none worthy of worship but Allāh), and Muhammad is the Messenger of Allāh."] [that] makes a person a Muslim and … begins the reconciliation with his original inbuilt faith in Allāh (*tawhîd*). Since *tawhid* is integral to *fitrah*, it is the principle which governs its metaphysical implications.
(Mohamed, 1996, p. 85).

Thus, it is in the nature of our own souls that we have the awareness about our Lord, Allāh, the Almighty. Ibn Kathir (2000) in his exegesis commented that

> Allāh stated that He brought the descendants of Adam out of their fathers' loins, and they testified against themselves that Allāh is their Lord and King and that there is no deity worthy of worship except Him. Allāh created them on this *Fitrah*, or way, just as He said in Ar-Rum 30:30.

The religious meaning of *Fitrah* is found in the following *Hadīth*:

- It is narrated by Abu Hurayrah that Allāh's Messenger (ﷺ) said, "Every child is born with a true faith of Islam (i.e., to worship none but Allāh Alone) but his parents convert him to Judaism, Christianity, or Magainism, as an animal delivers a perfect baby animal. Do you find it mutilated?" (Bukhari (a)).
- On the authority of al-Bara'b. 'Azib that Allāh's Messenger (ﷺ) said to a person: "O, so and so, as you go to your bed; the rest of the *Hadīth* is the same but with this variation of wording that he said: 'Thine Apostle whom Thou sent.' If you die that night you would die on *fitrah* [nature] and if you get up in the morning you would get up with a bliss" (Muslim (d)).

Allāh's Messenger (ﷺ) informed us that every child is born on the *Fitrah*; this means that the child submits to the laws of Allāh as his Lord and Creator, and his soul adheres to the correct beliefs and truth. His parents and the socialisation process make him follow the religion of the parent or significant others. The Messenger of Allāh (ﷺ) said:

> Allāh said: "I created My slaves as *haneefs* (believers in pure monotheism), then the *Shaytaan* [devil] misled them from their religion; he forbade them what I had permitted to them and commanded them to associate others with Me for which I had not sent down any authority."

This means that

> when it is said that a child is born as a Muslim [it means] that he is born inherently ready, when he reaches the age of discretion, if he is given the choice between Islam and its opposite, to prefer Islam over its opposite and to choose Islam as his religion, so long as there is nothing to prevent him from doing so, such as his whims and desires or tribalism. Following his desires makes him prefer falsehood so that he may attain some share of leadership or wealth, and tribalism or racial pride makes him follow his forefathers or elders, even if they are not following true guidance.
>
> (Islam Q&A, 2009)

EVIDENCE OF THE EXISTENCE OF THE *FITRAH*

There is evidence of the existence of the *Fitrah* in both Islāmic theology and empirical studies. In fact, Ibn Taymiyyah (1991) has argued what is necessitated by the *Fitrah* "requires no proof, because it is the most firmly-rooted of epistemologies, the most established of all knowledges, and the foundation of all foundations" (p. 72). However, the Qur'ān and the *Sunnah* mention the concept of the *Fitrah*. Allāh says in the Qur'ān:

وَلَئِنْ سَأَلْتَهُمْ مَنْ خَلَقَهُمْ لَيَقُولُنَّ اللَّهُ ۖ فَأَنَّىٰ يُؤْفَكُونَ

- *And if you asked them who created them, they would surely say: "Allāh." So how are they deluded?*

  (Az-Zukhruf 43:87, interpretation of the meaning)

وَلَئِنْ سَأَلْتَهُمْ مَنْ خَلَقَ السَّمَاوَاتِ وَالْأَرْضَ لَيَقُولُنَّ اللَّهُ ۚ قُلْ أَفَرَأَيْتُمْ مَا تَدْعُونَ مِنْ دُونِ اللَّهِ إِنْ أَرَادَنِيَ اللَّهُ بِضُرٍّ هَلْ هُنَّ كَاشِفَاتُ ضُرِّهِ أَوْ أَرَادَنِي بِرَحْمَةٍ هَلْ هُنَّ مُمْسِكَاتُ رَحْمَتِهِ ۚ قُلْ حَسْبِيَ اللَّهُ ۖ عَلَيْهِ يَتَوَكَّلُ الْمُتَوَكِّلُونَ

- *And if you asked them: "Who created the heavens and the earth?" They would surely say: "Allāh." Say: "Then have you considered what you invoke besides Allāh?"*

  (Az-Zumar 39:38, interpretation of the meaning)

According to Islāmic theology, the belief in God is built in human soul of the *Fitrah*. That is why an overwhelming majority of the people in the world believe in God in one form or another. A survey from the Pew Research Center shows that 62% of people say that religion plays an important role in their lives, while 61% agree that God plays an important role in their lives (Tamir et al., 2020). In addition, it is estimated that

> 84% of the world's population identifies with a religious group. Members of this demographic are generally younger and produce more children than those who have no religious affiliation, so the world is getting more religious, not less – although there are significant geographical variations.
>
> (Sherwood, 2018)

The findings of research studies suggest that children below the age of five find it easier to believe in some superhuman properties and may continue to believe in all-seeing, all-knowing supernatural agents, such as a god or gods (University of Oxford, 2011). Ibn Taymīyyah (1991) has noted that God is known to be All-Seeing and All-Hearing by one's *Fitrah*. In contemporary period, neuroscience research supports the idea that the brain is primed to "believe" (Azar, 2010). It has also been suggested that children naturally develop a belief in God because their mental mechanisms have properties that favour learning about God (Barrett, 2012). In an earlier publication, Barrett claimed that young people have a predisposition to believe in a supreme being and children are more likely to believe in creationism rather than evolution, despite what they may be told by parents or teachers (Beckford, 2008). He added that anthropologists have found that in some cultures children believe in God even when religious teachings are withheld from them.

Rottman and Kelemen (2012) suggest that "religion primarily stems from within the person rather than from external, socially organised sources … evolved components of the human mind tend to lead people towards religiosity early in life" (pp. 206–207). In addition, the authors claimed that "recent evidence from cognitive scientists of religion, anthropology, and psychologists suggest that there is strong evidence that young children can in fact be religious" (p. 205). There is also evidence to suggest that humans have an innate circuit with a sense of moral virtue and judgement. Babies, even before they can speak or walk, have been found to feel empathy and compassion, judge the good and bad, act to soothe those in distress, and have a rudimentary sense of justice (Bloom, 2013). The God gene hypothesis proposes that human spirituality is influenced by heredity and a specific gene (VMAT2) predisposes humans towards spiritual or mystic experiences (Hamer, 2004; Asadi et al., 2016).

SCHOLARS' UNDERSTANDING OF THE *FITRAH*

Ibn Taymīyyah (2000) stated,

> God created man with a particular nature, *fitrah*. The beliefs, values and the principles of Islāmic life and society have their roots in this *fitrah*. Islam is the religion of *fitrah*, and the whole purpose of Islam is the perfection of man on the lines of his *fitrah*. Reason is part of *fitrah*.
>
> (p. xxxiii)

Islam is also called *Dīn al-Fitrah*, the religion of human nature and the natural religion for humankind to believe in and submit to One Creator. Ibn Taymīyyah (2000) commented on the *Hādīth* of Allāh's Messenger (ﷺ), stating,

> What he [The Prophet] meant is that there is a certain nature with which God created man, and that is the nature of Islam. God endowed humankind with this essential nature the day He addressed them saying, "Am I not your Lord?" and they said, "Yes, You are" (Al-A'raf 7:172).
>
> (p. 3)

Abû Haytham stated, in the context of the *Hādīth* of Allāh's Messenger (ﷺ),

> And if his parents are Jews, they make him a Jew, with respect to his worldly situation [i.e., with respect to inheritance, etc.]; and if Christians, they make him a Christian, with respect to that situation; and if Magians, they make him a Magian, with respect

to that situation; his situation is the same as that of his parents until his tongue speaks for him; but if he dies before his attaining to the age when sexual maturity begins to show itself, he dies in a state of conformity to his preceding natural constitution, with which he was created in his mother's womb.

(Ibn Manzûr, 1988, p. 1109)

According to Mohamed (1996), citing Ibn Taymīyyah (1981),

The legal implication of this Hādīth is that all children are born pure, sinless and predisposed to belief in one God; moreover, they are of the inmates of Paradise; however, if their parents are non–Muslims, the religion of their parents will be applicable to them in this world.

(pp. 382–383)

Ibn Qutayba al-Daynuri (1983) suggested that

Islāmic theology does not teach that children are born Muslim, but rather that they are born with a simple spiritual and intellectual inclination towards God and towards good, for God took a covenant with humanity prior to their earthly existence (Al-A'raf 7:172) and it is this primordial affirmation of God that yields the tendency to journey towards Him and towards good in this earthly existence. Thus, every child is born with a natural spiritual, moral and intellectual constitution by which they make sense of reality, and this inborn tendency is affirmed and nourished by the revealed system of guidance known as Islam.

(pp. 58–59)

Table 5.1 presents the scholars' understanding of the *Fitrah*.

CHARACTERISTICS OF *FITRAH*

Fitrah has both spiritual and physical elements. Ibn Ashour

divided the *fitrah* (innate nature) into: Physical, such as sensory characteristics with which man was created; Mental, such as ability to comprehend the Lord's laws. The basic criterion for

Table 5.1 Scholars' understanding of the *Fitrah*

Scholars	Definition or Explanation of Fitrah
Al-Tabari	*Fitrah* is the *deen* (way or religion) of Allāh.
Abû Haytham	*Fitrah* means to be born either prosperous or unprosperous [in relation to the soul].
Abu Ishaaq az-Zajjaaj	"Allah, may He be glorified and exalted, created people with the inclination to believe in Him according to what is mentioned in the *hadith*. Allah, may He be exalted, took from the loins of Adam his progeny like tiny particles, and made them testify concerning themselves that He was their Creator [al-A'raaf 7:172]" (Islam Q&A, 2017).
Abu l-Lait as-Samarqandi	"Humans and *Jinn* are created with *fitrah*, and thus obligated (*taklīf*) to follow God's lawn" (p. 243).
Ibn Qutaybah	"'Every newborn is born in a state of *fitrah*' refers to the covenant that Allah took from them when they were in the loins of their father Adam, 'and made them testify concerning themselves (saying): "Am I not your Lord?" They said: "Yes"' [al-A'raf 7:172]" (Islam Q&A, 2017).
Al-Sayyuti	"The best explanation of *fitrah* is that it is the *Sunnah* (way) of all of the Prophets which is in agreement with (all of) the revealed Laws, indicating that it is a response to naturally created inclinations. In the Holy Qur'an, Almighty God, the Most High and Exalted, has identified the pure *fitrah* with which He created mankind" (Cited in www.missionislam.com).
Ibnu Ashur	*Fitrah* is equated with rational faculty or sound moral judgement, which is engraved in the human soul, that affirms moral laws (Ibnu Ashur, 2009, p. 62).
Imam Nawawi	*Fitrah* is the unconfirmed state which exists until the individual consciously acknowledges his belief (Cited in Mohamed, 1966).
Al-Faruqi	The *fitrah* or innate common sense is a faculty where people understand the quality dimension of reality. This is the faculty of people granted the knowledge to know Allāh (Al-Faruqi, 1980).

Table 5.1 Cont.

Scholars	Definition or Explanation of Fitrah
Al-Attas	"When we say that such a man is fulfilling the purpose for his creation and existence, it is obvious that that man's obligation to serve God is felt by him as normal because it comes as a natural inclination on the man's part to do so. This natural tendency in man to serve and worship God is also referred to as *Dín* … here in the religious context it has a more specific signification of the natural state of being called '*Fitrah*'. In fact, *Dín* also means '*Fitrah*'. It is the pattern according to which God has created all things" (Al-Attas, 1985, pp. 57–58).
Langgulung	"*Fitrah* can be viewed from two perspectives: Human potential (the nurture of the virtuous attributes of God in oneself) and Divine revelations (*wahy*) to His Prophets and Messengers in the form of Islam and *Tawhid*. This means that the religion revealed by Allāh to His messengers through His Revelations is suited to the basic potential or *fitrah* (nature) of mankind" (Cited in Bhat, 2016, p. 167).
Mohamed	"*Fitrah* may be defined as a natural predisposition for good and for submission to the One God" (Mohamed, 1966).
Badawi & Haleem	*Fitrah* is "the genesis of creation, the original unadulterated nature of things or in other words the unassailable natural disposition" (Badawi & Haleem, 2008, p. 717).
Utz	*Fitrah* is "the pristine nature within humans that leads them to acknowledge the truth of God's existence and to follow His guidance" (Utz, 2011, p. 47).

determining what is in accordance with the *fitrah* and what is inconsistent with it, are the rulings of the heavenly laws. Whatever those heavenly laws guided to, is *fitrah*, and whatever they prohibited, is against *fitrah*.

(Cited in Oziev, 2022)

The spiritual element is the natural inclination to worship God alone, and it includes compliance with what God and His Messenger explained. That is, human behaviour should adhere to the revealed Laws (the *Shari'ah*) and the *Sunnah* of the Allāh's Messenger (ﷺ). It is a natural compass of good and evil and for humankind to distinguish behaviours that are allowed (*halal*) and those who are forbidden (*haram*). In the Qur'ān, Almighty Allāh, the Most High and Exalted, has identified the pure *Fitrah* with which He created mankind:

فَأَقِمْ وَجْهَكَ لِلدِّينِ حَنِيفاً ۚ فِطْرَتَ اللَّهِ الَّتِي فَطَرَ النَّاسَ عَلَيْهَا ۚ لَا تَبْدِيلَ لِخَلْقِ اللَّهِ ۚ

ذَٰلِكَ الدِّينُ الْقَيِّمُ وَلَٰكِنَّ أَكْثَرَ النَّاسِ لَا يَعْلَمُونَ

- *So, direct your face toward the religion, inclining to truth. [Adhere to] the Fitrah of Allāh upon which He has created [all] people. No change should there be in the creation of Allāh. That is the correct religion, but most of the people do not know.*
(Ar-Rum 30:30, interpretation of the meaning)

In this verse, Allāh, the Almighty identifies the pure *Fitrah* with which He created mankind and for mankind to adhere to pure monotheism. It has been suggested that "Believing in Oneness of God, concept of healthy family (male and female only), etc., are the only correct *fitrah* (innate nature)" (Oziev, 2022). The belief in the Oneness and Unicity of Allāh inspires a person to complete obedience to Allāh and His Messenger (ﷺ). Believers who worship Allāh are in congruence with the natural inclination of their souls in service of Allāh. It has been suggested that this

spiritual and rational urge (to believe in Allāh) is the strongest factor that prompts man to believe in Allāh and affirm His Oneness, because it is usually stronger than any other impulses that may lead man to fall into ignorance and doubt. Often this urge (to believe) may overwhelm a person and make him realise the belief in divine Oneness (*Tawhîd*) deep in his heart at times of crisis and calamity, even if the one who still has that sound natural inclination (*fitrah*) is pretending today to be an atheist. The call of *Tawhîd* is still urging him from deep inside to believe, because of this natural inclination (*fitrah*) which is the first covenant taken from the sons of Adam.

(Islam Q&A, 2017)

It would be valuable to reflect on the statements made by Ibn Sina on the meaning of the *Fitrah* (Box 5.1).

Box 5.1   Ibn Sina on the meaning of the *Fitrah*

"The meaning of *Fitrah* is that a person imagines himself having happened in this world at once while he is sane, but he did not hear an opinion, did not believe a certain path, did not associate with a nation, did not know politics, but he witnessed the sensibilities and took them. Then he exposes a thing to his mind and doubts it. And if his doubt prevails, then *Fitrah* does not support it. And if his doubt did not prevail, then it is required by *Fitrah*."

(Cited in Oziev, 2022)

In the context of the statements made by Ibn Sina, it may be inferred that the "divine law is the only criterion to properly judge things!" (Oziev, 2022).

It is obligatory for Muslims to follow the commands of the Prophet Muhammad (ﷺ), as mentioned in the following verse from the Qur'ān. Allāh says:

وَمَآ ءَاتَىٰكُمُ ٱلرَّسُولُ فَخُذُوهُ وَمَا نَهَىٰكُمْ عَنْهُ فَٱنتَهُواْ ۚ وَٱتَّقُواْ ٱللَّهَ ۖ إِنَّ ٱللَّهَ شَدِيدُ ٱلْعِقَابِ

- *Whatever the Messenger has given you, take it. And whatever he has forbidden you – refrain from. And fear Allāh. Indeed, Allāh is severe in penalty.*

(Al-Hashr 59:7, interpretation of the meaning)

According to the exegesis of Ibn Kathir (2000), this verse means, "whatever the Messenger commands you, then do it and whatever he forbids you, then avoid it. Surely, He only commands righteousness and forbids evil." This clearly states that all Muslims should fulfil with and maintain the characteristics of *Fitrah*.

There are also the physical elements of the *Fitrah*, known as the *Sunan al-Fitrah*. It is narrated by Ammar b. Yasir,

> Allāh's Messenger (ﷺ) said: The rinsing of mouth and snuffing up water in the nose are acts that bear the characteristics of *fitrah* (nature). He then narrated a similar tradition (as reported by Aishah), but he did not mention the words "letting the beard grow". He added the words "circumcision" and "sprinkling water on the private part of the body". He did not mention the words "cleansing oneself after easing". Abu Dawud said: A similar tradition has been reported on the authority of Ibn 'Abbas. He mentioned only five *Sunnah* all relating to the head, one of them being parting of the hair; it did not include wearing the beard. Abu Dawud said: The tradition as reported by Hammad has also been transmitted by Talq b. Habib, Mujahid, and Bakr b. 'Abd Allāh b. al-Muzani as their own statement (not as a tradition from the Prophet (ﷺ)). They did not mention the words "letting the beard grow". The version transmitted by Muhammad b. Abd Allāh b. Abi Maryam, Abu Salamah, and Abu Hurairah from the Prophet (ﷺ) mentions the words "letting the beard grow". A similar tradition has been reported by Ibrahim al-Nakha'i. He mentioned the words "wearing the beard and circumcision".
>
> (Abu Dawud (b))

Al-Mu'tamir narrated that his father said:

> I heard Talq mentioning ten things that have to do with the *fitrah*: Using the *Siwak*, trimming the moustache, clipping the nails, washing the joints, shaving the pubes, rinsing the nose, and I am not sure about rinsing the mouth.
>
> (An-Nasa'i (a))

TRIALS, TRIBULATIONS, ALIENATION, AND THE *FITRAH*

Trials and tribulations are part of a Muslim's life, and they will endure many tests and hardships in order to validate the sincerity of their faith. Allāh mentions in the Qur'ān:

وَلَنَبْلُوَنَّكُم بِشَىْءٍ مِّنَ ٱلْخَوْفِ وَٱلْجُوعِ وَنَقْصٍ مِّنَ ٱلْأَمْوُلِ وَٱلْأَنفُسِ وَٱلثَّمَرُتِ ۗ وَبَشِّرِ ٱلصَّبِرِينَ

ٱلَّذِينَ إِذَآ أَصَبَتْهُم مُّصِيبَةٌ قَالُواْ إِنَّا لِلَّهِ وَإِنَّآ إِلَيْهِ رُجِعُونَ

- *And we will surely test you with something of fear, hunger, loss of wealth, lives and fruits, but give good tidings to As-Saabiroon (the patient).*

  Who, when disaster strikes them, say, "Indeed we belong to Allāh and truly, and indeed to Him we shall return."
  (Al-Baqarah 2:155–157, interpretation of the meaning)

Trials and tribulations are tests from Allāh in order to enable the individual to break through the clouded *Fitrah* embedded within the multiple layers of false beliefs that have accumulated due the strong influence of psychosocial factors, the acculturation of values incongruent with Islāmic beliefs, and practices that may lead the individual away from the *Fitrah*. Thus, the individual is alienated from his *Fitrah* because his purpose and meaning of life are in the service of something other than Allāh. For some individuals, the *Fitrah* remains clouded, but in moments of trauma and intense suffering some turn towards the Divine for help and support. Utz (2011) suggested,

Times of crisis are particularly likely to awaken our spiritual side and to uncover the *fitrah* that has been buried by false beliefs, principles, ideals and behaviours. During these times, we are likely to call upon Allāh to save us from hardship and suffering.
(p. 193)

This is reflected in the following verse of the Qur'ān:

وَإِذَا مَسَّ ٱلْإِنسَنَ ٱلضُّرُّ دَعَانَا لِجَنبِهِ أَوْ قَاعِدًا أَوْ قَآئِمًا فَلَمَّا كَشَفْنَا عَنْهُ ضُرَّهُ مَرَّ كَأَن لَّمْ يَدْعُنَا إِلَى ضُرٍّ مَّسَّهُ ۚ كَذَلِكَ زُيِّنَ لِلْمُسْرِفِينَ مَا كَانُواْ يَعْمَلُونَ

- *And when affliction touches man, he calls upon Us, whether lying on his side, sitting, or standing; but when We remove from him his affliction, he continues [in disobedience] as if he had never called upon Us to [remove] an affliction that touched him. Thus, is made pleasing to the transgressors that which they have been doing.*

(Yunus 10:12, interpretation of the meaning)

In the face of trials, tribulations, and prosperity, Muslims should be aware that Allāh does not decree anything but that which is good for their worldly and spiritual affairs. Suhaib reported that Allāh's Messenger (ﷺ) said:

Strange are the ways of a believer for there is good in every affair of his and this is not the case with anyone else except in the case of a believer for if he has an occasion to feel delight, he thanks (Allāh), thus there is a good for him in it, and if he gets into trouble and shows resignation (and endures it patiently), there is a good for him in it.

(Muslim (e))

There is also the understanding of the *Fitrah* as a state of intrinsic goodness and evilness (Al-Qarni, 2003). That is, the *Fitrah* oscillates between the common good and evil behaviours and practices. Allāh has endowed humankind with the inborn capacity, intellect, and free will to distinguish between what is right and lawful and what is not. However, due to psychosocial conditioning the *Fitrah* gets corrupted and primes humankind to evil and deviating from the teaching of Islām.

The dualistic dimension of *fitrah* indicates two equal tendencies of good and evil that are dynamic and have potentials to take humans to higher levels in harmony with the pre-existential *fitrah* and also to lower levels that may wipe out the purity inherent in one's original *fitrah* as a result of negative thinking and social influences.

(Haque, 2018, p. 139)

It has been suggested that "submission to it [the *fitrah*] brings harmony, for it means realisation of what is inherent in one's true nature; opposition to it brings discord, for it means realisation of what is extraneous to one's true nature" (Al-Attas, 1985, pp. 57–58). The *Fitrah* and divine revelation provide humankind with this sense or instinct to live according to the laws of Allāh, thus illuminating the *Fitrah* and keeping it alive for the development of spiritual and psychological health.

However, how does one distinguish between the moral good and wrong?

On the authority of an-Nawas bin Sam'an (may Allāh be pleased with him), the Prophet (ﷺ) said: "Righteousness is in good character, and wrongdoing is that which wavers in your soul, and which you dislike people finding out about." [Muslim]. And on the authority of Wabisah bin Ma'bad (may Allāh be pleased with him) who said: "I came to the Messenger of Allāh (ﷺ) said, 'You have come to ask about righteousness.' I said, 'Yes.' He (ﷺ) said, 'Consult your heart. Righteousness is that about which the soul feels at ease and the heart feels tranquil. And wrongdoing is that which wavers in the soul and causes uneasiness in the breast, even though people have repeatedly given their legal opinion [in its favour].'"

(An-Nawawi (a))

This *Hādīth* defines the role of our *Fitrah* in enabling our inner sense of right and wrong at play in our lives. In order for humankind to break away from the alienation from the *Fitrah* and actualise their spiritual potential, they need to reconnect spiritually through the Divine and *Sunnah* guidance in both material and spiritual matters. This is echoed in the following verse of the Qur'ān:

إِنَّ عَلَيْنَا لَلْهُدَىٰ

- *Indeed [incumbent] upon Us is guidance.*
(Al-Layl 92:12, interpretation of the meaning)

This is reinforced by the *Hādīth* narrated by Anas that Prophet Muhammad (ﷺ) said "Whoever turns away from my *Sunnah* is not of me" (An-Nasa'i (b)). Allāh also reminds us,

مَن يَهْدِ ٱللَّهُ فَهُوَ ٱلْمُهْتَدِى ۖ وَمَن يُضْلِلْ فَأُوْلَٰئِكَ هُمُ ٱلْخَٰسِرُونَ

- *Whoever Allāh guides – he is the [rightly] guided; and whoever He send astray – it is they are the losers.*
(Al-A'raf 7:178, interpretation of the meaning)

According to the exegesis of Ibn Kathir (2000), the above verse, according to a *Hādīth* narrated from `Abdullah bin Mas`ud, reads,

> All praise is due to Allāh, Whom we praise and seek help, guidance and forgiveness from. We seek refuge with Allāh from the evils within ourselves and from the burden of our evil deeds. He whom Allāh guides, will never be misled; and he whom He misguides, will never have one who will guide him. I bear witness that there is no deity worthy of worship except Allāh without partners and that Muhammad is His servant and Messenger.
>
> (The complete *Hādīth* was collected by Imam Ahmad and the collectors of Sunan and others)

THE CORRUPTION OF THE *FITRAH*

Without guidance, the *Fitrah* may become corruptible, but it cannot be destroyed. Shaykh Saalih bin Fawzaan bin Abdillaah al-Fawzaan (2013) suggested,

> The soul, if it is left upon its *fitrah* (natural state) affirms Allah's divinity and has love for Allah, worships Him alone, and does not ascribe partners to Him. However, the Shayaateen from the *Jinn* and the *Ins* (mankind) corrupts and deviates it from that with what they reveal to one another by way of beautification in speech and deceptions. *Tawhîd* is centered in the *fitrah*. *Shirk* is foreign and inserted into it.

But, this *Fitrah* sometimes becomes clouded because of corrupt societal and environmental factors that influence the degeneration of spirituality. In contemporary society, we are constantly bombarded with immoral messages and behaviours, which means most individuals are desensitised or they are acculturated with low ethical intelligence. Their moral compass is suppressed, thus they embrace immorality and deviant behaviours. Ibn Taymīyyah (1991) writes,

> The servants of God are inherently compelled by their *fitrah* to love God, though amongst them are those who corrupt this *fitrah* … and this love of God intensifies according to one's knowledge

of Him and the soundness of one's *fitrah*. And it diminishes with diminished knowledge, and the pollution of one's *fitrah* with corruptive vain desires.

(p. 67)

The balanced satisfaction of the needs of *Fitrah* is echoed in the following verses of the Qur'ān. Allāh says,

زُيِّنَ لِلنَّاسِ حُبُّ ٱلشَّهَوَٰتِ مِنَ ٱلنِّسَآءِ وَٱلْبَنِينَ وَٱلْقَنَٰطِيرِ ٱلْمُقَنطَرَةِ مِنَ ٱلذَّهَبِ وَٱلْفِضَّةِ وَٱلْخَيْلِ ٱلْمُسَوَّمَةِ وَٱلْأَنْعَٰمِ وَٱلْحَرْثِ ۗ ذَٰلِكَ مَتَٰعُ ٱلْحَيَوٰةِ ٱلدُّنْيَا ۖ وَٱللَّهُ عِندَهُۥ حُسْنُ ٱلْمَـَٔابِ

- *Beautified for people is the love of that which they desire – of women and sons, heaped-up sums of gold and silver, fine branded horses, and cattle and tilled land. That is the enjoyment of worldly life, but Allah has with Him the best return* [i.e., Paradise].

(Ali-'Imran 3:14, interpretation of the meaning)

يَٰبَنِىٓ ءَادَمَ خُذُواْ زِينَتَكُمْ عِندَ كُلِّ مَسْجِدٍ وَكُلُواْ وَٱشْرَبُواْ وَلَا تُسْرِفُوٓاْ ۚ إِنَّهُۥ لَا يُحِبُّ ٱلْمُسْرِفِينَ

- *O children of Adam, take your adornment* [i.e., wear your clothing] *at every masjid, and eat and drink, but be not excessive. Indeed, He likes not those who commit excess.*

(Al-A'raf 7:31, interpretation of the meaning)

According to Ibn Kathir (2000), the verse of Ali-'Imran 3:14, means that

Allāh mentions the delights that He put in this life for people, such as women and children, and He started with women, because the test with them is more tempting. But also "This is the pleasure of the present world's life' meaning, these are the delights of this life and its short-lived joys, That is the reward of the those who have *taqwa* is better than all joys of this world." The second verse (Al-A'raf 7:31), according to Ibn Kathir (2000), relates to the people who were commanded to wear their best clothes when performing every prayer. In addition, this verse is also about prohibiting extravagance. Al-Bukhari said that Ibn

`Abbas said, "Eat what you wish and wear what you wish, as long as you avoid two things: extravagance and arrogance." Ibn Jarir said that Muhammad bin `Abdul-A`la narrated to us that Muhammad bin Thawr narrated to us from Ma`mar from Ibn Tawus from his father who said that Ibn `Abbas said, "Allah has allowed eating and drinking, as long as it does not contain extravagance or arrogance." Ibn Jarir commented on Allah's statement, "Allah the Exalted says that He does not like those who trespass the limits on an allowed matter or a prohibited matter, those who go to the extreme over what He has allowed, allow what He has prohibited, or prohibit what He has allowed. But, He likes that what He has allowed be considered as such (without extravagance) and what He has prohibited be considered as such. This is the justice that He has commanded.'"

This means that Muslims should fulfil their needs and desires while remembering the Hereafter, so as to create a balanced satisfaction of the needs of *Fitrah* without transgression.

CONCLUSION: ROLE OF THE *FITRAH*

The *Fitrah* is an important concept in Islāmic psychology. Not only is it embedded in the human soul, it is an essential facet of human behaviour (Box 5.2). The *Fitrah* embodies the notion that humans are hardwired with a moral compass and an innate sense of morality and truth.

Box 5.2

- *Fitrah* is our natural moral compass to guide us towards the truth.
- The *Fitrah* is the natural inclination towards the affirmation of *Tawhîd*.
- It enables humans to enjoin what is good and forbid what is wrong (At-Tawbah 9:71).
- It is an essential part of Islamic ethics and ethical intelligence.
- It is essential in the development of personality.
- *Fitrah* entails that we are moral beings at our core (Elqabbany, 2021, p. 255).

- *Fitrah* acts as an anchor and contributes to psychological and spiritual health.
- It helps to cope with adversity during trials and tribulations by seeking help from Allāh.
- *Fitrah* makes humankind motive-driven, as they are aware that this life has a purpose and meaning.

FURTHER READING

Mohamed, Y. (1996). *Fitrah: The Islamic Concept of Human Nature*. London: TA-HA Publishers Ltd.

6

THE INNER WORLD OF A HUMAN BEING (PART 1)
The *Nafs* and *Rûh*

INTRODUCTION

In Islāmic psychology, the metaphysical elements and the inner psyche that influence human behaviours are the self (*Nafs*), the soul (*Rûh*), the heart (*Qalb*), and the intellect (*'Aql*). From an Islāmic perspective, these elements are in the inner world (*Alam-e-Batin*) of humans. However, only Allāh, the Almighty, knows the truth of the inner world of a person and His knowledge encompasses generalities and minor details of the essence of man.

> Allāh Almighty has called Himself Names which reflect this attribute, such as *Al-Khabeer* (the All-Aware), which entails that Allāh Knows what will be before it happens; *Al-Hakeem* (the Wise), which entails that Allāh Knows the details of things; *Ash-Shaheed* (the Witness), which entails that Allāh Knows what is unseen and what is seen, i.e., that nothing is unknown to Him; and *Al-Muhsiy* (the Reckoner), which entails that the fact that Allāh Knows so much does not distract Him from knowing the tiniest details, such as the light of the day and how strong the wind is, and when the leaves fall. Allāh Knows the numbers and the movements of each leaf.
>
> (IslamWeb, 2012)

Allāh says in the Qur'ān:

$$\text{إِنَّهُ هُوَ ٱلسَّمِيعُ ٱلْعَلِيمُ}$$

- *Indeed, He is the Hearing, the Knowing.*

(Ash-Shu'arâ 26:220)

DOI: 10.4324/9781003312956-6

The concepts of self (*Nafs*), the soul (*Rûh*), the heart (*Qalb*), and the intellect ('*Aql*) are the metaphysical elements of the spiritual being based on the work of the Islamic scholar Abu Hamid al-Ghazālī and derived from Qur'anic sources. It has been noted by Keshavarzi and Haque (2013) that Al-Ghazālī viewed the four aspects of the human being (*Nafs*, *Rûh*, '*Aql*, and *Qalb*) as interconnected and having an interdependent holistic relationship with one another, which makes up the soul of the human being. However, it would be valuable not only to distinguish between these concepts, due to their distinct purposes, but also to identify the kinds of characteristics divine revelation gives to the entities in this constellation. This and the following chapter examine the concepts of the self (*Nafs*), the soul (*Rûh*), the heart (*Qalb*), and the intellect ('*Aql*) in the development of personality and provides an analysis of the multifaceted relationship between these concepts. Let us first examine the nature of the *Nafs* (self) and the soul (*Ruh*).

NAFS (SELF)

The study of the *Nafs* is a major element of Islāmic psychology. *Nafs* (pl. *Anfus* or *Nufus*) (نَفْس) is an Arabic word that lexically means self, soul, the psyche, the ego, life, person, heart, or mind. (Al-Akiti, 1997). In the literature, the *Nafs* is synonymous with the concepts of "self," "psyche," or "soul". In the Qur'ān, the word *Nafs* appears 295 times as a noun and is used in two ways. Ahmed (2015) suggested that the first way in which the word *Nafs* is used is to indicate our own self. The second explanation refers to the elements of the self, which include desires, appetite, anger, passion, and lust. The three levels or states of the *Nafs* described in the Qur'ān are: *Nafs Ammāra* (Yusuf 12:53), *Nafs Lawwāma* (Al-Qiyamah 75:2), and *Nafs Muṭma'innah* (Fajr 89:27–28). The concept of *Nafs* is also predominant in Sufi literature, and it has been referred as the lowest facet of an individual's inner animal and satanic psyche (Chittick, 1983, p. 12).

There is a general misconception in the literature on Islāmic psychology that equates the *Nafs* with the Freudian psychosexual development of the id, ego, and super-ego. Keshavarzi and Ali (2021) proposed that "it is possible to liken the *nafs* in this sense to Freud's conceptualization of the id" (p. 28). This notion has been rejected by contemporary Islāmic psychology scholars and thinkers because of its Orientalist approach, including the doyen of Islāmic psychology, Malik Badri. Badri (2021) stated,

A good and widely held example at the time was their proposition that the Freudian seminal theory of the three structures of personality – namely the id, ego, and superego – are the same as the three spiritual ego states of the soul that are mentioned in the Qur'ān. They claimed that the commanding soul *Nafs ammārah* stands for the id, the soul *nafs* is exemplified by the ego, and the tranquil soul *Nafs muṭma'innah* stands for the superego. This undermined the richer and metaphysical nature of these Qur'ānic concepts. In the late 1950s I personally witnessed many Muslim psychologists strongly defend this false belief as if Freud were a spiritually motivated scholar.

(p. xxi)

Students of Islāmic psychology, however, should be aware of the literature on Islāmic psychology, both print and web-based, from contemporary thinkers who equate Freud's psychoanalytic theory of personality with the states of the *Nafs* as stated in the Qur'ān. An additional explanation of the *Nafs* (self) is presented in Box 6.1.

Box 6.1   Additional explanation of the *Nafs* (self)

- In Islāmic tradition, the spiritual soul is referred to as *Nafs* (Al-Raghib; Ibn Sina; Ibn al-Arabi).
- The *Nafs* is simply related to the human soul, the entire soul, and the self (Ahmad, 1992).
- Al-Ghazālī (2009) refers to the paradigm of the spiritual self as the "lower" part of the self/soul.
- Ibn al-Qayyim Al-Jawziyyah (b), commenting on the states of *Nafs*, said that the "*Nafs* is a single entity, although its state may change from the *Nafs al-Ammara*, to the *Nafs al-Lawwama*, to the *Nafs al-Mutma`innah*, which is the final aim of perfection" (p. 308).
- The concept is interchangeable with terms like the "soul," "spirit," "body," or "self."
- The *Nafs* has been defined as "something internal in the entity of a human whose exact nature is not perceived. It is ready to accept direction towards good or evil. It combines together a number of human attributes and characteristics that have a clear effect on human behaviour" (Karzoon, 1997, p. 60).

- The *Nafs* is an internal entity or drive that shapes or directs human behaviour, in combination with personality, towards good or evil (Rassool, 2021a, p. 60).
- The *Nafs* is the totality of the human self/human psyche.

AL-GHAZĀLĪ'S CONCEPT OF *NAFS*

Al-Ghazālī has two distinct meanings for the *Nafs*. The first meaning is the principle that "unites the irascible and appetitive faculties, and constantly enjoins evil" (Al-Ghazālī, 1995, p. 233). The second meaning is the soul, which is a person's essence, free of matter. Al-Ghazālī (2010) refers to the *Nafs* as the appetitive soul, which "united man's blameworthy qualities" (p. xvi), as opposed to his rational soul. He speaks of the *Nafs* as the vehicle (*markab*) of the heart and states that that Sufis call the *Nafs* the animal spirit (*al-riih al-hayawdni an nafs*). He also views the *Nafs* as the "subtle spiritual substance which is the real essence of man" (p. xvii). He describes the two meanings of the *Nafs*. One consists of both the faculty of anger (*ghadab*) and of appetence (*shahwa*) [appetites, desires] in man. This, in simplistic terms, is the principle in man that includes his blameworthy qualities. He uses the saying that your worst enemy is your *Nafs*. The other consists of that which is "the soul of man and his essence". But it is identified by different descriptors according to its differing states.

> When it is at rest under His command, and agitation has left it on account of its opposition to the fleshly appetites, it is called "the soul at rest" (*al-nafi al-mufma'inna*). Of such a soul did God, the Exalted, say, Oh, you soul at peace, return to your Lord, pleased, and pleasing Him (Al-Fajr 89:27–28).
>
> (Al-Ghazālī, 2010, p. 8)

He said, "Never have I dealt with anything more difficult than my own soul, which sometimes helps me and sometimes opposed me" (Cited in Abu Zainab, 2015). Imam al-Ghazālī categorised the *Nafs* into three stages as identified in the Qur'ān.

TYPES OF *NAFS*

Allāh says in the Qur'ān,

وَيَسْأَلُونَكَ عَنِ الرُّوحِ ۖ قُلِ الرُّوحُ مِنْ أَمْرِ رَبِّي وَمَا أُوتِيتُمْ مِنَ الْعِلْمِ إِلَّا قَلِيلًا

• *And they ask you, [O Muhammad], about the soul. Say, "The soul is of the affair of my Lord. And mankind has not been given of knowledge except a little."*

(Al–Isrā 17:85, interpretation of the meaning)

The knowledge of the *Nafs* is based on the Qur'ān, traditional knowledge, and scholarly interpretation of the Qur'ān. There is a general consensus among the scholars that Allāh has described at least three main types of the *Nafs*, namely *Nafs al-Ammara Bissu'* (the *Nafs* that urges evil), *Nafs al-Lawwama* (the *Nafs* that Blames), and *Nafs al-Mutma'innah* (the *Nafs* at Peace) (Figure 6.1).

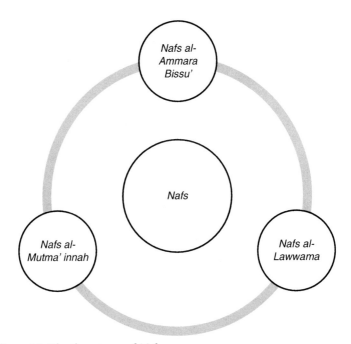

Figure 6.1 The three types of *Nafs*

Nafs al-Ammara Bissu' (the Nafs that urges evil)

The *Nafs al-Ammara Bissu'* is found Surah Yusuf verse 53. Allāh says in the Qur'ān:

إِنَّ النَّفْسَ لَأَمَّارَةٌ بِالسُّوءِ

• *Indeed, the soul is a persistent enjoiner of evil.*
(Yusuf 12:53, interpretation of the meaning)

This *Nafs*, by its very nature, directs the individual towards every wrong action. This evil can only be relieved by the help of Allāh, who refers to this *Nafs* in the story of the wife of al-Aziz (Zuleika) and Prophet Yusuf [Qur'ān, Chapter 12]. The behavioural intention of this *Nafs* is inclined towards wants and desires in an impulsive way towards enjoining evil. This evil, based on conceptualisation of the *Nafs* by Al-Ghazālī, "is contained within the aspect of the human being as a social animal with survival/aggressive instincts (*quwwat ghaḍabiyyah*) and appetitive/carnal drives (*Quwwat shahawiyyah*)" (Keshavarzi & Ali, 2021, p. 28). Imam Al-Tabari, in his exegesis of the above verse [Yusuf 12:53], commented that it is this *Nafs* that brings punishment itself. He further commented that Allāh also says:

يَـٰٓأَيُّهَا ٱلَّذِينَ ءَامَنُوا۟ لَا تَتَّبِعُوا۟ خُطُوَٰتِ ٱلشَّيْطَـٰنِ ۚ وَمَن يَتَّبِعْ خُطُوَٰتِ ٱلشَّيْطَـٰنِ فَإِنَّهُ يَأْمُرُ بِٱلْفَحْشَآءِ وَٱلْمُنكَرِ ۚ وَلَوْلَا فَضْلُ ٱللَّهِ عَلَيْكُمْ وَرَحْمَتُهُ مَا زَكَىٰ مِنكُم مِّنْ أَحَدٍ أَبَدًا وَلَـٰكِنَّ ٱللَّهَ يُزَكِّى مَن يَشَآءُ ۗ وَٱللَّهُ سَمِيعٌ عَلِيمٌ

• *O you who have believed, do not follow the footsteps of Satan. And whoever follows the footsteps of Satan – indeed, he enjoins immorality and wrongdoing. And if not for the favor of Allāh upon you and His mercy, not one of you would have been pure, ever, but Allāh purifies whom He wills, and Allāh is Hearing and Knowing.*
(An-Nur 24:21, interpretation of the meaning)

Imam Al-Tabari explained the above verse by stating that

this *Nafs* resides in the world of the senses and is dominated by earthly desires (*shahwat*) and passions ... Evil lies hidden in the *nafs* and it is this that leads it on to do wrong. If Allāh were to leave the servant alone with his self, the servant would be destroyed between its evil and the evil. This particular soul, at the lowest level, is prone to disobedience and sinful behaviours because of its attractions towards evil and fails to submit to Allāh.

Zarabozo (2002) maintains that if individuals allow the soul to exert a significant control, they start losing a sense of remorse or guilt for their sinful behaviours (pp. 62–63). This state has been described as having their hearts blocked from believing in the truth. Allāh also says:

كَلَّا ۖ بَلْ رَانَ عَلَى قُلُوبِهِمْ مَا كَانُوا يَكْسِبُونَ

- *No! Rather, the stain has covered their hearts of that which they were earning.*

    (Al-Mutaffifin 83:14, interpretation of the meaning)

According to exegesis of Ibn Kathir (2000), "It is the dark covering that cast over it from the many sins and wrong they committed that has covered up their hearts." (*And if not for the favor of Allāh upon you and His mercy, not one of you would have been pure*), meaning, if He did not help whomever He wills to repent and come back to Him and be purified from *Shirk*, evil and sin, and whatever bad characteristics each person has according to his nature, no one would ever attain purity and goodness. In this context, Zarabozo (2002) commented that "since the soul is already predisposed to those kinds of evil acts, *Satan* will whisper to them and easily persuade them to do evil deeds" (p. 63).

Nafs al-Lawwama *(the* Nafs *that blames)*

This type of self is also viewed as the self-reproaching soul and as having an awareness of evil deeds. It is a self-critical stage during which an individual blames himself for his bad deeds or not doing more good deeds and feels a sense of guilt or remorse. It is reported by Ibn Kathir (2000) that "'Ikrimah Ibn Abi Najih reported from Mujahid: 'He is sorry for what he missed (of good deeds) and he blames himself for it.'" This may be regarded as the policing of "ethical intelligence" of the soul. Allāh mentions in the Qur'ān:

وَلَا أُقْسِمُ بِالنَّفْسِ اللَّوَّامَةِ

- *And I swear by the reproaching soul.*
(Al-Qiyamah75:2, interpretation of the meaning)

Hasan al-Basri said, "You always see the believer blaming himself and saying things like 'Did I want this? Why did I do that? Was this better than that?'" (Cited in Al-Akiti, 1997). In this stage, the *Nafs*, being conscious of its own imperfections, means that individuals have a sense of guilt and would seek repentance from Allāh or attempt to address their transgressions [*Fahishah* (immoral sin)].

وَٱلَّذِينَ إِذَا فَعَلُوا۟ فَٰحِشَةً أَوْ ظَلَمُوٓا۟ أَنفُسَهُمْ ذَكَرُوا۟ ٱللَّهَ فَٱسْتَغْفَرُوا۟ لِذُنُوبِهِمْ وَمَن يَغْفِرُ ٱلذُّنُوبَ إِلَّا ٱللَّهُ وَلَمْ يُصِرُّوا۟ عَلَىٰ مَا فَعَلُوا۟ وَهُمْ يَعْلَمُونَ

- *And those who, when they commit an immorality or wrong themselves [by transgression], remember Allāh and seek forgiveness for their sins — and who can forgive sins except Allāh? — and [who] do not persist in what they have done while they know.*
(Ali 'Imran 3:135, interpretation of the meaning)

This is the stage of contemplation and spiritual awakening in repentance and seeking forgiveness. Anas (May Allāh be pleased with him) reported that the Messenger of Allāh (ﷺ) said,

Allāh, the Exalted, has said: "O son of Adam, I forgive you as long as you pray to Me and hope for My forgiveness, whatever sins you have committed. O son of Adam, I do not care if your sins reach the height of the heaven, then you ask for my forgiveness, I will forgive you. O son of Adam, if you come to Me with an earth load of sins, and meet Me associating nothing to Me, I would match it with an earth load of forgiveness."
(Tirmidhî (i))

Nafs al-Mutma`innah *(the* Nafs *at peace)*

This is the *Nafs* at peace, serenity, or in a tranquil state as a consequence of spiritual health. This is the stage where the *Nafs* has earned the pleasure of Allāh and the person displays goodness, piety, and righteousness. It was narrated that 'Â'ishah (may Allāh be pleased with her) said: "I heard the Messenger of Allāh (ﷺ) said: 'Enjoin what is good and forbid what is evil, before you call and you are not answered'" (Ibn Majah (d)). About this stage of the *Nafs*, Allāh mentions in the Qur'ān,

يَا أَيَّتُهَا النَّفْسُ الْمُطْمَئِنَّةُ

ارْجِعِي إِلَى رَبِّكِ رَاضِيَةً مَرْضِيَّةً

فَادْخُلِي فِي عِبَادِي

وَادْخُلِي جَنَّتِي

- *[To the righteous it will be said]: O reassured soul, return to your Lord, well pleased and pleasing [to Him]. And enter among My [righteous] servants. And enter My paradise.*
  (Al-Fajr 89:27–30, interpretation of the meaning)

According to Imam Al-Tabari, Ibn Abbas said that "It is the tranquil and believing soul." Al-Qatadah said,

It is the soul of the believer, made calm by what Allāh has promised. Its owner is at rest and content with his knowledge of Allāh's Names and Attributes, and with what He has said about Himself and His Messenger, and with what He has said about what awaits the soul after death: about the departure of the soul, the life in the *Barzakh* [designates a place between hell and heaven, where the soul resides after death], and the events of the Day of *Qiyamah* [Day of Judgment] which will follow. So much so that a believer such as this can almost see them with his own eyes. So, he submits to the will of Allāh and surrenders to Him contentedly, never dissatisfied or complaining, and with his faith never wavering. He does not rejoice at his gains, nor do his afflictions make him despair – for he knows that they were decreed long before they happened to him, even before he was created.
(Imam Al-Tabari, cited in Al-Akiti, 1997)

Ibn al-Qayyim Al-Jawziyyah (b) stated,

It has been said that the *Nafs al-Lawwama* is the one, which cannot rest in any one state. It often changes, remembers and forgets, submits and evades, loves and hates, rejoices and become sad, accepts and rejects, obeys and rebels. *Nafs al-Lawwama* is also the *nafs* of the believer ... It has also been mentioned that the *nafs* blames itself on the Day of *Qiyamah* – for everyone blames himself for his actions, either his bad deeds, if he was one who had many wrong actions, or for his shortcomings, if he was one who did good deeds. All of this is accurate.

(p. 308)

Imam al-Ghazālī (2010) suggests, "When it is at rest under His command, and agitation has left it on account of its opposition to the fleshly appetites, it is called 'the soul at rest' (*al-nafī al-mufma'inna*)" (p. 10). Thus, being in strong connection with the Creator is a level that we need to strive to attain in this life. This is our 'self-actualisation', but it is through the purification of the soul that we are able to, in essence, fulfil the rationale of our creation, which is the worship of and obedience to Allāh.

DISCIPLINING THE *NAFS*

Despite the evil nature of the *Nafs*, according to Al-Ghazālī, the *Nafs* is the essence by which man can get to know God. Khan (2020) suggested that "contrary to the popular usage of the term among Muslims, the *nafs*, by its very nature, is not intrinsically evil. It can be trained and disciplined, leading to its ultimate state: *Mutma'innah*" (p. 119). The Qur'ān and *Sunnah* repeatedly emphasise purifying the soul. This is reflected in the following verse:

قَدْ أَفْلَحَ مَن تَزَكَّىٰ

* *He has certainly succeeded who purifies himself.*
(Al A'la 87:14, interpretation of the meaning)

Jihaad al-nafs is the struggle against self in relation to evil ideas, desires, lust, anger, and deviant behaviours. Discipling the self is considered to be a major struggle and is compared to fighting in the battlefield (*al-jihad al-akbar*). In order to overcome this struggle, there is a need to purge all animalistic and satanic ideas and influences from one's soul. Ibn al-Qayyim Al-Jawziyyah (c) said:

Jihad al-nafs means striving to make oneself learn true guidance, and to follow it after coming to know it, calling others to it, and bearing with patience the difficulties of calling others to Allāh. *Jihad al-Shaytaan* means striving against him and warding off the doubts and desires that he throws at a person, and the doubts that undermine faith, and striving against the corrupt desires that he tries to inspire in a person.

(pp. 9–12)

Skinner (2019) cited Al-Ghazālī's analogy of a rider on a horse to show how the *Nafs* can be disciplined. According to Skinner (2019),

In this analogy, the horse is the *hawā* [animal self], healthy and operating in its *fiṭrah*; guided by *aql* (the reins), under the control of the rider who is centered in the *Qalb* under divine guidance. From this analogy, psychopathology can be seen in different manifestations. For example, the horse out of control; the horse under control but by the reins directing it in an irrational way; the horse firmly under control and being firmly guided by the reins to where the rider wants to go but being contrary to *Fiṭrah* and destructive.

(p. 24)

In some way, it is the *hawā* of the *Nafs* (self) that need to be restrained or disciplined. Al-Ghazālī describes how a believer must protect himself against these enemies, saying:

Know that the body is like a city and the intellect of the mature human being is like a king ruling that town. All the forces of the external and internal senses he can muster are like his soldiers and his aides. The soul/self that enjoins evil (*nafs ammāra*), that is, lust and anger, is like an enemy that challenges him in his kingdom and strives to slaughter his people. The body thus becomes like a garrison-town or sea-outpost, and the soul like its custodian posted in it. If he fights against his enemies, defeats them, and compels them to do what he likes, he will be praised when he returns to God's presence, as God said: " ... [who strive and fight] in the way of God with their wealth and their lives over those of remained [behind], by degrees. And to all God has promised the best [reward]." [An-Nisa' 4:95]

(sunnahonline.com)

The purification of the soul means to purify and cleanse the heart of vices and immoral traits by minimising the effect of the *hawā*. The purification of the soul is found in the fabric of Islāmic beliefs and practices in order to overcome and discipline the corrupted *Nafs*. Some of the approaches in training and disciplining the *Nafs* include seeking authentic religious knowledge, making sincere intentions, reading the Qur'ān and reflecting on its teachings, providing the soul with beneficial nourishment by the remembrance of Allāh (*zikr*), enjoining what is good and forbidding what is wrong, performing obligatory prayers, increasing small acts of kindness; not enriching the self with sins and evil deeds, not succumbing to the *Nafs* by obeying and fulfilling every dictate and demand of fantasies and desires rather than meeting basic needs, making supplications (the weapon of the believer), and being charitable. Allāh says in the Qur'ān,

$$قَدْ أَفْلَحَ مَن تَزَكَّىٰ$$

$$وَذَكَرَ اسْمَ رَبِّهِ فَصَلَّىٰ$$

* *He has certainly succeeded who purifies himself*

And mentions the name of his Lord and prays.
(Al A'la 87:14–15, interpretation of the meaning)

On the authority of Abu Abbas Abdullah bin Abbas (may Allāh be pleased with him) who said: One day I was behind the Prophet (ﷺ) [riding on the same mount] and he said, "O young man, I shall teach you some words [of advice]: Be mindful of Allāh and Allāh will protect you. Be mindful of Allāh and you will find Him in front of you. If you ask, then ask Allāh [alone]; and if you seek help, then seek help from Allāh [alone]. And know that if the nation were to gather together to benefit you with anything, they would not benefit you except with what Allāh had already prescribed for you. And if they were to gather together to harm you with anything, they would not harm you except with what Allāh had already prescribed against you. The pens have been lifted and the pages have dried."

(An-Nawawi (b))

The Messenger of Allāh (ﷺ) commanded us to say:

اللَّهُمَّ إِنِّي أَعُوذُ بِكَ مِنَ الْعَجْزِ وَالْكَسَلِ وَالْبُخْلِ وَالْجُبْنِ وَالْهَرَمِ وَعَذَابِ الْقَبْرِ اللَّهُمَّ آتِ نَفْسِي تَقْوَاهَا وَزَكِّهَا أَنْتَ خَيْرُ مَنْ زَكَّاهَا أَنْتَ وَلِيُّهَا وَمَوْلَاهَا اللَّهُمَّ إِنِّي أَعُوذُ بِكَ مِنَ نَفْسٍ لَا تَشْبَعُ وَمِنْ قَلْبٍ لَا يَخْشَعُ وَمِنْ عِلْمٍ لَا يَنْفَعُ وَدَعْوَةٍ لَا تُسْتَجَابُ

O Allāh, I seek refuge in You from incapacity, laziness, miserliness, cowardice, old age, the torment of the grave. O Allāh, make my soul obedient and purify it, for You are the best One to purify it, You are its Guardian and Lord. O Allāh, I seek refuge in You from a soul that is not satisfied, a heart that is not humble, knowledge that is of no benefit and a supplication that is not answered.

(An–Nasa'i (c))

Thus, it is through the process of the purification of the soul (*Tazkiyah-an-Nafs*) that thebehavioural inclinations of *Nafs* can be controlled and disciplined.

THE *RÛH* (SPIRIT): AN INTRODUCTION

The word *Rûh* is mentioned 21 times in Qur'ān in 20 verses. The Qur'ān uses the concepts of both the *Nafs* and the *Rûh* to highlight the notion of the soul. The term *Rûh* (also known as spirit, soul, or breath of life) is used in the Qur'ān in various ways to refer to metaphysical entities such as angels, revelation, or divine inspiration. It is also used to signify the inner human nature or soul, which is the constituent that gives life to the mind and body by spreading throughout the physical limbs. It drives the feelings, thoughts, behaviours, and volition of human beings. However, the *Nafs* and *Rûh* (spirit) are regarded as synonyms and, depending on the context of use, are interchangeable by the majority of Islāmic scholars. Allāh says in the Qur'ān:

وَلَوْ تَرَىٰ إِذِ الظَّالِمُونَ فِي غَمَرَاتِ الْمَوْتِ وَالْمَلَائِكَةُ بَاسِطُو أَيْدِيهِمْ أَخْرِجُوا أَنْفُسَكُمْ

- *And if you could but see when the wrongdoers are in the overwhelming pangs of death while the angels extend their hands, [saying], "Discharge your souls!"*

(Al An'ām 6:93, interpretation of the meaning)

$$\text{لَّهُ يَتَوَفَّى الْأَنْفُسَ حِينَ مَوْتِهَا وَالَّتِي لَمْ تَمُتْ فِي مَنَامِهَا ۖ فَيُمْسِكُ الَّتِي قَضَىٰ عَلَيْهَا}$$

$$\text{الْمَوْتَ وَيُرْسِلُ الْأُخْرَىٰ إِلَىٰ أَجَلٍ مُسَمًّى ۚ}$$

- *Allāh takes the souls at the time of their death, and those that do not die [He takes] during their sleep. Then He keeps those for which He has decreed death and releases the others for a specified term.*
  (Surah Az-Zumar 39:42, interpretation of the meaning)

Knowledge about the *Rūh*'s true essence belongs exclusively to Allāh. This is exemplified in a *Hādīth* that was narrated by Ibn 'Abbas.

The Quraysh said to the Jews: "Give us something that we can ask this man about." So, he said: "Ask him about the *rūh*." So, they asked him about the *rūh*. So, Allāh Most High, revealed: They ask you concerning the *rūh*. Say: "The *rūh* is one of the things, the knowledge of which is only with my Lord. And of knowledge, you have been given only a little" (Al-Isrā 17:85).
(Tirmidhî (i))

Allāh says in the Qur'ān:

$$\text{وَيَسْأَلُونَكَ عَنِ ٱلرُّوحِ ۖ قُلِ ٱلرُّوحُ مِنْ أَمْرِ رَبِّى وَمَآ أُوتِيتُم مِّنَ ٱلْعِلْمِ إِلَّا قَلِيلًا}$$

- *And they ask you [Muhammad] about the soul. Say: The soul is of the affair [i.e., concern] of my Lord. And you [i.e., mankind] have not been given of knowledge except a little.*
  (Al-Isra' 17:85, interpretation of the meaning)

In the exegesis of Ibn Kathir (2000), it is noted that Al-Bukhari recorded in his Tafsir of this Ayah [verse] that `Abdullah bin Mas`ud said,

While I was walking with the Prophet on a farm, and he was resting on a palm-leaf stalk, some Jews passed by. Some of them said to the others, "Ask him about the *rūh*." Some of them said, "What urges you to ask him about that?" Others said, "Do not ask him, lest he gives you a reply which you do not like." But they said, "Ask him." So, they asked him about the *rūh*. The Prophet kept quiet and did not give them an answer, and I knew that he was receiving revelation, so I stayed where I was. When the revelation was complete, the Prophet said: "And they ask you concerning the *rûh* (the spirit). Say: 'The *rûh* (the spirit) is one of the things, the knowledge of which is only with my Lord .... '''

QUR'ĀNIC EVIDENCE: RANGE OF MEANINGS FOR MAN'S SOUL

Allāh says in the Qur'ān:

يَا أَيُّهَا النَّاسُ اتَّقُوا رَبَّكُمُ الَّذِي خَلَقَكُمْ مِنْ نَفْسٍ وَاحِدَةٍ وَخَلَقَ مِنْهَا زَوْجَهَا وَبَثَّ مِنْهُمَا رِجَالًا كَثِيرًا وَنِسَاءً ۚ

- *O mankind, fear your Lord, who created you from one soul and created from it its mate and dispersed from both of them many men and women.*
  (An-Nisā 4:1, interpretation of the meaning)

هُوَ الَّذِي خَلَقَكُمْ مِنْ نَفْسٍ وَاحِدَةٍ وَجَعَلَ مِنْهَا زَوْجَهَا لِيَسْكُنَ إِلَيْهَا ۖ

- *It is He who created you from one soul and created from it its mate that he might dwell in security with her.*
  (Al-A'rāf 7:189, interpretation of the meaning)

خَلَقَكُمْ مِنْ نَفْسٍ وَاحِدَةٍ

- *He created you from one soul.*
  (Az-Zumar 39:6)

وَهُوَ الَّذِي أَنْشَأَكُمْ مِنْ نَفْسٍ وَاحِدَةٍ فَمُسْتَقَرٌّ وَمُسْتَوْدَعٌ ۗ

- *And it is He who produced you from one soul and [gave you] a place of dwelling and of storage.*
  (Al-An'ām 6:98, interpretation of the meaning)

The soul is the one that tastes death, and this is explained in the following verses. Allāh says in the Qur'ān:

كُلُّ نَفْسٍ ذَائِقَةُ الْمَوْتِ ۖ ثُمَّ إِلَيْنَا تُرْجَعُونَ

- *Every soul shall taste death, then to Us will you be returned.*
  (Al-'Ankabūt 29:57, interpretation of the meaning)

كُلُّ نَفْسٍ ذَائِقَةُ ٱلْمَوْتِ ۗ وَنَبْلُوكُم بِٱلشَّرِّ وَٱلْخَيْرِ فِتْنَةً ۖ وَإِلَيْنَا تُرْجَعُونَ

- *Every soul will taste death. And We test you with evil and with good as trial; and to Us you will be returned.*
  (Al-Anbiya 21:35, interpretation of the meaning)

كُلُّ نَفْسٍ ذَائِقَةُ الْمَوْتِ ۗ وَإِنَّمَا تُوَفَّوْنَ أُجُورَكُمْ يَوْمَ الْقِيَامَةِ ۖ

- *Every soul will taste death, and you will only be given your [full] compensation on the Day of Resurrection.*
  (Ali 'Imran 3:185, interpretation of the meaning)

The above verses indicate that all souls will taste death, but this cannot happen without the decree or permission of God. The soul has also attributes, both positive and negative, which include:

- Desires (Al-Anbya 21:102; Fussilat 41:31, Az-Zukhruf 43:71);
- Needs and desires (Yusuf 12:68);
- Stinginess (Al-Hashr 59:9; An-Nisā 4:12; At-Taghabun 64:16);
- Constraint or restriction (At-Tawbah 9:118);
- Regret (Az-Zumar 39:56); and
- Purification (Ash-Shams 91:7–10).

NAFS AND RÛH

The scholars of *Ahlus-Sunnah wal Jamaah* (Ibn Taymīyyah and Ibn Qayyim of Jawziyyah) maintained that the terms *Nafs* and *Rûh* are interchangeable. Their rationale is that the three states of *Nafs* mentioned in the Qur'ān – *Nafs Ammara*, *Nafs Lawwama*, and *Nafs Mutma'innah* – can also apply to *Rûh*. Other scholars say that *Nafs* and *Rûh* are two different things. That is, life exists in humans when *Rûh* has entered inside his heart (*Qalb*). Simply, when the soul as an entity is in the body it is referred as *Nafs,* but when the soul is separated or apart from the body it is known as *Rûh*. According to Sharfuddin (2021),

nafs is the name of the state of man when his *rûh* is inside his corpus. *Nafs* is also the heart (*qalb*). *Nafs* is the arrogant 'I' or the 'self' inside every person. It is the ego. Arrogance or excess of ego can destroy a person.

Al-Tuwaijri (2016) suggested that the essence of the *Rûh* is "different from that of the physical body, and once the soul is removed, the physical body ceases to function."

However, there are several *Hadīth* that indicate that the *Nafs* and the *Rûh* are the same thing. Umm Salamah reported that the Messenger of Allāh (ﷺ) said: "When the *rûh* is taken out, the eyesight follows it." (Muslim (f)). In another *Hadīth*, Abu Hurayrah reported that the Messenger of Allāh (ﷺ) said, "Do you not see that when a person dies his gaze is fixed intently? That occurs when his eyesight follows his *nafs* [as it comes out]" (Muslim (g)). However, as "these terms may be used interchangeably in relation to their essence, the difference between them is merely a difference in attributes and usage" (Al-Kanadi, 1996). Box 6.2 provides an overview of different perspectives on the interchangeability of *Nafs* and *Rûh*.

Box 6.2 *Nafs* and *Rûh*

Ibn Taymīyyah and Ibn Qayyim of Jawziyyah	*Nafs* and *Rûh* are interchangeable. *Nafs Ammara*, *Nafs Lawwama*, and *Nafs Mutma'innah* can also apply to *Rûh*.
Other scholars	*Nafs* and *Rûh* are two different things:
	1. *Nafs* = the soul as an entity is in the body.
	2. *Rûh* = the soul is separated or apart from the body.
Sharfuddin (2021)	*Nafs* is the name of the state of man when his *Rûh* is inside his corpus. *Nafs* is also the heart (*Qalb*).
Al-Tuwaijri (2016)	The essence of the *Rûh* is different from that of the physical body, and once the soul is removed, the physical body ceases to function.
Al-Kanadi (1996)	*Nafs* and *Rûh* are used interchangeably in relation to their essence; the difference between them is merely a difference in attributes and usage.
Hadīths (Muslim)	When the *Rûh* is taken out, the eyesight follows it: "Do you not see that when a person dies his gaze is fixed intently? That occurs when his eyesight follows his *Nafs* [as it comes out]".

NAFS OR *RŪH*: SLEEP, BIRTH, AND DEATH

Both the Qur'ān and *Hadīth* provide explanations for when the *Rūh* or soul enters the human body and what happens to a soul when it departs the body after a person's death. Ibn Sulaymaan explains the view of the role of the *Rūh* during sleep as follows:

> Man has life [*hayaah*], a spirit [*rūh*] and a soul [*nafs*]. When he sleeps, his *nafs* – with which he senses and understands things – emerges from his body; however, it doesn't completely separate from the physical body. Rather, it extends from it, radiating outward like a cable. While both life and the *rūh* remain in his body (being the two means by which he breathes as well as tosses and turns during sleep), man sees visions by means of the *nafs* which emerges from him. When he is about to awaken, his *nafs* returns to him faster than the blinking of an eye. However, if Allah wills that he die in his sleep, He seizes that *nafs* which had come out as described.

This position is based on the following verse of the Qur'ān:

$$ ٱللَّهُ يَتَوَفَّى ٱلْأَنفُسَ حِينَ مَوْتِهَا وَٱلَّتِى لَمْ تَمُتْ فِى مَنَامِهَا ۖ فَيُمْسِكُ ٱلَّتِى قَضَىٰ عَلَيْهَا ٱلْمَوْتَ وَيُرْسِلُ ٱلْأُخْرَىٰ إِلَىٰ أَجَلٍ مُّسَمًّى ۚ إِنَّ فِى ذَٰلِكَ لَءَايَـٰتٍ لِّقَوْمٍ يَتَفَكَّرُونَ $$

- *God takes the souls at the time of their death, and those that do not die [He takes] during their sleep. Then He keeps those for which He has decreed death and releases the others for a specified term. Indeed, in that are signs for a people who give thought.*

  (Az–Zumar 39:42, interpretation of the meaning)

It is narrated by Abu Qatada that when the people slept so late that they did not offer the (morning) prayer, the Prophet (ﷺ) said, "Allah captured your souls (made you sleep) when He willed and returned them (to your bodies) when He willed" (Bukhari (g)). Ibn Rajab (c) (may Allāh have mercy on him) comments that the above verse indicates that

> sleep is a death, and the Hadīth indicates when a person sleeps his soul is taken. They both indicate that the soul that is taken in death is the soul that is taken during sleep. The taking of the soul from the body does not necessarily mean that it has departed from the body altogether; rather it may be taken

whilst some kind of connection is still present, as in the case of one who is sleeping.

(pp. 325–326)

There is a *Ḥadīth* that describes when the soul first enters the human body in the mother's womb. Ibn Mas'ud said that God's messenger, who spoke the truth and whose word was believed, told them the following:

> 'Abd Allah b. Mas'ud said: The Messenger of Allah (ﷺ) who spoke the truth and whose word was belief told us the following: The constituents of one of you are collected for forty days in his mother's womb, then they become a piece of congealed blood for a similar period, then they become a lump of flesh for a similar period. Then Allah sends to him an angel with four words who records his provision the period of his life, his deeds, and whether he will be miserable or blessed; thereafter he breathes the spirit into him. One of you will do the deeds of those who go to Paradise so that there will be only a cubit between him and it or will be within a cubit, then what is decreed will overcome him so that he will do the deeds of those who go to Hell and will enter it; and one of you will do the deeds of those who go to hell, so that there will be only a cubit between him and it or will be within a cubit, then what is decreed will overcome him, so that he will do the deeds of those who go to Paradise and will enter it.

(Abu Dawud (c))

The soul after death is described in the following *Ḥadīth*:

> He reported God's messenger as saying, "When the soul of a believer comes out, two angels meet it and take it up." Hammad said he mentioned some of the fragrance of its odour and made mention of musk, and said, "The inhabitants of heaven will say, 'A good soul has come from the earth. God bless you and a body which you inhabited!' He will then be taken to his Lord who will tell them to take him away till the end of the appointed time" [a reference to the day of resurrection. Cf. Qur'ān, vi, 2]. He said, "When an infidel's soul comes out (Hammad saying that he mentioned some of its stench and made mention of cursing), the

inhabitants of heaven say, 'A wicked soul has come from the earth,' and they will be told to take him away till the end of the appointed time." Abu Hurairah said that God's messenger then put a seamless garment he was wearing over his nose thus [this would be indicated by putting his garment over his nose].

(Muslim (h))

CONCLUSION

In the context of Islāmic psychology, the *Nafs* and *Rûh* are two components of the inner world of the human being. The *Nafs* is considered the self and the *Rûh* is considered the soul. However, depending on the context of use, the two terms are considered interchangeable by the majority of Islāmic scholars.

FURTHER READING

Dalhat, Y. (2015). The Concept of *Al-Rûh* (Soul) In Islam. *International Journal of Education and Research*, 3(8), 431–440.

Ibn Taymīyyah, A.A. (1988). *Risalah fi al-Aql wa al-Rûh*. Beirut: Darr al-Hijrah.

7

THE INNER WORLD OF A HUMAN BEING (PART 2)

The *Qalb* and *'Aql*

INTRODUCTION

In Islāmic tradition the heart (قلب) (*Qalb*) refers to the spiritual heart, which is the "inner self" of an individual. Al-Ghazālī (1995) suggested that the heart has a dual nature. The first is the physical heart, "which contains a cavity filled with blood and is the locus of the Spirit" (*Rûh*); the second meaning is the spiritual heart, which is a "spiritual, divine subtlety connected to the physical heart, which is the reality or real essence of man, which perceived, knows, and intuits" (p. 234). He went on to maintain that the spiritual heart is

> the essence of a man. In man, it is what perceives, knows, is aware, is spoken to, punishes, blames, and is responsible. It has connection with the corporeal heart, and the minds of most men have been baffled in trying to grasp the mode of the connection ... It [the heart] is like king and the soldiers are like servants and helpers.
>
> (Al-Ghazālī, 1980 p. 3)

The first part of this chapter focuses on the *Qalb* and the second part focuses on the *'Aql* (intellect). The chapter also examines the complex relationship between the self (*Nafs*), the soul (*Rûh*), the heart (*Qalb*), and the intellect (*'Aql*).

IBN AL-QAYYIM'S TYPES OF HEARTS

Ibn al-Qayyim classified the *Qalb* into three types due to its functional aspects of life and death:

DOI: 10.4324/9781003312956-7

the first type of heart is the living, humble, soft, attentive and heedful heart. The second type is the brittle, dry and dead heart. The third type is the diseased heart, either it is closer to securing itself or it is closer to its devastation.

(Ibn al-Qayyim Al-Jawziyyah (d), p. 141)

It is narrated by An-Nu'man bin Bashir that I heard Allāh's Messenger (ﷺ) saying, "Beware! There is a piece of flesh in the body if it becomes good (reformed) the whole body becomes good but if it gets spoilt the whole body gets spoilt and that is the heart" (Bukhari (f)).

The first: The healthy or sound heart

The sound or healthy heart is one that is psychologically robust and untainted by false doubts and hindrance about Allāh and His Messenger. Ibn al-Qayyim (d) states that this is "the truthful and sound (*Salīm*) heart" (p. 136). The meaning of *Salīm* is having security, and this "is characterised so because this attribute of truthfulness and security has become a constant and established description of it" (Shafi, 2011). Due to its soundness, this type of heart is secure from committing any form of *shirk* (the sin of idolatry or polytheism). According to Ibn al-Qayyim (d), this type of heart is free from carnal desires and adheres to the order and prohibitions of Allāh:

Therefore, it becomes sound through loving Allāh and seeking the ruling of His Messenger (ﷺ); It becomes sound through showing Him fear, hope, trust, and reliance; penitence; and humility; it prefers what pleases Him in every circumstance-and distances itself from everything that would displease Him in every possible way. This is the reality of servitude (*'Ubūdiyyah*) which can only be directed to Allāh Alone. This type of heart's actions are purely for Allāh sake. The focus of its loves is for the sake of Allāh; if it hates, it hates for the sake of Allāh. This means that the heart's desire, love, trust and reliance, repentance, humbleness, dread, and reverential hope are only for the love and sake Allāh.

(p. 137)

This is the sole type of heart than an individual can bring to Allāh on the Day of Judgement. Allāh says in the Qur'ān:

$$\text{يَوْمَ لَا يَنْفَعُ مَالٌ وَلَا بَنُونَ}$$

$$\text{إِلَّا مَنْ أَتَى اللَّهَ بِقَلْبٍ سَلِيمٍ}$$

- *The Day when there will not benefit [anyone] wealth or children. But only one who comes to Allāh with a sound heart.*
  (Ash-Shu'arâ 26:88–89, interpretation of the meaning)

In addition, the heart needs to follow the teaching and role model of the Messenger of Allāh (ﷺ), obeying in sayings and actions. Allāh says in the Qur'ān:

$$\text{يَا أَيُّهَا الَّذِينَ آمَنُوا لَا تُقَدِّمُوا بَيْنَ يَدَيِ اللَّهِ وَرَسُولِهِ}$$

- *O you who have believed, do not put [yourselves] before Allāh and His Messenger.*
  (Al-Ĥujurāt 49:1, interpretation of the meaning)

The second: The dead heart

This type of heart is spiritually dead and contains no life, which is the opposite of the sound heart. This heart is devoid of the knowledge of His Lord and His commands, and it delves into temptations, fantasies, desires, and pleasures of the material world. Of this type of heart, Ibn al-Qayyim (d) suggests,

> Therefore, it worships other than Allāh. It directs its love, dread, reverential hope, pleasure, displeasure, glorification, and submission to other than Him. If it loves, it loves for the sake of its base desires; if it hates, it hates for the sake of its base desires; if it gives, it gives for the sake of its base desires; if it withholds, it withholds for the sake of its base desires. It gives preference to its base desires and these are more beloved to it than the Pleasure of its Master.
>
> (p. 140)

It is interesting how Ibn al-Qayyim describes the features of this dead heart.

The third: The diseased heart

This type of heart is living but has some faulty lines inherent in it, which are based on two contradictory dimensions. On one hand, it has sincerity towards Him, reliance upon Him, and faith in and love for Allāh, and these are what give it life; however, on the other hand, this heart also has a craving for lust and pleasure, prefers them, and strives to experience them. Basically, this type of heart responds to the call of whichever one of the two dimensions happens to have most control over it at a particular time. Shafi (2011) stated,

> It is constantly being tried by two callers, one calling it to Allāh, His Messenger and the abode of the Hereafter and the other calling it to temporal, worldly matters. It responds to the one that is closest and most predominant at that time.

This means that this type of heart oscillates between the moral good and deviant behaviours.

QUR'ĀNIC AND *HADĪTH* VIEWS OF THE TYPES OF HEART

Allāh mentioned these types of heart in His saying in the Qur'ān:

وَمَا أَرْسَلْنَا مِنْ قَبْلِكَ مِنْ رَسُولٍ وَلَا نَبِيٍّ إِلَّا إِذَا تَمَنَّىٰ أَلْقَى الشَّيْطَانُ فِي أُمْنِيَّتِهِ فَيَنْسَخُ اللَّهُ مَا يُلْقِي الشَّيْطَانُ ثُمَّ يُحْكِمُ اللَّهُ آيَاتِهِ ۗ وَاللَّهُ عَلِيمٌ حَكِيمٌ

لِيَجْعَلَ مَا يُلْقِي الشَّيْطَانُ فِتْنَةً لِلَّذِينَ فِي قُلُوبِهِمْ مَرَضٌ وَالْقَاسِيَةِ قُلُوبُهُمْ ۗ وَإِنَّ الظَّالِمِينَ لَفِي شِقَاقٍ بَعِيدٍ

وَلِيَعْلَمَ الَّذِينَ أُوتُوا الْعِلْمَ أَنَّهُ الْحَقُّ مِنْ رَبِّكَ فَيُؤْمِنُوا بِهِ فَتُخْبِتَ لَهُ قُلُوبُهُمْ ۗ وَإِنَّ اللَّهَ لَهَادِ الَّذِينَ آمَنُوا إِلَىٰ صِرَاطٍ مُسْتَقِيمٍ

- *And We did not send before you any messenger or prophet except that when he spoke [or recited], Satan threw into it [some misunderstanding]. But Allāh abolishes that which Satan throws in; then Allāh makes precise His verses. And Allāh is Knowing and Wise. [That is] so He may make what Satan throws in a trial for those within whose hearts is disease and those hard of heart. And indeed, the wrongdoers are in extreme dissension. And so those who were given knowledge may know that it is the truth from your Lord and [therefore] believe in it, and their hearts humbly submit to it. And indeed, is Allāh the Guide of those who have believed to a straight path.*

(Al-Haj 22:52–54, interpretation of the meaning)

Ibn al-Qayyim (d) comments on the above three verses by suggesting that

Allāh, the Glorious and Exalted, has mentioned two types of hearts put to trial and one type that is victorious. The two types of heart that are put to trial are the diseased and the harsh and dry. The victorious heart is the heart of the believer that is humble before its Lord, it is at rest and satisfaction with Him, submissive and obedient to Him.

(pp. 142–143)

That is, having a sound heart follows the natural inclination | (*Fitrah*) to the worship of God. A summary of Ibn al-Qayyim's types of hearts and characteristics is presented in Table 7.1.

Ibn al-Qayyim (d) mentions that the Companions of the Messenger of Allāh (ﷺ) (may Allāh be pleased with them) divided the hearts into four categories. Table 7.2 presents the Companions' four types of heart, their characteristics, and their meaning.

Table 7.1 Ibn al-Qayyim's types of heart

Healthy/Sound Heart	Dead Heart	Diseased Heart
Has no impediment	Is spiritually dead	Joins the ranks of the diseased hearts
Recognises and accepts truth	Is harsh	
	Does not accept the truth	Joins the ranks of the truthful and secure hearts
Submits to Allāh	Does not submit to Allāh	
Is loving	Succumbs to *Shaytān*'s whispering and creation of doubts	Hears *Shaytān*'s whispering
Opposes *Shaytān*		
Rejects *Shaytān*'s whispering and creation of doubts		Notices *Shaytān*'s creation of doubts
Is shielded or protected against the work of *Shaytān*		

Source: Adapted from Rassool (2021a).

Table 7.2 Companions' four types of heart, characteristics, and meaning

Types of heart	Characteristics	Meaning
Believer	A heart that has solely ... Illuminated by a blazing torch Polished	Detached of everything besides Allāh and His Messenger
		Separated and secured from everything save the truth
		Secure from false doubts and misguiding carnal desires
		Situated in the niche of faith
		Illuminated by the light of knowledge and faith
Disbeliever	Encased	Immersed in a veil or covering
		Cannot be reached by the light of knowledge and faith
Hypocrite	Inverted [he knew and then rejected; he saw only to become blind]	Most evil of hearts
		Allāh causes them to relapse and return to falsehood
		Believes falsehoods to be the truth and feels allegiance to those who follow falsehoods
		Believes the truth to be a falsehood and displays enmity towards those who follow truth
Faith vs. Hypocrisy	Has two desires/ inclinations	Has not become established upon faith
		Its torch is not illuminated because it has not devoted itself solely to the truth that Allāh sent His Messenger with
		Contains some faith and some of its opposite
		Is sometimes closer to disbelief than faith
		At other times, is closer to faith than disbelief
		Follows whatever is predominant within it

Source: Adapted from Ibn al-Qayyim (d).

There needs to be a clarification regarding the four categories of the heart (Table 7.2). Shafi (2011) cited that Ibn Abî Shaybah commented, "The heart that has two urges: an urge calling it to faith and an urge calling it to hypocrisy. It belongs to the need that predominates it." In relation to the 'encased heart' immersed by a veil covering the light of knowledge and faith, Allāh said in the Qur'ān:

وَقَالُوا قُلُوبُنَا غُلْفٌ

- *And they said, "Our hearts are wrapped."*
  (Al-Baqarah 2:88, interpretation of the meaning)

In his exegesis Ibn Kathir (2000) explained that this verse also relates to "Allāh has set a seal upon their hearts because of their disbelief, so they believe not but a little." According to the explanation given by Ibn al-Qayyim (d), this is a punishment from Allāh, who covered their hearts with a veil because they [the Jews] did not accept the truth: "Therefore, it is a covering upon the hearts, a seal for the ears and blindness for the eyes. This is the obscuring screen upon the eyes" (p. 146). This is reflected in the following verse of the Qur'ān,

وَإِذَا قَرَأْتَ الْقُرْآنَ جَعَلْنَا بَيْنَكَ وَبَيْنَ الَّذِينَ لَا يُؤْمِنُونَ بِالْآخِرَةِ حِجَابًا مَسْتُورًا

وَجَعَلْنَا عَلَى قُلُوبِهِمْ أَكِنَّةً أَنْ يَفْقَهُوهُ وَفِي آذَانِهِمْ وَقْرًا ۚ وَإِذَا ذَكَرْتَ رَبَّكَ فِي الْقُرْآنِ

وَحْدَهُ وَلَّوْا عَلَى أَدْبَارِهِمْ نُفُورًا

- *And when you recite the* Qur'ān, *We put between you and those who do not believe in the Hereafter a concealed partition. And We have placed over their hearts coverings, lest they understand it, and in their ears deafness.*
  (Al-Isra' 17:45–46, interpretation of the meaning)

Ibn al-Qayyim (d) comments that people with these types of hearts are rebuked "to purify their *Tawhīd*, and following innovation or imitation (*ittibāʿ*) they turn on their heels and run! The 'inverted heart' refers to the heart of the hypocrite." The individual with the characteristics of a dead heart is exemplified in the following verse. Allāh said in the Qur'ān:

صُمٌّ بُكْمٌ عُمْيٌ فَهُمْ لَا يَرْجِعُونَ

- *Deaf, dumb, and blind-so they will not return [to the right path].*
  (Al-Baqarah 2:18, interpretation of the meaning)

According to the exegesis of Ibn Kathir (2000), "deaf" means that they cannot hear the guidance, "dumb" means they cannot utter the words that might benefit them, and "blind" means they are in total darkness and deviation. This is one with the dead heart. It was narrated that 'Abdullah bin 'Amr said:

> It was said to the Messenger of Allāh (ﷺ) "Which of the people is best?" He said: "Everyone who is pure of heart and sincere in speech." They said: "Sincere in speech, we know what this is, but what is pure of heart?" He said: "It is (the heart) that is pious and pure, with no sin, injustice, rancour, or envy in it."
>
> (Ibn Majah (e))

There is a *Hadīth* relating to the four kinds of hearts based in faith, unbelief, and hypocrisy, as is authentically reported from Hudhayfah b. al-Yamān. Abu Sa'id reported: The Messenger of Allāh (ﷺ) said,

> There are four kinds of hearts: a polished heart as shiny as a radiant lamp, a sealed heart with a knot tied around it, a heart that is turned upside down, and a heart that is wrapped. As for the polished heart, it is the heart of the believer and its lamp is the light of faith. The sealed heart is the heart of the unbeliever. The heart that is turned upside down is the heart of a pure hypocrite, for he had knowledge, but he denied it. As for the heart that is wrapped, it is the heart that contains both faith and hypocrisy. The parable of faith in this heart is the parable of the herb that is sustained by pure water, and the parable of the hypocrisy in it is the parable of an ulcer that thrives upon puss and blood; whichever of the two is greater will dominate.
>
> (Ahmad (a))

TRIALS AND TRIBULATIONS OF THE HEART

The heart (*Qalb*) is subjected to trials and tribulations, is debased through deviation, and suffers punishment. However, the heart also undertakes responsibilities, receives rewarded, and is elevated through true Divine guidance. This is the heart that is like a "polished mirror" in which Divine knowledge is reflected. The diseased or dead heart will be hardened, sick, blind, sealed, and devoid or it will have limited spiritual inclinations. Thus, the individual needs to constantly check his heart to identify the nature and cause of any problem and start purifying the soul as a matter of urgency. Hudhyafah b. al-Yamān said:

> I heard the Messenger of Allāh (ﷺ) observing: Trials and tribulation will be presented to the heart [one after another] in the same way that the mat is knitted together, reed by reed. Any heart that accepts them will have a black spot form on it. Any heart that rejects them will have a white spot put on it until the hearts end up being one of two types: a black heart, murky and like an overturned vessel, it does not know the good and does not reject the evil, [all it seeks] is that which its base desires seek; and a white heart which will not be harmed by trials for as long as the heavens and the earth remain.
>
> (Muslim (i))

According to Ibn al-Qayyim (d):

> The trials that are presented to the hearts are the causes of its disease. They are the trials of carnal desires and doubts, the trials of aimless wandering and misguidance, the trials of sins and innovations and the trials of oppression and ignorance. The first type [i.e., carnal desires] leads to the corruption of desire and intent and the second type [i.e., doubts] leads to the corruption of knowledge and belief.
>
> (p. 145)

Despite its negative elements of satanic and carnal temptations, it also has another function in bringing the connection of Divine guidance to reach the individual through the *Fitrah*. This is the polished mirror.

Table 7.3 Trials and tribulations: Reactions of the heart

Types of heart	Reactions to trials and tribulations	Disease(s) of the heart
Type 1: Black heart	Is similar to a sponge soaking in water Forms a black spot Accepts trials until it becomes totally black and inverted Is like an "overturned vessel" (i.e., inverted)	Confusing good and evil Not knowing what is good or evil Believing good to be evil Believing evil to be good Believing truth to be falsehood Believing falsehood to be truth Giving precedence to basic desires when seeking judgement
Type 2: White heart	Is set ablaze with the light of faith and its niche has been illuminated Rejects trials presented to it and represses them, hence its light, blaze, and strength increase	No diseases

Source: Adapted from Rassool (2021a).

'AQL (INTELLECT): AN INTRODUCTION

The term *'Aql* originally meant "to restrain" or "to tie." It is derived from the root *'aqala'*, which means to possess intelligence, to comprehend, and to understand. Eventually it came to mean reason or intellect. *'Aql* in Islāmic psychology is the rational faculty of the soul or mind. It has also been translated as "dialectical reasoning" (Esposito, 2004, p. 22). "The root meaning of the word *'aql'* is shackle. *Aql* is normally understood as the faculty that shackles, or reins in, the forces in the *Hawā* [the animal self]" (Skinner, 2019, p. 23). The *'Aql* is regarded as one of the gifts bestowed to humans by God, the Almighty. We use our intellect to maintain our moral good, and it is essential in the development of ethical intelligence. Box 7.1 provides further explanation of *'Aql*.

Box 7.1   Explanation of *'Aql*

- The meaning of *'Aql* from Qur'ānic verses and *Sunnah*: A quality when a person has the capacity to reason, undertakes reflective practice, and acts.
- Imam Ahmad and al-Muhasibi both described *'Aql* as an innate property of man or an inborn light for perception.
- Ibn Taymīyyah (1988): Those who acted contrary to his knowledge, deserve not to be called *al-aqil* (wise or intelligent).
- Al-Jawzi (2004) suggested that the concept is restricted to only four meanings: (1) sensory-cognitive processing of information; (2) to designate self-evident things or truths; (3) that which is gained through experience; and (4) restraining oneself from the heart's vain desires [ethical intelligence].
- Dalhat (2015): "The intellectual ability to comprehend evidence of factual knowledge in an information or message received or discovered" (p. 78).

QUR'ĀN AND *'AQL*

There are a number of verses in the Qur'ān that focus on those with an absence of intellect or the power of reasoning or those who fail to use the intellect for guidance. Those who have deficit in intellect or an absence of intellect or reason would be absolved from accountability, responsibility, and liability under Islāmic *Shari'ah* [jurisprudence]. However, Allāh rebukes those who fail to use this ability. Allāh says in the Qur'ān,

إِنَّ شَرَّ ٱلدَّوَآبِّ عِندَ ٱللَّهِ ٱلصُّمُّ ٱلْبُكْمُ ٱلَّذِينَ لَا يَعْقِلُونَ

- *Indeed, the worst of living creatures in the sight of Allāh are the deaf, dumb who do not use reason.*

(Al-Anfal 8:22, interpretation of the meaning)

Allāh also mentions the individuals who failed to use their intellect to understand and be guided. Allāh mentions in the Qur'ān,

وَقَالُوا لَوْ كُنَّا نَسْمَعُ أَوْ نَعْقِلُ مَا كُنَّا فِي أَصْحَابِ ٱلسَّعِيرِ

- *And they will say, "If only we had been listening or reasoning, we would not be among the companions of the Blaze."*

    (Al-Mulk 67:10, interpretation of the meaning)

أَفَلَمْ يَسِيرُوا فِي الْأَرْضِ فَتَكُونَ لَهُمْ قُلُوبٌ يَعْقِلُونَ بِهَا أَوْ آذَانٌ يَسْمَعُونَ فَإِنَّهَا لَا تَعْمَى الْأَبْصَارُ وَلَٰكِنْ تَعْمَى الْقُلُوبُ الَّتِي فِي الصُّدُورِ

- *So, have they not travelled through the earth and have hearts by which to reason and ears by which to hear. For indeed, it is not eyes that are blinded, but blinded are the hearts which are within the breasts.*

    (Al-Haj 22:46, interpretation of the meaning)

In his exegesis, the explanation given by Ibn Kathir (2000) for "If only we had been listening or reasoning" is that

> "If we would have benefited from our intellect or listened to the truth that Allāh revealed, we would not have been disbelieving in Allāh and misguided about Him. "Have they not travelled through the land" means, "have they not travelled in the physical sense and also used their minds to ponder." "And have they hearts wherewith to understand and ears which to hear" meaning, "let them learn a lesson from that." "For indeed, it is not eyes that are blinded, but blinded are the hearts which are within the breasts" means, "the blind person is not the one whose eyes cannot see, but rather the one who has no insight. Even if the physical eyes are sound, they still cannot learn the lesson."

The following verse of the Qur'ān sums up the failure of these people to use their faculties of the heart, vision, and hearing as a means of gaining guidance or denying the truth.

لَهُمْ قُلُوبٌ لَّا يَفْقَهُونَ بِهَا وَلَهُمْ أَعْيُنٌ لَّا يُبْصِرُونَ بِهَا وَلَهُمْ ءَاذَانٌ لَّا يَسْمَعُونَ بِهَآ

- *They have hearts with which they do not understand, they have eyes with which they do not see, and they have ears with which they do not hear.*

    (Al-A'raf 7:179, interpretation of the meaning)

Al-Ghazālī (2010) describes *'Aql* as having five functions. Four of these functions essentially describe cognitive operations, such as logical reasoning. The fifth function articulates the knowledge of the heart (*Qalb*).

ANATOMICAL SEAT OF *'AQL*

There are divergent of opinions among Islāmic scholars concerning the anatomical seat of intellect. Some believe it is in the brain, while others believe it is in the heart. A brief overview of scholars and their positions is shown in Box 7.2.

Box 7.2   Anatomical seat of *'Aql*

'Aql in the brain

- Muslim physicians and jurists seem to assume that the *'Aql,* or cognition, is the function of the physical brain (Al-Bayjūrī, 2002, pp. 272–273).
- Imam Ahmad.
- Imam Abu Hanifa.

'Aql in the heart (*Qalb*)

- Imam al-Shafi'ee based on the verses in Al-Haj 22:46 and Qaf 50:37.
- Ibn al-Jawzi.
- Al-Ghazālī (2010).
- Some Hanbali scholars of jurisprudence consider the organ of intellect to be centrally in the heart.

Al-Ghazālī (2010) stated that "'Intellect' may be used with the force of knowledge (*'ilm*) of the real nature of things and is thus an expression for the quality of knowledge whose seat is the heart" (p. 9). Ibn Taymīyyah (1988) observed,

"Where does intellect, reason (*aql*) reside within it (the body)?" Then reason is established with the soul that displays reason (grasps, understands). And as for the body, then it is connected to his heart, just as Allāh, the Most High said, "Do they not traverse through the Earth wherewith they have hearts with which they understand" (Al-Haj 22:46). And it was said to Ibn Abbas, "How did you acquire knowledge?" He said, "With an inquisitive tongue and an understanding heart."

(pp. 53–55)

It is valuable to clarify the position of Ibn Taymīyyah (1988) on the relationship between the heart and the brain. He stated,

However, that which is correct (in the matter) is that the spirit, which is the soul, it has a connection to this (the heart) and to that (the brain), and that which it is described of intellect is connected to both this and that.

(pp. 53–55)

What Ibn Taymīyyah attempts to do is synthesise the two opposite views by explaining that "cognition is related to both heart and brain. He said the foundation of the will and decision making is in the heart, and the foundation of thought is the brain" (Dalhat, 2015, p. 81). Other authors also commented on the relationship between the intellect and the combination of the heart and the brain. It has been suggested that '*Aql*

is not exclusive to any organ but is connected to the soul, heart and brain that collectively play a role in producing the attribute of intellect (*aql*) in a person, and within those roles, the heart is in the driver's seat and the brain is an accomplice and without the soul there is no life (*hayaat*), hence reason (*aql*) is said of all three.

(Abu Iyaad, 2013)

However, a review of the evidence from the Qur'ān, *Sunnah*, the Arabic language, and other collateral evidence identifies the heart as the central seat of intelligence rather than the brain (Dalhat, 2015). There is now evidence from the relatively new field of neurocardiology about the role of the cardiac neurons, which are about 40,000 neurons called 'sensory neurites' that communicate with the brain (Armour, 2007), the complex nervous network of the heart (Kukanova & Mravec, 2006), and the intracardiac nervous system (Durães Campos et al., 2018).

INTERRELATIONSHIP BETWEEN THE *QALB*, '*AQL*, AND *NAFS*

It is through the purification of the self (*Nafs*) that there is sense of equilibrium and synthesis between these three elements, giving rise towards the *Fitrah*. Allāh mentions in the Qur'ān,

$$وَنَفْسٍ وَمَا سَوَّىٰهَا$$

$$فَأَلْهَمَهَا فُجُورَهَا وَتَقْوَىٰهَا$$

$$قَدْ أَفْلَحَ مَن زَكَّىٰهَا$$

$$وَقَدْ خَابَ مَن دَسَّىٰهَا$$

- *And [by] the soul and He who proportioned it*

  And inspired it [with discernment of] its wickedness and its righteousness, He has succeeded who purifies it,

  And he has failed who instils it [with corruption].
  (Ash-Shams 91:7–10, interpretation of the meaning)

The commentaries on the above verses from Saheeh International (n.d.) suggest,

That God after giving the human self powers of the body, sense and mind has not left it uninformed in the world but has instilled into his unconscious by means of a natural inspiration the distinction between good and evil, right and wrong, and the sense of the good to be good and of the evil to be evil. That the future of man depends on how by using the powers of discrimination, will and judgment that God has endowed him with, he develops the good and suppresses the evil tendencies of the self. If he develops the good inclination and frees his self of the evil inclinations, he will attain to eternal success, and if, on the contrary, he suppresses the good and promotes the evil, he will meet with disappointment and failure.

(Al-Mehri, 2010, p. 617)

In his exegesis Ibn Kathir (2000) explained that verses 7 to 10 indicate that

> Allāh created it sound and well-proportioned upon the correct nature (*Al-fitrah*). Allāh He explained the good and the evil to it (the *Nafs*). He showed him to his transgression and his *Taqwa* [God consciousness]. This means that He clarified that for it and He guided it to what has been ordained for him.

Al-Ghazālī (1993) provides an analogy to explain the relationship between these three elements:

> Soul is a king over body as a king over an empire. In the empire of soul, hands, feet and other organs are like different businessmen and industrialists in town. Greed is a collector of revenue in that town, anger is its police, intellect is it minister and soul is its king. The collector greed is like one who collects food and anger is like a police who keeps guard over it. The collector greed is a downright liar and a deceiver. It ostensibly wishes good but there is destructive poison in it. The reign of soul over the region of body is similar. It goes on well if all organs and attributes are under the rule of soul. When soul takes the help of its minister intellect, it rules over greed keeping anger in control.

(pp. 5–6)

This means that a mature *'Aql* will enable the *Qalb* to make connection with God. In contrast, an *'Aql* with limited knowledge will find it trickier to control the *Nafs* of its impulsiveness and desires, and it will cause the *Qalb* to become rusty and not shining, like a mirror that reflects evils rather than virtues.

Gulam (2018) examines the *Qalb* in relation to the *Nafs* and *'Aql* in the development and make-up of human nature. That is, its role in the development of human personality and characteristics. Just like the self needs to be polished like a mirror, the "*qalb* may be polished by struggling against desires, acquiring good characteristics, seclusion, solitude and continually remembering (*zikr*) Allāh" (Cited in Solihin, 2012). This means that after the purification of the *Nafs*, the *Qalb* also needs to be purified, to be shined as a polished mirror will reflect the right virtues and absence of evils. Al-Ghazālī cites a famous saying from the Prophet (ﷺ):

> An-Nu'man b. Bashir reported God's Messenger as saying, "In the body there is a piece of flesh, and the whole body is sound if it is sound, but the whole body is corrupt if it is corrupt. It is the heart."
>
> (Bukhari & Muslim (d))

This means that the sound *Qalb* acts as a shield protecting both the *'Aql* and the *Nafs* from evil temptations. It has been suggested that "a strong *qalb* can protect the *aql* from deviation and wrongful thought and raise the *nafs* in status to *al-Muṭma'innah*" (Gulam, 2018, p. 207). It is through the process of purification of the *Nafs* and the *Qalb* that the *'Aql*, *Nafs*, and *Qalb* can be bound, despite their inequalities and function, in an integrated whole.

CONCLUSION

In the context of Islāmic psychology, the *Qalb and 'Aql* are two additional components of the inner world of the human being: the spiritual heart and the rational mind. The process of purification of the self (*Nafs*) ensures that they exist in equilibrium and synthesis, even in world of trials and tribulations.

FURTHER READINGS

Al-Ghazālī, A.H. (2016). *Disciplining the soul, refining the character, and curing the sicknesses of the heart.* Cambridge: The Islamic Texts Society.

8

ISLĀMIC HEALING

INTRODUCTION

Islāmic psychologists are increasingly aware that for mental health problems their patients may utilise faith-based healing practices rooted in their Islāmic worldview in place of psychotropic medications and/or traditional psychotherapy. The holistic dimension of health is integrated and unified within the Qurʾān and *Sunnah* of Islām. *Ash-shifa'* is one of the names of the Qurʾānic and *Surah Al-Fātiḥah*, which has the meaning of "that which heals" or "the restorer of health." Healing is regarded as an intervention, an outcome, a process, and, at times, all three components (Levin, 2018). From an Islāmic perspective, healing originates from the divine source, and it is through this divine connection with sacredness that healing takes place. In addition, healing is obtained through the individual process and from natural substances (e.g., herbs and medicines). It is Allāh that is *As-Shafi* (The Healer) and not the psychologist or healthcare practitioner. It was narrated by ʿAisha (May Allāh be pleased with her) that Allāh's Messenger (ﷺ) used to treat with a *Ruqyah* [prayers for healing or protective purposes] saying, "O the Lord of the people! Remove the trouble The cure is in Your Hands, and there is none except You who can remove it (the disease)" (Bukhari (b)). In this context, the Islāmic psychologist or health care practitioner is the facilitator and not the healer. It is Almighty Allāh that knows the diseases of the soul, heart, body, and mind as well as their cures. Surely Allāh has testified this in the Qurʾān.

DOI: 10.4324/9781003312956-8

وَإِن يَمْسَسْكَ ٱللَّهُ بِضُرٍّ فَلَا كَاشِفَ لَهُ إِلَّا هُوَ

- *And if Allāh should touch you with adversity, there is no remover of it except him.*

(Al-'An`am 6:17, interpretation of meaning)

Healing has been defined as "a positive, subjective, unpredictable process involving transformation to a new sense of wholeness, spiritual transcendence, and reinterpretation of life. Operational definition: Healing is the personal experience of transcending suffering and transforming to wholeness" (McElliott, 2010, p. 251). This means that there are contemplation-, reflection-, and action-oriented approaches in the healing process.

Firth et al. (2015) have suggested that the concept of healing has several defining attributes: "Healing is a holistic transformative process; it is personal; it is innate or naturally occurring; it is multidimensional; and it involves repair and recovery of mind, body, and spirit" (p. 46). Healing is a process that transforms the individual in progressive stages on the healing journey, moving on a continuum from illness behaviour to wellness. This is a personal and subjective experience of trials and tribulations at the emotional, psychological, social, and spiritual levels. Muslims endure many trials throughout their lives. It has been suggested that healing involves repair and recovery of the wholeness for the total person (Carlson & Shield, 1989). From an Islāmic perspective, healing involves the purification of multiple dimensions: mind, body, and soul. The focus of this chapter is on an examination of the concept of Islāmic healing; the relationship between body, mind, and soul; and how to heal the body and soul using Islāmic spiritual interventions.

HEALING FROM THE QUR'ĀN

وَنُنَزِّلُ مِنَ ٱلْقُرْءَانِ مَا هُوَ شِفَآءٌ وَرَحْمَةٌ لِّلْمُؤْمِنِينَ

- *And We send down of the Qur'ān and that which is healing and mercy for the believers.*

(Al-Isrā' 17:82, interpretation of the meaning)

In Islām, the Qur'ān is not just a guidance but a healing for humankind. The above verse echoes the focus of the Qur'ān. Al-Haafiz Ibn Kathir (2000) said in his commentary on this verse:

> Here Allāh tells us about His Book, which He revealed to His Messenger Muhammad (ﷺ) and it takes away the diseases in the heart such as doubt, hypocrisy, *shirk*, deviation and misguidance; the Qur'ān heals all of that. And it is also a mercy which brings about faith, wisdom and the pursuit of and desire for goodness. This is only for those who believe in it and follow it; for such it will be a healing and a mercy.

Though the complete Qur'ān is a source of healing, there are five other verses that address healing and are referred to as *Ayat Ash-Shifa* or the Qur'ānic verses of healing. In one verse, Allāh says:

قُلْ هُوَ لِلَّذِينَ ءَامَنُواْ هُدًى وَشِفَآءٌ

- *Say: It is for those who believe, a guidance and cure.*
(Fuṣṣilat 41:44, interpretation of the meaning)

The following verse also reflects the power of the Qur'ān:

يَـٰٓأَيُّهَا ٱلنَّاسُ قَدْ جَآءَتْكُم مَّوْعِظَةٌ مِّن رَّبِّكُمْ وَشِفَآءٌ لِّمَا فِى ٱلصُّدُورِ وَهُدًى وَرَحْمَةٌ لِّلْمُؤْمِنِي

- *O mankind, there has to come to you instruction from your Lord and healing for what is in the breasts and guidance and mercy for the believers.*
(Yunus 10:57, interpretation of the meaning)

The other verses relating to Qur'ānic healing include At-Tawba 9:14, An-Nahl 16:69, and Ash-Shu'arâ 26:80. There is guidance in the Qur'ān that contains innumerable benefits, so everyone who wishes to maintain physical, psychological, and spiritual health (mind, body, and soul) in this world and in the Hereafter must refer to it for judgement and follow its commands. In Islāmic thought, human nature and behaviour and emotions are inherent holistic processes that integrate physical, psychological, social, and spiritual dimensions. Accordingly, the Islāmic nature of the human being is whole, comprehensive, and complete according to the Qur'ān and *Sunnah*. In essence,

> Islam provides a balanced focus between universal principles of human behaviours (with its universal laws and *Shar'iah* or divine laws) and individual differences. The universal laws may include biological, social, psychological and economic dimensions based on empirical research. The Qur'ān and *Hadīth* provide guidance and basis to the laws of human nature. These laws can be used as the foundation to develop theories about human nature based upon the writings of Muslim scholars and contemporary research findings.
>
> (Rassool, 2021a, p. xv)

This shows us that the Qur'ān has many benefits, including good advice and guidance, cures for our hearts and for all diseases, and a Mercy for mankind. So, the Qur'ān is the complete source of healing for all mental, spiritual, and physical diseases – all diseases of this world and the Hereafter. However, Ibn al-Qayyim Al-Jawziyyah (c) (May Allāh have mercy on him) said:

> Not everyone is guided to use it for the purpose of healing. If the sick person uses the Qur'ān for healing in the proper way, and applies it to his disease with sincerity, faith, complete acceptance and firm conviction, fulfilling all its conditions, then no disease can resist it. There is no sickness, spiritual or physical, but in the Qur'ān there is that which indicates its remedy, its cause and how to protect against it for those who are blessed with understanding of His Book. The Qur'ān contains the treatment for hearts and souls, and as such it is a means of expelling all sicknesses from the body. In this regard the Qur'ān is a healing and a remedy for many diseases.
>
> (Vol. 1, pp. 164–165)

IMPORTANCE OF HEALTH IN ISLĀM

The Islāmic perspective on the key to health (physical, mental, and spiritual) is "to maintain the connection with our Creator, Allāh, the Exalted and the Almighty; to fully submit to Him and His decree; to subsequently purify the soul and cleanse the heart; and to enjoy what is good and forbid what is evil" (Rassool, 2020, p. 11). In the Western tradition, the word 'health' is derived from an Anglo-Saxon word meaning "whole, holy, and healthy." 'Heal' means "to make sound or whole" and stems from the root, *haelan*, literally "to make whole" (Merriam-Webster, n.d.). Optimal health is attained when all of the dimensions (physical, social, emotional, intellectual, spiritual, and environmental/occupational) are interrelated and in equilibrium. The Muslim scholar Alâ' ad-Deen Abul Haasan 'Ali ibn Abi Haazm al-Qarshi ad-Dimashqi, also known as Ibn an-Nafees (n.d.), defined health as a "state of the body in which functions are normal per se while disease is the opposite state." Thus, health is perceived as the body's baseline condition, and disease is a reaction of the body due to abnormal functioning. Health becomes the norm, and disease is the imbalance of the body's functions.

Thus, Islām places health as a blessing. Ibn Abbas (May Allāh be pleased with him) reported that the Messenger of Allāh (ﷺ) said, "There are two blessings in which many people incur loss. (They are) health and free time (for doing good)" (Bukhari (c)). Another *Hadīth* gives us the proper perspective of the essential things in life:

> 'Ubaidullah bin Mihsan Al-Ansari (May Allāh be pleased with him) reported that the Messenger of Allāh (ﷺ) said, "Whosoever begins the day feeling family security and good health; and possessing provision for his day is as though he possessed the whole world."
>
> (Tirmidhi (c))

In another *Hadīth*, the Prophet (ﷺ) defines the relative importance of health and wealth: "There is no harm in wealth for someone who has *taqwa* (God consciousness), but health for the person who has *taqwa* is even better than wealth. Cheerfulness is a blessing" (Al-Adab Al-Mufrad (b)). The importance of health is also echoed in the following *Hadīth*: The Prophet (ﷺ) said, "Ask God for forgiveness and health, for after being granted certainty, one is given nothing better than health" (Tirmidhî (d)). In Islām the maintenance of good health is part of our responsibility and accountability. Abu Hurairah narrated that the Messenger of Allāh (ﷺ) said: "Indeed the first of what will be asked about on the Day of Judgment – meaning the slave (of Allāh) being questioned about the favours – is that it will be said to him: 'Did We not make your body, health, and give you of cool water to drink?'" (Tirmidhî (e)).

The factors contributing to health and illness are multi-dimensional, including spiritual, ecological, psychological, emotional, and nutritional dimensions as well as exercise and physical activity, sleep, and wakefulness. The maintenance of harmony with the laws of God in body and soul is between the individual, the family, and the community. The preservation of health is enjoined, and it involves maintaining a moderate health balance in a state of dynamic equilibrium. That is, adherence to Islāmic lifestyles is a realisation of the true nature of the human being (*Fitrah*) by establishing positive behavioural patterns to promote health and rejecting any behaviours that are contradictory to health. This is reflected in the statements made by Kasule (2008):

The Muslim must keep his body physically fit to be able to undertake the functions of vicegerency and building a civilisation. Poor health not only deprives society of the contributions of an individual, but also creates a burden for others. Neglect of one's health is a sin. It is a religious obligation for the sick to seek treatment. It is also obligatory to undertake disease-preventing measures such as dietary regulation, general and oral hygiene, avoiding violence, avoiding spiritual diseases that precede mental illness, or in general avoiding anything that impairs good health. Prevention and public health of physical, psychological and spiritual health, in Islam, is given high priority. However, there is a greater need to give serious consideration to the spiritual dimension and the role it plays in health and disease. There is a need to show our gratitude to Allāh by worshipping Him and doing good things. Imam Al-Ghazālī (n.d.) stated that "A proper understanding and implementation of religion, from the standpoint of both knowledge and worship, can only be arrived at through physical health and life preservation."

SPIRITUALITY AND HEALTH

Spirituality is an important aspect of healing. In some Western nations, spirituality, as a concept, is perceived as not being interchangeable with religion. From an Islāmic perspective, the concept of spirituality has a broader meaning than religion and encompasses philosophical ideas about life, the code of behaviour, ethics, the meaning of life, and purpose. Rassool (2000) stated,

> In Islām and following the Qur'ān and *Hādīth*, there is no distinction between religion and spirituality. The concept of religion is embedded in the umbrella of spirituality. In the Islāmic context, there is no spirituality without religious thoughts and practices, and the religion of Islām provides the spiritual path for salvation and a way of life. Central to Islāmic teachings are the connections between knowledge, health, holism, the environment, and the "Oneness of Allāh," the unity of God in all spheres of life, death, and the hereafter. Islāmic teachings and practice have enabled the development of a holistic framework in meeting the physical, spiritual, psycho-social, and environmental needs of the individuals and communities.
>
> (p. 1479)

The spiritual model health in Islām is an interrelation between the mind, the spirit and the body, because the essence of the human being is holistic in nature: biologically, psychologically, socially, and spiritually (transcendentally). The concept of self is expressed by body, mind, and soul connection. In Islāmic tradition, there are interconnections between the soul (*al-Nafs*), the spirit (*al-Rûh*), the intellect (*al-'Aql*), and the heart (*al-Qalb*) (see Chapter 6) as well as the body (*jism*), and all find their respective roots in the Qur'ān. All of these entities have a strong and significant influence on the healing process. It is the harmony between mind, body, and soul that enables the process of healing to occur.

For Muslims, their concerns are not only about physical and psychological health but also spiritual health. Al-Ghazālī divided illness into physical and spiritual. According to Fidanboylu (2017), Al-Ghazālī

> stated that spiritual illnesses are far more dangerous than physical, which results from the ignorance and deviation from The All-Mighty

Allāh. He determined some of the spiritual illnesses as: self-centeredness, addiction to wealth, fame and status, ignorance, cowardice, cruelty, lust, doubt (*Waswâs*), malevolence, calumny, envy, deceit, and avarice.

(p. 5)

All of these dimensions of health are interwoven and holistic, and any repair or cure cannot be devoid of spiritual healing.

From an Islāmic worldview, the real purpose of life for Muslims is to know, worship, and obey Allāh. The theme of spirituality is embedded with subthemes and dimensions that include the meaning of life, the purpose of life in this world and hereafter, hopes and fears, having absolute trust in Allāh (*Al-Tawakkul Allāh*), and trials and tribulations. The dimension of trials and tribulations involves suffering. Muslims believe that Allāh tests us with hardships as well as prosperity in order to validate the sincerity of our faith. It is normal that we experience stress during the tests and trials that Allāh presents to us in this life. Allāh says in the Qur'ān,

وَلَنَبْلُوَنَّكُم بِشَىْءٍ مِّنَ ٱلْخَوْفِ وَٱلْجُوعِ وَنَقْصٍ مِّنَ ٱلْأَمْوَٰلِ وَٱلْأَنفُسِ وَٱلثَّمَرَٰتِ وَبَشِّرِ

وَلَنَبْلُوَنَّكُم بِشَىْءٍ مِّنَ ٱلْخَوْفِ وَٱلْجُوعِ وَنَقْصٍ مِّنَ ٱلْأَمْوَٰلِ وَٱلْأَنفُسِ وَٱلثَّمَرَٰتِ وَبَشِّرِ

ٱلصَّٰبِرِينَ

- *And We will surely test you with something of fear and hunger and a loss of wealth, lives, and fruits but give good tidings to the patient.*
  (Al-Baqarah 2:155, interpretation of the meaning)

During trials and tribulations, a Muslim must show endurance, resilience, and patience as faith will be tested, as identified by the following verse of the Qur'ān:

لَقَدْ خَلَقْنَا ٱلْإِنسَٰنَ فِى كَبَدٍ

- *We have certainly created man into hardship.*
  (Al-Balad 90:4, interpretation of the meaning)

So, when any disease befalls a Muslim, it can be expiation for his/her sins. For this reason, many Muslims do not seek help, as they believe illness can and will purify the body (Rassool, 2000). Sometimes, the intensity of the suffering is related to their level of faith or connection with Allāh. Eltaiba (2007) suggested that the "stronger the connection with Allāh, the more a person would be subject to trials. Trials in this sense are considered a chance to get rewarded for the level of endurance" (p. 125). It is a fact that in time of trials and tribulations our spirituality is awakened, and we experience the transcendence of suffering. In simpler terms, it is the realisation of the truth of our existence and our potential for spiritual growth by seeking divine intervention. Trials and tribulations are part of the process in the purification of the soul. The purification of the soul is a kind of 'self-actualisation' of the soul by striving to move closer to becoming as much of a complete and truthful servant of Allāh as possible depending on potential. The purification of the soul goes beyond the ritual acts of worship to become complete as a servant of Allāh. Shaykh Ibn 'Uthaymeen (2001) categorises people into four distinct levels based on their reactions to trials and tribulations (Box 8.1).

Box 8.1   Shaykh Ibn 'Uthaymeen (2001) on people's reactions to trials and tribulations

- First Level: Discontent (Forbidden). Involves discontent with the Lord, showing anger, and may even lead to disbelief. People may invoke woe, cause destruction (striking the cheeks, tearing the clothes, and pulling out the hair), and the like, and this is forbidden.
- Second Level: Patience (Obligatory). Faith protects the person from discontent.
- Third Level: Acceptance (Highly preferred): A person accepts misfortune so that its presence or absence are the same to him.
- Fourth Level: Gratitude (Highest Level). The person thanks Allāh for the misfortune that has befallen him. Trials and tribulations are expiations of sins, and the person's reward is increased.

ISLĀMIC HEALING

Islāmic healing and genuine restoration and repair are always an act of Divine intervention. Mohamed (2020) suggested that

Islamic psycho-spiritual healing is not only concerned with restoring the psyche to a state of balance, or helping a person become socially well-adjusted, but will help the psyche transcend itself and enter the higher spiritual domain that aligns with innate human nature (*fiṭrah*).

The healing process is a continuum ranging from illness behaviour to wellness behaviour that involves both a protective dimension and a dimension of repairing and restoring.

The Qurʾān and the *Sunnah* are the central sources of references for the prevention and protection of Muslims in relation to evil eyes, *Jinn* possession, and witchcraft. Box 8.2 provides a summary of preventive measures from Shaykh Ibn al-Qayyim al-Jawziyya (n.d.) (May Allāh have mercy on him).

Box 8.2   Summary of preventive measures from Shaykh Ibn Qayyim

- One has to observe pure *Tawhid* [Unicity of God].
- Seek Allāh's protection.
- Observe *Taqwa* [God consciousness].
- Patience is the key to safety.
- Put one's trust in Allāh.
- Ignore or dismiss them from one's thoughts.
- Get nearer to Allāh.
- Repent of one's sins.
- Seek Allāh's forgiveness.
- Give charity.
- Treat others well.

Source: Adapted from *Bada'iʿ al-Fawa'id*, Shaykh Ibn al-Qayyim al-Jawziyyah (n.d.)

PREVENTION OF EVIL EYE AND *JINN* POSSESSION

The general intervention is to seek refuge with Allāh, and this is the most important aspect of Islamic interventions to fight against all human and *Jinn* evils. Seeking refuge in Allāh is both an action of the heart and of the tongue. The term *Isti'adha* is an abbreviation for saying "I seek refuge in Allāh" (*Aoothubillah*). The most common way of seeking refuge with Allāh is to say:

أعوذ بالله من الشيطان الرجيم

* *I seek refuge with Allāh, from the accursed Shaytān.*

According to Ibn Kathir (2000), *Isti'adha* means:

I seek refuge with Allāh from the cursed *Satan* so that he is prevented from affecting my religious or worldly affairs or hindering me from adhering to what I was commanded or luring me into what I was prohibited from.

Qamar (2013) suggested that "seeking refuge with Allāh gives a powerful feeling of security that acts like a psychological shield" (p. 48). However, for this shield to be effective, the two fundamental dimensions of the belief system – namely, belief in the Oneness of Allāh and trust in Allāh – must be adhered to. In terms of prevention, this is done by seeking Allāh's blessings. "[I]t is narrated in the al-Sahihayn that 'Aishah (may Allah be pleased with her) said: 'The Messenger of Allāh (ﷺ) used to tell me to recite *Ruqyah* (incantation) for protection against the evil eye'" (Islam Q&A, 2003b). It was narrated that Sahl ibn Haneef said: "The Messenger of Allāh (ﷺ) said: 'If one of you sees something that he likes in himself or his wealth, let him pray for blessing for it, for the evil eye is real" (Ibn Al-Sunni, Imam Ahmad & Al-Haakim, n.d.). Al-Qurtubi (n.d.) stated that "Every Muslim who likes something must pray for blessing, for if he prays for blessing, that will ward off any potential harm, beyond a doubt."

The fortress against the devils, *Jinn*, and witchcraft is to adhere to the teachings of the of the Qur'ān and the *Sunnah*. That is, for protection people should recite the *Al-Mu'awwidhatayn* (*Surahs Al-Falaq* and *An-Nas*, *Surah Al-Ikhlas*, Surah *Al-Fatihah*, and *Ayat-ul-Kursiy* (the Qur'anic Verse of the Throne, *Surah Al-Baqarah*, 2:255); the whole chapter of *Surah Al-Baqarah*; the last two verses of *Surat Al-Baqarah* at night; the remembrance of Allāh (*Dhikr*); and the call to prayer (*Adhan*). Shaykh Ibn 'Uthaymeen (n.d.) stated that "if a person recites *Ayat al-Kursiy* [*Surat al-Baqarah* 2:255] at night, he will continue to have protection from Allāh, and no *Shaytān* will come near him until morning. And Allāh is the Protector." In addition to the above shields, for protection against evils it is important to strengthen one's faith and remember Allāh often (*Dhikr*). It was narrated from al-Harith al-Ash'ari that the Prophet (ﷺ) said:

> Allāh commanded Yahya ibn Zakariya (peace be upon him) five things to follow and to enjoin upon the Children of Israel … and he commanded them to remember Allāh, and the likeness of that is a man who was being pursued by the enemy, until he reached a strong fortress in which he found protection; similarly, a man cannot find protection from the Shaytān except by remembering Allāh.
>
> (Tirmidhî (f))

The call of prayer (the *Adhan*) is also a fortress against evils. It was narrated by Abu Hurairah (may Allāh be pleased with him) that the Messenger of Allāh (ﷺ) said: "When the Shaytān hears the call to prayer, he runs away fast" (Muslim (b)). The regular recitation of the Qur'ān offers protection against the devil.

There is also a recommendation to eat a special kind of date, the *Ajwah*, which is grown in the city of Madinah, Saudi Arabia, and costs around 70 Saudi Riyals per kilogram. There are many *Hādīths* relating to the use of *Ajwah* dates for protection. It is narrated that the Messenger (ﷺ) said, "If Somebody takes seven *Ajwah* dates in the morning, neither magic nor poison will hurt him that day" (Bukhari (g)); "*Ajwah* dates are from paradise" (Tirmidhî (g)); and in reference to someone eating seven *Ajwah* dates, "He will not be harmed by anything until he reaches the evening" (Muslim (c)).

A summary of the protective measures against evils and *Jinns* is presented in Table 8.1.

HEALING INTERVENTIONS: REPAIR AND RESTORATION

The following Islamic healing interventions can be used as a protective shield and also as therapeutic interventions for spiritual diseases, evil eye, *Jinn* possession, and witchcraft. Muslim clients are

Table 8.1 Protections and supplications against evil eye and *Jinn* possession

	Protections and supplications
General interventions	• Seek refuge with Allāh: "I seek refuge with Allāh, from the accursed Shaytān."
	• "O Allāh! I seek refuge with You from worry and grief, from incapacity and laziness, from cowardice and miserliness, from being heavily in debt and from being overpowered by (other) men" (*Allaahumma inni a'oodhu bika min al-hammi wa'l-hazani, wa a'oodhi bika min al-'ajzi wa'l-kasali, wa a'oodhu bika min al-jubni wa'l-bukhli, wa a'oodhi bika min ghalabat il-dayn wa qahri al-rijaal*) (Bukhari (d)).
	• "O Allāh! I seek Refuge with Your Perfect Words from every devil and from poisonous pests and from every evil, harmful, envious eye" (*U'eethukumaa bikalimaatil-laahit-taam-mati min kulli shaitaanin wa haam-matin, wa min kulli 'ainin laammatin*) (Bukhari (e)).
Evil eye	• The Messenger of Allāh (ﷺ) supplicated: *Baarik Allaahu fih (May Allāh bless it)* or *Allaahumma baarik 'alayhi (O Allāh, bless it)*.
	• And one may say: *MaSha' Allāh (that which Allāh wills will come to pass)*.
	• "I seek refuge with the Perfect Words of Allāh from the evil of what He has created" (*A'oodhu bi kalimat-illah il-tammati min sharri ma khalaqa*).
	• "I seek refuge with the Perfect Words of Allāh from His Anger and Punishment, and from the evil of His creatures, and the incitements of devils and their presence" (*A'oodhu bi kalimat-illah il-tammati min ghadabihi wa 'iqabihi, wa min sharri 'ibadihi wa min hamazat al-shayateeni wa an yahduroon*).
Jinn possession	• Recite *Al-Mu'awwidhatayn (Surahs Al-Falaq and Al-Nas), Surah Al-Ikhlas, Surah Al-Fatihah*, and *Ayat-ul-Kursiy* (the Qur'ānic Verse of the Throne, *Surah Al-Baqarah*, 2:255).
	• "I seek refuge with the Perfect Words of Allāh from the evil of what He has created (*A'oodhu bi kalimat-illah il-tammati min sharri ma khalaqa*).

(*Continued*)

Table 8.1 Cont.

Protections and supplications
• "I seek refuge with the Perfect Words of Allāh from His Anger and Punishment, and from the evil of His creatures, and the incitements of devils and their presence" (*A'oodhu bi kalimat-illah il-tammati min ghadabihi wa 'iqabihi, wa min sharri 'ibadihi wa min hamazat al-shayateeni wa an yahduroon*). • Qur'ān 2:255: "None has the right to be worshipped but He ... Allāh!" (*La ilaha illa Huwa*). • Read the whole chapter of Qur'ān 2. • Qur'ān 2:285–286: Read the last two verses of *Surat al-Baqarah* at night. • Recite [100 times]: "There is no god except Allāh Alone with no partner or associate; His is the Sovereignty and His is the praise, and He is able to do all things" (*La ilaha ill-Allāh wahdahu la shareeka lah, lahu'l-mulk wa lahu'l-hamd wa huwa 'ala kulli shayin Qadeer*). • Remember Allāh often: *Dhikr*. • Call to prayer. The *Adhan*. • Reciting the Qur'ān offers protection against the *Shaytān*: Allāh says (interpretation of the meaning): "And when you (Muhammad) recite the Qur'ān, We put between you and those who believe not in the Hereafter, an invisible veil (or screen their hearts, so they hear or understand it not)" [Qur'ān 17:45]. • Eat seven dates daily (morning): *Ajwa* (or other dates).

encouraged to heal themselves through prayers, supplications or *Du'as*, reading the Qur'ān, and trusting Allāh.

Remembrance of Allāh

The concept of remembrance of Allāh (*Dhikr*) is central to Islamic practices in the form of glorifying, exalting, and praising. For example, Allāh says in the Qur'ān (interpretation of the meaning):

"So remember Me; I will remember you. And be grateful to Me, and do not deny Me" (Al-Baqarah 2:152). Those who have believed and whose hearts are assured by the remembrance of Allāh. Unquestionably, by the remembrance of Allāh hearts are assured" (Ar-Ra`d 13:12), and so "remember the name of your Lord and devote yourself to Him with [complete] devotion" (Al-Muzzammil 73:8).

It is stated that

all scholars of Islam have agreed on the acceptance and permissibility of the remembrance of Allāh by heart and by tongue, for the adult men and women, for children, for the one who has ablution, and for the one without ablution, even for the woman during her menses. Moreover, *Dhikr* is allowed by all scholars in the form of *Tasbih* (glorifying), *Tahmid* (praising), *Takbir* (exalting), and praising for the Prophet (ﷺ).

(Imam Nawawi, n.d.)

The Prophet (ﷺ) said: "The example of the one who remembers his Lord (God) in comparison with the one who does not remember his Lord is that of the living and the dead" (Bukhari & Muslim (a)). Qadhi (2009) suggested, "If you truly have spirituality, if your heart is alive, it will be manifested in *Dhikr*." One of the blessings of *Dhikr* is that it purifies the heart and makes it alive. Shaykh al-Islam Ibn Taymiyah (n.d.), one of the great scholars of medieval Islām, said that

the example of *Dhikr* to the heart is that of fish to water; and if you do not do *Dhikr*, your heart will die. It was the Prophet (ﷺ) that told Mu'ādh Ibn Jabal, the famous companion never forgets to say *Dhikr* after the prayer (*Salaat*).

Prayer as a healing strategy

Prayer is the strategy most frequently used by believers and non-believers to cope with personal problems and to seek spiritual guidance. From an Islāmic perspective, prayer (*As-Salah*) is a direct communication with Allāh and the second pillar of Islam. The nearest a person is to His Lord is when he is in a state of prostration (*Sajdah*) in prayer. *Sajdah* is the highest degree of humility that an individual can exhibit before his Creator. The main purpose of prayer is the remembrance of God, as stated in the Qur'ān:

إِنَّنِى أَنَا ٱللَّهُ لَاۤ إِلَٰهَ إِلَّاۤ أَنَا۠ فَٱعۡبُدۡنِى وَأَقِمِ ٱلصَّلَوٰةَ لِذِكۡرِىٓ

- *Indeed, I am Allāh. There is no deity except Me, so worship Me and establish prayer for My remembrance.*

(Ṭāhā 20:14, interpretation of the meaning)

The Prophet (ﷺ) said "The first thing among their deeds for which the people will be brought to account on the Day of Resurrection will be prayer" (Abu Dawud (a)). The other functions of prayer include acting as a shield or protection against evil, prohibiting immorality and wrongdoing, wiping out sins or evil deeds, building the ideal Muslim character, and serving as a source of comfort and tranquillity (Rassool, 2019).

Making supplications (Du'as)

Supplications have the enormous potential to help us ask for forgiveness and other things. The following are some of the Prophet's sayings about making *Du'ah* to Allāh. The Prophet (ﷺ) said: "The *Du'as* of any one of you will be answered so long as he does not seek to hasten it, and does not say, 'I made *Du'as*, but I had no answer'" (Bukhari & Muslim (b)). The Messenger of Allāh (ﷺ) said:

"There is no man who prays to Allāh and makes *Du'as* to Him and does not receive a response. Either it will be hastened for him in this world, or it will be stored up for him in the Hereafter, so long as he does not pray for something sinful, or to cut the ties of kinship, or seek a speedy response." They said, "O Messenger of Allāh, what does seeking a speedy response mean?" He said, "Saying, 'I prayed to my Lord, and He did not answer me.'"

(Tirmidhî (h))

The Prophet (ﷺ) said:

> If a person who is afflicted by anxiety or sorrow says: "*Allaahumma inni 'abduka wa ibnu 'abdika wa ibn ammatika naasiyati bi yadika maadin fiyya hukmuka 'adlun fiyya qadaa'uka as'aluka bi kulli ismin huwa laka sammayta bihi nafsaka aw 'allamtahu ahadan min khalqika aw anzaltahu fi kitaabika aw asta'tharta bihi fi 'ilm il-ghaybi 'indaka an taj'al al-Qur'aana rabee'a qalbi wa noora sadri wa jalaa'a huzni wa dhahaaba hammi*" ("O Allah, I am Your slave, and the son of Your male slave, and the son of your female slave. My forehead is in Your Hand (i.e., you have control over me). Your Judgment upon me is assured, and Your Decree concerning me is just. I ask You by every Name that You have named Yourself with, revealed in Your Book, taught any one of Your creation or kept unto Yourself in the knowledge of the unseen that is with You, to make the Qur'an the spring of my heart, and the light of my chest, the banisher of my sadness, and the reliever of my distress").

(Ahmad (a))

Ruqyah

Ruqyah (incantation) in Islām is the recitation of the Qur'ān, seeking of refuge in Allāh, remembrance, and supplications that are used as a means of treating sicknesses and other problems, and the Qur'ān is a source of healing (Shaykh Assim Al-Hakeem, n.d.). The main purpose of *Ruqyah* is to treat and cure evil eye, possession of *Jinn*, envy, and black magic. The essence is to place full trust, reliance, and dependence only on Allāh, the source of all healing and cure. The Scholars advise Muslims who are sick,

> whether that is spiritual (mental) illness such as anxiety and depression, or physical illness such as various kinds of pain, to hasten first of all to treat the problem with *Ruqyah* as prescribed in *Shari'ah*. Then we advise treating it with natural materials which Allāh has created, such as honey and plants, for Allāh has created special properties in them which may treat many kinds of diseases. We think that you should not take artificial chemical remedies for anxiety. For this disease, a person needs a spiritual

remedy rather than a chemical one. So, he needs to increase his faith and his trust in his Lord; he needs to make more *Du'as* and pray more. If he does that, his anxiety will be removed. Seeking to relax by means of doing acts of worship has a great effect on the soul, dispelling many kinds of psychological disease. Hence we do not see any benefit in going to a psychologist whose beliefs are corrupt, let alone one who is a *Kaafar* [a person who disbelieves in God]. The more the doctor knows about Allāh and His religion, the best advice he will give to his patient.

(Islam Q&A, 2002a).

Self-*Ruqyah* is acceptable and permissible. It is stated that "There is nothing wrong with the Muslim reciting *Ruqyah* for himself. That is permissible; indeed, it is a good *Sunnah*, for the Messenger (ﷺ) recited Ruqyah for himself, and some of his companions recited Ruqyah for themselves" (Islam Q&A, 2002b). It was narrated that: "When the Messenger of Allāh was ill, he would recite *al-Mu'awwidhatayn* over himself and spit drily. When his pain grew intense, I recited over him and wiped him with his own hand, seeking its barakah (blessing)" (Bukhari & Muslim (c)). With regard to the supplications that are prescribed for the Muslim to say if he wants to recite *Ruqyah* for himself or for someone else, there are many such supplications, the greatest of which are *al-Fātihah* and *al-Mu'awwidhatayn*. Shaykh Ibn 'Uthaymeen (n.d.) was asked: Can a believer become mentally ill? What is the treatment for that according to *Shari'ah*? He replied:

Undoubtedly a person may suffer from psychological or mental diseases, such as anxiety about the future and regret for the past. Psychological diseases affect the body more than physical diseases affect it. Treating these diseases by means of the things prescribed in *Shari'ah* – for example, *Ruqyah*, is more effective than treating them with physical medicines, as is well known.

(Islam Q&A, 2002a).

CONCLUSION

The Islāmic approach to psychological and spiritual illnesses is to discover the best possible therapeutic methods by using a combination of traditional psychotherapeutic methods and spiritual healing interventions. Spiritual interventions are recommended for all physical, psychological, and spiritual problems or disorders. Ibn Al-Qayyim Al-Jawziyyah (d) stated that once a person abandons the Qur'ān, they abandon all means of healing the sick through it as well.

It is recommended to use *Ruqyah* as an Islāmic healing intervention with Muslim patients regardless of the specificities of psychological illness. Spiritual interventions, including *Ruqyah*, become a therapeutic tool in an Islāmic psychotherapist's repertoire of therapeutic healing modalities. The challenge for Islāmic psychotherapists is to incorporate Islāmic healing interventions in traditional therapies for both non–Muslim and Muslim patients.

FURTHER READINGS

Rassool, G. Hussein. (2016). *Islāmic Counselling: An introduction to theory and practice*. Hove, East Sussex: Routledge.

Rassool, G. Hussein. (2019). *Evil Eye, Jinn Possession, and Mental Health Issues: An Islāmic Perspective*. Oxford: Routledge.

9

RESEARCH METHODOLOGY IN ISLĀMIC PSYCHOLOGY

INTRODUCTION

This chapter focuses on the methods and techniques of academic research in the context of Islāmic psychology and psychotherapy from an Islāmic integrated perspective. An overview of research methodology based on the Western scientific paradigm and the Islāmic integrated research perspective is presented. The Islāmisation of knowledge development has stressed the importance of both the epistemological (theoretical content of human thought) and the methodological dimensions (research) of approaches in knowledge integration. Muslim researchers and scholars have two approaches or methodologies in studying human behaviours and experiences. The first method, based on the Western paradigm, is the use of intuition, empirical evidence, and rationality. However, this research methodology does not recognise divine Islāmic revelation as a proper source of scientific knowledge and espouses the values of Judaeo-Christian cultures and religions. In contrast, the alternative methodology of research is to adopt the methodology of the classical Muslim scholars based on the *Tawhîdic* paradigm and the Islāmic worldview. In this context and at this stage, it would be invaluable to briefly examine the concept of 'knowledge integration' and integrated research.

KNOWLEDGE INTEGRATION AND INTEGRATED RESEARCH

Since the late 20th century, 'knowledge integration' and integrated research have been used in contemporary Islāmic philosophy to

DOI: 10.4324/9781003312956-9

reconcile Islām and modernity as well as to integrate Islāmic ethics and epistemological values in social sciences. 'Knowledge integration', according to Kasule (2015), "involves integrating Islāmic moral and epistemological values in the various disciplines of knowledge that are taught" (p. 124). In the context of research from an Islāmic perspective, it is the process of synthesising research methodologies and approaches (empirical, rational) with Islāmic sciences and methodologies. Both 'knowledge integration' and integrated research focus on the integration of empirical evidence (*Ilm 'aqli*) with revealed knowledge (*Ilm 'naqli*) as well as the synthesis of both sources of knowledge into an integrated model based on *Tawhīdic* paradigm. According to Shafii (1985),

> The task of integration is ... rather a systematic reorientation and restructuring of the entire field of human knowledge in accordance with a new set of criteria and categories, derived from, and based on [the] Islāmic worldview.
>
> (p. 6)

Thus, the essence of integrated research, from an Islāmic perspective, is to bring knowledge from the different compartments and sources under one umbrella to achieve a given goal or a set of objectives. This is reflected in the statement made by Al-'Alwani (2005), who suggested that Allāh commands humanity to undertake

> two different kinds of readings ... the Book of Allah for religious guidance and the book of existence, which is the created universe. Only this kind of understanding, which takes into consideration the two sources of knowledge, can be considered as comprehensive.
>
> (p. 30)

The sources of knowledge are from *Ilm naqli*, which is revealed and transmitted knowledge from the Qur'ān and *Sunnah*, and from *Ilm 'aqli*, which is rational knowledge based on intuition, human intellect, observation, and experimentation. In relation to conflicting knowledge from the two sources, Kasule (2021) suggested,

> There is no essential contradiction between transmitted knowledge (*'Ilm naqli*) and rational empirical knowledge (*'Ilm 'aqli*).

Any apparent contradictions are either due to incorrect empirical observations or due to human intellectual deficiency in understanding *'Ilm naqli*. There have been confusions about what source of knowledge to use. *'Ilm naqli* is used exclusively in matters of ethics and morality. *'Ilm 'aqli* is used to answer questions of an empirical nature but requires the guidance of *'Ilm naqli* regarding fundamentals like objectivity (*Istiqamat*), ethics (*Akhlaq*), and purposiveness (*Gha'iyyat*).

There is no contradiction in using both the Divine and acquired knowledge, as they both are from the same source. So, the problem of duality in Islāmic research methodology is resolved. Islāmic research in psychology also needs to exercise *ijtihad* (independent reasoning), which has been a significant process in the development of Islāmic thought and knowledge. The definition of *Ijtihad* "would mean that one has spent so much effort in pursuit of the knowledge of *Shariah* that further pursuit is humanly impossible" (Aboobackaer, 2019). According to Imam Al-Ghazālī, "*Ijtihad* means to expand once [*sic*] capacity in certain matter [*sic*] and use it to the utmost" (Cited in Aboobackaer, 2019). *Ijtihad* has always been an important tool and resource for Muslims to resolve psychosocial issues. Figure 9.1 depicts the integrated research methodology in Islāmic psychology and psychotherapy.

OVERVIEW OF SCIENTIFIC METHOD

There are different methods for the acquisition of knowledge. It may be based on the process of insight (i.e., based on awareness or instinct), authority (i.e., based on the knowledge of experts or what authorities say), rationalism (i.e., based on reasoning), and empiricism (i.e., based on sensory experience). An empirical method is a research model in psychology that aims to obtain knowledge through our senses (e.g., sight, hearing, etc.), and through experience and measurement. This means it is a method of inquiry that uses careful observation and experiments to document or collect facts and evidence on behaviours. Psychologists prefer to learn about behaviours and experiences through direct observation or experience. For example, in psychology behaviourism is the clearest example of empiricism. There are several steps in the empirical

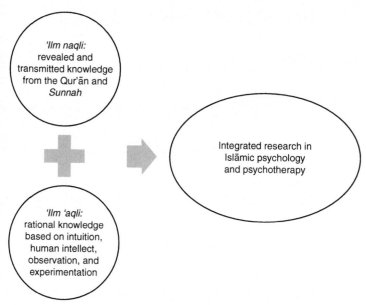

Figure 9.1 Integrated research methodology in Islāmic psychology and psychotherapy

approach: observation, formulation of the hypothesis, testing of the hypothesis, formation of a theory, and theory construction. The aim of the modern scientific method is to build knowledge about the natural world in order to describe, explain, predict, and control. Figure 9.2 presents the philosophy of scientific research.

It is important to note the historical development of the experimental method during the Golden Age of Islām. Both Abu Yusuf Yaqub Ibn Ishâq Al-Kindī (Al-Kindī) and Jābir ibn Hayyān placed great emphasis on the use of experimentation as a source of knowledge. Al-Kindī was a pioneer in experimental psychology, which led to his discovery that sensation is proportionate to the stimulus. He proposed several theories on perception, sleeping and dreams, and emotional processes (Awaad et al., 2019). Al-Hasan ibn al-Haytham (Ibn al-Haytham) used experimentation to obtain the results in his *Book of Optics* (1021 CE). Methodologically, Ibn al-Haytham combined observations, experiments, and rational arguments to support

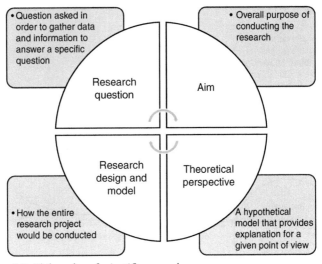

Figure 9.2 Philosophy of scientific research

his theory of vision and, therefore, to discuss the psychology of visual perception (Dhanani, 2018).

Within the research paradigm, it is also important to identify the research philosophy (Figure 9.2) and define the philosophical position of a researcher. This is related to

> a system of the researcher's worldview, aims, thought, following which new, reliable knowledge about the research object is obtained. It is the basis of the research, which involves the choice of research strategy, formulation of the problem, data collection, processing, and analysis.
>
> (Akhmetova & Rafikov, 2021)

The philosophy and worldview (discussed in Chapter 1) are also embedded in the orientation of the researcher, as these factors will influence research questions, methodology, and interpretation of findings. In this context the Islāmic research philosophy/aim is to "Understand the Power and Creation of Allah (nature, universe to know the Creator and understand the purpose of creation" (Akhmetova & Rafikov, 2021).

METHODS OF RESEARCH

Research methodology involves specific procedures for collecting and analysing data. Two decisions need to be made regarding the collection and analysis of data. Data collection depends on the research question and design. Research methods can be qualitative (they deal with concepts, subjective experiences, wordings, or ideas) or quantitative (they deal with numbers and statistics). Table 9.1 shows various research methods; indicates whether they are qualitative, quantitative, or either; and provides a brief explanation of their aims or focus.

Table 9.1 Research methodologies: Qualitative and quantitative

Research method	Primary or secondary?	Qualitative or quantitative?	Explanation/use
Action research	Primary	Qualitative	Collaborative research links theory to practice
Case studies	Either	Either	To gain an in-depth understanding of a single case or a specific group or context to test a theory or hypothesis
Ethnography	Primary	Qualitative	Description of peoples and cultures
Experiment	Primary	Quantitative	To test cause-and-effect relationships
Focus group	Primary	Quantitative	To gain a more in-depth understanding of a topic by asking questions and generating discussion with a group of people
Grounded theory	Primary	Either	Appropriate when little is known about a phenomenon; the aim being to produce or construct an explanatory theory that uncovers a process inherent to the substantive area of inquiry (Tie et al., 2010)

(Continued)

Table 9.1 Cont.

Research method	Primary or secondary?	Qualitative or quantitative?	Explanation/use
Interviews	Primary	Quantitative	To gain a more in-depth understanding of a topic by asking people questions in face-to-face conversations
Narrative	Primary	Qualitative	Collecting and analysing stories people tell about their experiences
Observations	Primary	Either	Recording data to understand how something occurs in its natural setting
Phenomenological	Primary	Qualitative	Describing and interpreting participants' lived experiences
Secondary research	Secondary	Either	Collecting existing data or data from previous scientific studies in the form of texts, audio, or visual recordings
Surveys	Primary	Quantitative	To understand the general characteristics of a population by distributing questionnaires with open-ended questions

The collection of data is the initial step in the research process. The second step is the analysis of data. Table 9.2 provides an overview of data analysis for qualitative and quantitative methods. There are several ways to do qualitative data analysis, and these include content analysis (noting common themes or words), thematic analysis (identifying and interpreting patterns or themes), textual analysis (identifying information about how other human beings make sense of the world), and discourse analysis (examining language in social contexts). In contrast, quantitative analysis is used for assessing relationships between variables, measuring differences between groups, or testing scientific hypotheses. Two main branches of statistics are used in quantitative data analysis: descriptive statistics and inferential statistics. The common descriptive statistical

Table 9.2 Data analysis for qualitative and quantitative data

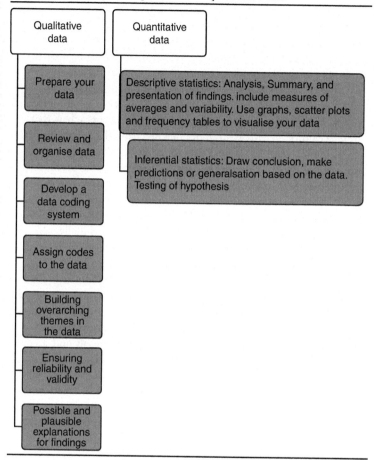

methods include mean (average), median, standard deviation, and skewness. The common inferential statistical methods include t-tests, ANOVA, correlation, and regression analysis. The choice of the right statistical method or technique depends on the type of data, the research question, and the hypotheses.

One of the main strengths of the qualitative method of research is that data collection occurs in the natural world and in social contexts. This type of research may be useful during the preliminary stages of a study or in a pilot study to provide data and information about what the focus of the research should be. This may generate new ideas or patterns that can be used in the proper study. In addition, using open-ended questions in qualitative research generates detailed descriptions of human experiences, feelings, perceptions, and worldviews. It also enables the study of complex or unexplored areas or the uncovering of novel issues and problems. The limitations of qualitative research include the role and involvement of the researcher in the research process. A central assumption of the qualitative approach is that researchers cannot be truly neutral or detached from data generation and analysis, which leads to skewed data. In addition, this type of research cannot be replicated, as research in the natural world involves uncontrolled factors or variables, which makes qualitative research unreliable. There is also the question of the generalisability of the data and its application to the wider population because small samples are often used to examine specific issues or problems. Finally, this approach may be time consuming due to the need to record, process, and analyse substantial amounts of data.

The strengths of the quantitative research method include the use of larger sample sizes; the faster collection of data; the use of randomised samples, which it is more objective (being anonymous); and the focus on facts or a series of information. Study replication is possible because standardised data-collection protocols and analysis are used. The findings of a quantitative research study may be generalisable because of the use of a large, randomised sample of the population. In addition, the same study can be used in cross–cultural research. That is, researchers may compare phenomena or behaviours across two or more cultures. The findings can be analysed and compared using both descriptive and inferential statistics. The main limitation of quantitative research is that often the context of the study or experiment is ignored. That is, the researcher does not consider the meaning behind social and environmental phenomena.

Quantitative research does not study things in a natural setting. Having predetermined variables and a specific methodology means that other relevant variables or contextual factors are disregarded. In addition, for robust statistical analysis and significance, there is a need to study a large sample of the population. Other limitations include missing data or inappropriate sampling methods that can confound variables and amplify biases, which may lead to incorrect findings.

Both quantitative and qualitative research methodologies are used in Islāmic psychology. The processes of data analysis for qualitative and quantitative research are presented in Table 9.2.

RESEARCH METHODOLOGY IN TRADITIONAL ISLĀMIC SCHOLARSHIP

This section focuses on an overview of the research methodology in traditional Islāmic scholarship and Islāmic studies. The word 'research' (*Bahth*) in the Arabic language means "to seek out or investigate a thing." Muslims have a duty to seek and convey knowledge based on the text of the Qur'ān and the authority of the Prophet (ﷺ). There is a consensus among Muslim scholars and academics that revealed knowledge "cannot be excluded from science because it constituted the presuppositions that lie at its foundation. This is particularly true with regard to the area of scientific research known as social or human sciences" (Safi, 2014, p. 81). The following verses of the Qur'ān exemplify the statements.

وَلَا تَقْفُ مَا لَيْسَ لَكَ بِهِ عِلْمٌ ۚ إِنَّ ٱلسَّمْعَ وَٱلْبَصَرَ وَٱلْفُؤَادَ كُلُّ أُو۟لَٰٓئِكَ كَانَ عَنْهُ مَسْـُٔولًا

- *And do not pursue that of which you have no knowledge. Indeed, the hearing, the sight and the heart — [about] all those [one] will be questioned.*
    (Al-Isra' 17:36, interpretation of the meaning)

قُلْ سِيرُوا۟ فِى ٱلْأَرْضِ فَٱنظُرُوا۟ كَيْفَ بَدَأَ ٱلْخَلْقَ ۚ

- *Say, [O Muhammad], "Travel through the land and observe how He began creation."*
    (Al-'Ankabut 29:20, interpretation of the meaning)

ٱللَّهُ ٱلَّذِينَ ءَامَنُوا۟ مِنكُمْ وَٱلَّذِينَ أُوتُوا۟ ٱلْعِلْمَ دَرَجَٰتٍ

- *God will raise those who have believed among you and those who were given knowledge, by degrees.*
    (Mujadilah 58:11, interpretation of the meaning)

قُلْ هَلْ يَسْتَوِى ٱلَّذِينَ يَعْلَمُونَ وَٱلَّذِينَ لَا يَعْلَمُونَ ۗ إِنَّمَا يَتَذَكَّرُ أُوْلُواْ ٱلْأَلْبَٰبِ

- *Say, Are those who know equal to those who do not know? Only they will remember [who are] people of understanding.*
(Az-Zumar 39:9, interpretation of the meaning)

Muslim academics and researchers have a collective duty (*Fard Kifayah*) to produce and disseminate authentic knowledge on behalf of the *Ummah*. This is reflected in the statement by Imam Zarkashi (n.d.):

It is a collective duty to produce books on whoever Allāh has given understanding and insight. Despite its short lifetime, the Muslim community continues to grow and develop with regard to its intellectual capabilities and knowledge is not permitted to be concealed. If writing books were abandoned, knowledge would be lost for people.

Safi (2014) has proposed a methodological approach that recognises revealed knowledge as a primary source of knowledge and aims to employ both text and action analysis techniques as necessary tools for theory building. So, our challenge and task is to produce knowledge and not just be consumers of knowledge.

Traditional methods of research in Islāmic studies are presented in Figure 9.3.

STEPS OF UNDERTAKING RESEARCH IN ISLĀMIC PSYCHOLOGY

The steps of undertaking research are presented in Figure 9.4. The research steps for Islāmic studies have been adapted for research in Islāmic psychology.

COMPETENCE AND PREPARATION FOR RESEARCH

First, the researcher begins with research competence and preparation for research. There are two conditions attached to this category. The researcher must be acquainted with and have a good grounding

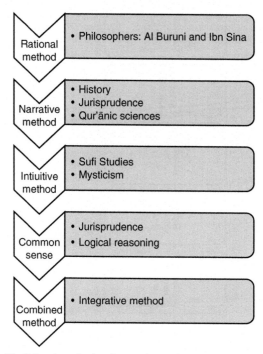

Figure 9.3 Traditional methods of research in Islāmic studies
Source: Adapted from Akhmetova & Rafikov (2022).

in the Qur'ān and *Sunnah* as well as a basic grasp of the Arabic language. This is reflected in a Prophetic report:

> This knowledge will be carried by the trustworthy ones in every time, they purge from it the distortions of the extremists and the interpretations of those who see [*sic*] to make the Book of Allāh false and the interpretations of the ignorant.
>
> (Dar al-Iftaa Al-Missriyyah, 2022)

It is important to first rely on the Qur'ān and *Sunnah* as your primary sources of truth. The researcher must also be well grounded in research methodologies in the social sciences, including quantitative, qualitative, and mixed methodologies.

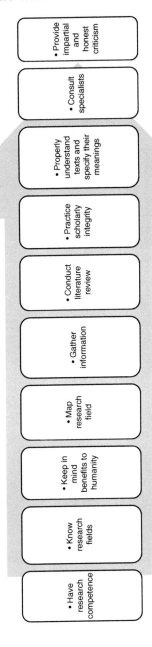

Figure 9.4 Steps of undertaking research
Source: Adapted from Dar al-Iftaa Al-Missriyyah (2022).

What is observed in the Islāmic literature and research in psychology is a lack of knowledge of the Qur'ān, *Sunnah*, and Islāmic studies among students and researchers.

> What we observe in terms of the inadequacy of students and training … [is that] such kinds of students … either sabotage the way by appropriating the works of their predecessors or by producing ideas that are lowly and immature. … They randomly pick out verses from the Qur'ān or *Ḥadīth* reports and derive rulings that God did not sanction.
>
> (Dar al-Iftaa Al-Missriyyah, 2022)

Inadequately educated authors and researchers usually misuse verses from the Qur'ān as evidence to support their opinions or findings without referring to the context in which the verses are used or without a proper understanding of *Tafsir*. Ibn Sirin (n.d.) said, "This knowledge is a religion, so consider from whom you receive your religion." It is narrated by `Abdullah bin `Amr:

> I heard the Prophet (ﷺ) saying, "Allāh will not deprive you of knowledge after he has given it to you, but it will be taken away through the death of the religious learned men with their knowledge. Then there will remain ignorant people who, when consulted, will give verdicts according to their opinions whereby they will mislead others and go astray."
>
> (Bukhari (d))

Muslim psychologists' lack of adequate preparation in Islāmic studies and Islāmic psychology are impeding scholarship and the development of Islāmic thought. So, it is of utmost importance to prepare for research with the right intention and have competence in the Qur'ān, *Sunnah*, and the necessary research methodologies.

KNOWING RESEARCH FIELDS AND MASTERING THEM

It is incumbent on every researcher to have acquired the fundamental knowledge in psychology and in Islāmic psychology using sound research skills. The researcher should be acquainted with the literature, methods of conducting research, research design, research frameworks, sampling procedures, measurement, and the format of research reports. Researchers may use intuition, authority, rationalism, and empiricism to generate new theories of knowledge; however, the scientific method can only be used to address empirical questions. Researchers also need to master earlier classical works on the science of the soul (*Ilm an Nafs*) and research traditions in Islāmic studies. Researchers should examine the literature on the subject of research with a critical lens. Ibn Khaldun (n.d.) stated,

> Proficiency and mastery in a field is only achieved by obtaining a skill in comprehending the principles and rules of the field, and understanding its problems, and deriving solution from its principles. As long as this skill is not obtained, proficiency in that field will not be obtained.

BENEFITS OF MUSLIM SCHOLARLY RESEARCH FOR HUMANITY

Researchers should keep in mind that a new work should have "ecological validity" and should bring value and benefit to humanity. The research findings should be generalisable to real life. A research activity that consumes or wastes time and resources and offers no benefit is itself a problem. In Islāmic traditions, the classical scholars, when asked about rulings or the details of an issue, would respond, "Is this an actually existing issue?" Research outcomes should benefit society and discover new ways of improving people's health and socio-economic conditions. This is an indication of the strong connection between knowledge gained from research, deriving human benefits, and the importance of knowledge in guiding people.

PROPER STRUCTURING, MAPPING, AND CLASSIFICATION OF THE RESEARCH FIELD

In the field of *Hādīth* and jurisprudence, scholars have explained the importance of properly structuring and mapping the research field:

> They call it in Arabic "*Al-sabr wa'l-taqseem*". *Al-sabr* is following the routes of *Hadith* to know its narrators, and *Al-taqseem* is

distinguishing every issue from the others in order to make it easier to think about it. They added *Al-taqseem* in an effort to clarify and explain in detail.

(Dar al-Iftaa Al-Missriyyah, 2022)

In Islāmic psychology, mapping may be used as a methodological research strategy. Concept mapping has also been used primarily as a means to assess knowledge integration (Besterfield-Sacre et al., 2004). A concept map "is a schematic device for representing a set of concept meanings embedded in a framework of propositions" (Novak & Gowin, 1984, p. 15). Daley (2004) suggested,

> Concept maps are created with the broader, more inclusive concepts at the top of the hierarchy, connecting through linking words with other concepts than can be subsumed. Concept maps are an important strategy in qualitative inquiry because they help the researcher focus on meaning. The maps support researchers in their attempts to make sure that qualitative data is embedded in a particular context.

In this context a concept map can be used as a visual representation of the relationships between various factors or concepts in the research, to provide a framework for a research project, to provide a synthesis of the data, to analyse the relationship of themes and interconnections in a study, or as a means of presenting the research findings.

GATHERING INFORMATION WITH AWARENESS AND FORETHOUGHT

The literature review is the beginning of any purposeful research on a particular theme. This is a critical step for appraising the landscape of the subject and for placing research findings into context. Unfortunately, students of psychology tend to produce a description of the literature rather than a critical appraisal of the research findings that includes the limitations of previous research on the subject. Writing a literature review requires a range of skills, including collection, identification, evaluation, critical examination, and summarisation of peer-reviewed published data in a cohesive, informative, and unbiased narrative. The sources of the literature review include the Qur'ān, *Ḥadīth*, research papers, academic texts, review articles, and databases. Some sources are accessible online. It should be noted that "researchers must exercise caution, for knowledge of the value of any given source is very important for helping arrive at the truth" (Dar al-Iftaa Al-Missriyyah, 2022). The task of a literature review is to make a critical review of the literature and build an argument or statement of the problem.

THOROUGHLY ANALYSING THE INTELLECTUAL MATERIAL, ITS ORDERING, AND FRAMEWORK

The collection and review of the existing literature should be presented in a systematic way. This also relates to the evaluation and critical examination of the literature. In the context of Islāmic studies,

> Each issue should be prefaced by a Qur'ānic passage and a sound prophetic report. There should also be an exegesis [explanation] of these texts from reliable sources. This methodology clarifies for us the development of thinking of the people of knowledge, their status, and what they have contributed over generations. From this, we may come to realise the impact of time and place.
>
> (Dar al-Iftaa Al-Missriyyah, 2022)

SCHOLARLY INTEGRITY IN RELATING IDEAS

Muslim researchers should adhere to the Qur'ānic concept of integrity when relating and attributing ideas to people. Qadi 'Iyad (n.d.) stated,

> Scholarly integrity in attributing sayings and ideas to people is to be done without even the slightest shortcoming, whether the attribution is to a great person or not, to a Muslim or not, to a pious person or not, to an early personality or a later one.
>
> (Cited in Dar al-Iftaa Al-Missriyyah, 2022)

In Islāmic psychology, researchers should adhere to the Islāmic ethical principles in addition to the professional standards essential for the responsible practice of research. The concept of ethical competence can be defined "in terms of character strength, ethical awareness, moral judgement skills and willingness to do good. Virtuous professional, experience of a professional, human communication, ethical knowledge and supporting surroundings in the organisation can be seen as prerequisites for ethical competence" (Kulju et al., 2016, p. 401). Ethical principles are examined in Chapter 4.

Adhering to those principles goes beyond attributing ideas and theories to previous scholars; it also involves implementing the principles of the Islāmic ethics ('Akhlaq), which is derived from the Qur'ān and *Sunnah*. The characteristics of the researcher include truth, integrity, honesty, fairness, disclosure of conflicts of interest, and the care and protection of human subjects and animals in the conduct of research. In addition, the researcher should not engage in unscholarly behaviour, plagiarise texts from other authors, omit authors who do not share the same ideologies as the author, or omit parts of texts so as to remove material that disagrees with the researcher's viewpoint. It has been suggested that the

> scholars of Islam have set a great example in such scholarly integrity because the Qur'ān itself has laid down this principle. This is of great benefit in the Islāmic sciences, like the science of *Hadith*, which has set out a methodology for authentic reports narrated from the Prophet (ﷺ).
>
> (Dar al-Iftaa Al-Missriyyah, 2022)

PROPER UNDERSTANDING OF THE TEXTS AND SPECIFYING THEIR MEANINGS

Properly understanding texts and specifying their meanings is appropriate and relevant to both Islāmic studies and Islāmic psychology. The danger in Islāmic psychology is that a scholar or researcher follows his own ideology and subjective notions while disseminating knowledge. Hassan (2022) noted that in Islāmic psychology and counselling "people are marshalling themselves to offer what is Islāmic and what is not without the requisite tools and knowledge [of the Qur'ān and *Sunnah*]." That is why the Qur'ān has warned against falsehood.

وَلَا تَقُولُواْ لِمَا تَصِفُ أَلْسِنَتُكُمُ ٱلْكَذِبَ هَٰذَا حَلَٰلٌ وَهَٰذَا حَرَامٌ لِّتَفْتَرُواْ عَلَى ٱللَّهِ ٱلْكَذِبَ ۚ

إِنَّ ٱلَّذِينَ يَفْتَرُونَ عَلَى ٱللَّهِ ٱلْكَذِبَ لَا يُفْلِحُونَ

- *And do not say about what your tongues assert of untruth, "This is lawful, and this is unlawful," to invent falsehood about Allāh. Indeed, those who invent falsehood about Allāh will not succeed.*
  (An-Nahl 16:116, interpretation of the meaning)

It is narrated by `Abdullah bin `Amr bin Al-`As that the Prophet (ﷺ) stated:

> Allah does not take away the knowledge, by taking it away from (the hearts of) the people but takes it away by the death of the religious learned men till when none of the (religious learned men) remains, people will take as their leaders' ignorant persons who when consulted will give their verdict without knowledge. So, they will go astray and will lead the people astray.
>
> (Bukhari (e))

Imam Malik (1983) (may Allāh be pleased with him) remarked, "Whoever is asked about a religious matter, before responding he should imagine both Heaven and Hell before him and consider his outcome in the Hereafter. Only then should he respond." The problem with this inauthentic knowledge is that it is based on weak arguments and deviant opinions about or explanations of the text. On the topic, Ibn Hazm al-Andalusi (1985), the great polymath, said: "There is nothing more harmful to knowledge and its people than those who enter into it, yet are not from it. They are ignorant, but think they are knowledgeable; they cause corruption while they think they are rectifying matters" (p. 24). In sum, we need to be objective and neutral and rely on authentic text.

RESORTING TO SPECIALISTS

Resorting to specialists means consulting the work of experts who are authorities in the area of study. That is, researchers should take information from trustworthy original sources. For example, in Islāmic sciences or Islāmic psychology, the researcher needs to consult specialists in the field who have a sound understanding of the methodological framework, not 'wannabe' scholars. In summary, references to or interpretation of the text and its meaning should be from trustworthy original sources, and specialists in the subject of the text should be given prominence.

IMPARTIAL AND HONEST CRITICISM

It is important provide impartial and honest criticism without creating violations of professional behaviours. Accordingly, the accomplished and trained researcher "has the right to understand and explain his own understanding of the Qur'ān, *Sunnah* and deriving intellectual production from them. He has the right to criticise and evaluate constructively" (Dar al-Iftaa Al-Missriyyah, 2022). The principle for this right to evaluate is found in the golden statement of Imam Malik bin Anas, "Everyone's opinion may be accepted or rejected except for the person in this grave," pointing to the grave of the Prophet (ﷺ). This is because in the Islāmic paradigm only the Prophet is infallible. However, the self-criticism should start with the researcher or scholar as well as providing constructive criticism of the works of other scholars. As the scholars would say, "Beware of putting forth your works before they have been refined and looked over many times" (Dar al-Iftaa Al-Missriyyah, 2022).

In summary, it is valuable for the researcher or scholar in Islāmic psychology to engage with the Islāmic traditions in scholarship and research and have a good comprehension of the discipline's methodologies. Understanding of the texts of the Qur'ān and *Sunnah* is crucial in any research in Islāmic studies. However, the Qur'ān and *Sunnah* should be used as a primary source of knowledge because of their absolute truth. Finally, the aim of the scholar is to identify and explain the truths (or proofs) that are revealed in the text and the natural world.

THE AIMS OF RESEARCH WRITING IN ISLĀMIC STUDIES

The aims and objectives of research writing in Islāmic studies have been proposed by Dar al-Iftaa Al-Missriyyah (2022) based on the works of Ibn Hazm and Ibn Khaldūn (Figure 9.5).

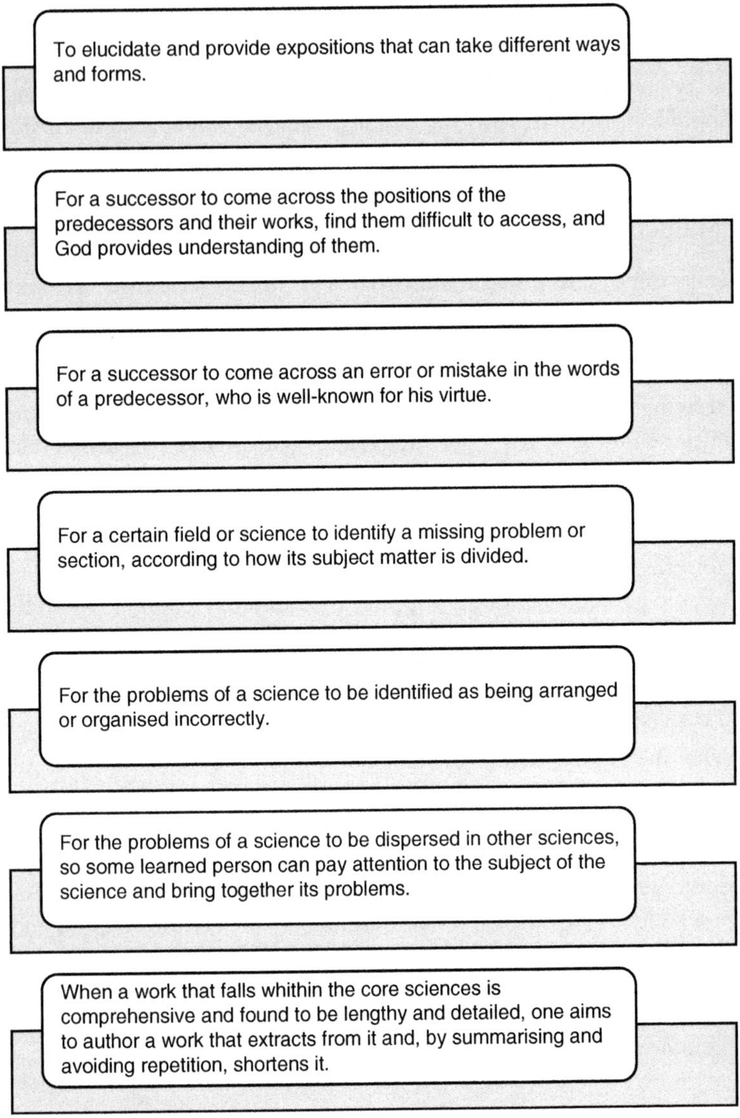

To elucidate and provide expositions that can take different ways and forms.

For a successor to come across the positions of the predecessors and their works, find them difficult to access, and God provides understanding of them.

For a successor to come across an error or mistake in the words of a predecessor, who is well-known for his virtue.

For a certain field or science to identify a missing problem or section, according to how its subject matter is divided.

For the problems of a science to be identified as being arranged or organised incorrectly.

For the problems of a science to be dispersed in other sciences, so some learned person can pay attention to the subject of the science and bring together its problems.

When a work that falls whithin the core sciences is comprehensive and found to be lengthy and detailed, one aims to author a work that extracts from it and, by summarising and avoiding repetition, shortens it.

Figure 9.5 Aims of research writing in Islāmic studies
Source: Dar al-Iftaa Al-Missriyyah (2022).

Imam Abu Bakr ibn al-Arabi (n.d.) summarised the seven aims by stating,

A judicious person, who undertakes the writing of a book, should not stray from two goals: Either to produce a meaning or devise a new order and structure, according to what we have set out in *Qanun al-Tawil* and determined in *al-Tahsil* in a general and detailed manner. Whatever is not included in these two aspects is simply putting ink on paper and adorning pages by plagiarism.

(Cited in Dar al-Iftaa Al-Missriyyah, 2022)

Some commentaries on the aims of research writing in Islāmic studies are found in Box 9.1.

Box 9.1   Aims of research writing in Islāmic studies

- "Elucidation and expositions can take different ways and forms" means the writing provides a clear explanation or interpretation and meaning of the text.
- "Deriving knowledge of the subject" means setting out the chapters and sections of the science, apprehending the problems of the science, or deriving them. This also may suggest making an additional commentary on the text from a different perspective without any form of changing or restructuring.
- "To come across the positions of the predecessors and their works and find them difficult to access and God provides understanding of them" means that the focus is on producing new research or knowledge to provide better understanding of the text. Previous research or understanding of the text may have been changed, for example due to linguistic shifts, which may make it difficult for contemporary researchers to understand or attach meanings to the text.
- "For a successor to come across an error or mistake in the words of a predecessor, who is well-known for his virtue" means there is a need to produce a new meaning or devise a new order or structure for the text. The error identified in the text should be

subjected to thorough examination to be certain, by clear evidence, that it is an error. This clarification should be made known to all.

- "For a certain field or science to be missing a problem or section, according to how its subject matter is divided" means that new research is needed to fill a knowledge gap by adding new text that is in line with the existing scholarship.

- "For the problems of a science to be arranged or organised incorrectly" focuses on producing a new structure or organisation of the text to correct a previous deficiency.

- "For the problems of a science to be dispersed in other sciences, so some learned person pays attention to the subject of the science and brings together its problems" focuses on integrating the sciences in a new field and making it available for others to adopt.

- "For a work that falls within the core sciences and is comprehensive to be lengthy and details, so one aims to author a work that extracts from it by summarising and avoiding repetition – shortens it" focuses on producing a new, shortened version of a core sciences text.

Source: Adapted from Dar al-Iftaa Al-Missriyyah (2022).

TOWARDS AN INTEGRATED METHODOLOGY OF RESEARCH IN ISLĀMIC PSYCHOLOGY

The aims of the task of developing an integrated methodology of research in Islāmic psychology are five-fold. First, the new methodology should recognise the Qur'ān and *Sunnah* as the primary source of knowledge. Second, Muslim scholars developing the research methodology in Islāmic psychology should use the methodologies of the Islāmic tradition as a paradigm. Third, scholars should use historical works from Islāmic classical scholars and the works of contemporary scholars as sources of psychology knowledge. Fourth, researchers need to use both qualitative and quantitative research methodologies, which provide a holistic and multidisciplinary approach. Fifth, the desired methodology must allow the integration of both revealed knowledge and knowledge derived from quantitative and qualitative research methodologies (Box 9.2).

Box 9.2   Summary of the aims of an integrated methodology

- The Qur'ān and *Sunnah* are the primary sources of knowledge.
- The methodologies of the Islāmic tradition should also be used by Muslim scholars as a paradigm to develop research methodologies in Islāmic psychology.
- Historical works from Islāmic classical scholars and contemporary scholars are useful sources of psychology knowledge.
- Researchers need to use both qualitative and quantitative methodologies.
- Both revealed knowledge and knowledge from quantitative and qualitative research methodologies should be integrated.

Rafikov and Akhmetova (2020) suggested,

The call for the integration of knowledge comes from the idea of the unity of knowledge. All knowledge comes from and is caused by the One God. Therefore, there is no distinction in Islām between religion and science, because all true knowledge points to the same source – the All-Knowing God (*Al-'Alim*).

(p. 123)

Both quantitative and qualitative research methods have different approaches and are often contrasted as representing two different worldviews, each with its own strengths and limitations. A mixed-methods approach capitalises on the advantages of the quantitative and qualitative methods while neutralising the drawbacks of each. However, great care should be taken to ensure that there is a clear rationale for using both quantitative and qualitative methodologies. In Islāmic psychology, for example, a qualitative approach can be used to generate hypotheses and a quantitative approach can be used for hypothesis testing. There are two ways of using the two methods: sequentially or in parallel. The sequential approach combines the methodologies in a purposeful, staged manner. A quantitative methodology (stage 1) may be followed by a qualitative study (stage 2) or vice versa. Ordering would depend on the research context, purpose, and design. In the parallel approach both methodologies are used. For example, a large survey may be accompanied by a focus group. Hammarberg et al. (2016) maintained,

> Qualitative and quantitative methods may be used together for corroboration (hoping for similar outcomes from both methods), elaboration (using qualitative data to explain or interpret quantitative data, or to demonstrate how the quantitative findings apply in particular cases), complementarity (where the qualitative and quantitative results differ but generate complementary insights) or contradiction (where qualitative and quantitative data lead to different conclusions).
>
> (p. 499)

The strengths of an integrated research approach (qualitative and quantitative methodologies) are that it provides both a vertical and horizontal understanding of the phenomenon being examined, it provides convergent outcomes, and it is applicable to the type of research used in Islāmic psychology. It is also possible that integrated research may lead to divergent outcomes. The dilemma is how do you reconcile the two sets of data. In addition, collecting and processing comprehensive data and interpretations may be challenging, time consuming, and labour intensive. Those who wish to apply an integrated approach need to have a sound knowledge of and well-developed research skills in both methodologies. Guidelines for conducting integrated research are presented in Box 9.3.

Box 9.3   Guidelines for conducting integrated research

- Be proficient in Islāmic sciences.
- Understand traditional Islāmic scholarship.
- Have knowledge in both quantitative and qualitative methodologies.
- Have skills in quantitative and qualitative methodologies.
- Understand the integrated research approach in Islāmic psychology.
- Think "outside the box" for designing research in Islāmic psychology.

- Use a qualitative approach for hypothesis generation.
- Use a quantitative approach for hypothesis testing.
- Use a serial or parallel approach when implementing an integrated research methodology.
- Consider alternative ways of analysing data based on the Islāmic research tradition.
- Use concept mapping in qualitative research.
- Use the integrative research method for corroboration, elaboration, complementarity, contradiction, or a mixture of purposes depending on the research design that best fits the hypotheses.
- Be aware of the limitations of the research design.
- Keep up to date with the latest techniques, software, articles, and manuals.
- Adopt research integrity based on Islāmic ethics and professional standards.
- Ensure the research is of value and benefit for the *Ummah*.

CONCLUSION

The paradigm of scientific research consists of ontology, epistemology, methodology, and methods based on revealed knowledge and empirical evidence. The worldview of Muslims plays a vital role in the research process as well as in the design and purpose of the research. The integrated research method is a framework based on quantitative and qualitative methodologies complemented by Islāmic traditions and scholarship. Islāmic research and scholarship is governed by the *Tawhîd* paradigm and it seeks to identify and disseminate the absolute truth, which can be found in Divine revelation and the universe.

FURTHER READING

Safi, L. (2014). *The foundation of knowledge: A Comparative Study in Islamic and Western Methods of Inquiry*. Herndon, VA: The International Institute of Islamic Thought.

Wheeldon, J., & Åhlberg, M.K. (2012). Concept maps and mind maps: Theory, definitions, and approaches. In *Visualizing social science research: Maps, methods, & meaning* (pp. 21–38). Thousand Oaks, CA: Sage Publications, Inc.

REFERENCES

Abbasi, S.S., Brasiliense, L.B.C., & Workman, R.K. (2007). The fate of medical knowledge and the neurosciences during the time of Genghis Khan and the Mongolian Empire. *Neurosurgical Focus*, 23(1), 1–6.

Abdul-Rahman, Z. (2017, 20 September). *The Lost Art of Contemplation*. Yaqeen Institute for Islāmic Research. https://yaqeeninstitute.org/en/zohair/the-lost-art-of-contemplation-spiritual-psychology-series/#ftnt_ref53 (accessed 23 March 2022).

Abdullah, M., & Nadvi, M.J. (2011). Understanding the Principles of Islamic Worldview. *The Dialogue*, 4(3), 268–289.

Abidi, M.H. (2021). Sufism and Jungian Psychology: Ways of Knowing and Being. In N. Pasha-Zaidi (Ed.), *Toward a Positive Psychology of Islam and Muslims: Spirituality, struggle and social justice*, vol. 15 of Cross-Cultural Advancements in Positive Psychology (pp. 399–416). Champs: Springer.

Aboobackaer, A.A. (2019). *Institution of Ijtihad and Modern World*. https://www.researchgate.net/profile/Anas-Aboobackaer (accessed on 18 March 2022).

Abu Dawud (a). *Sunan Abu Dawud 864*; classed as Sahih by al-Albani in Sahih Abi Dawud, 770. Cited in http://islamqa.info/en/22203 (accessed 28 March 2022).

Abu Dawud (b). *Sunan Abu Dawud 54*. In-book reference: Book 1, Hadith 54. English translation: Book 1, Hadith 53.

Abu Dawud (c). *Sunan Abi Dawud 4708*. In-book reference: Book 42, Hadith 113. English translation: Book 41, Hadith 4691. Sahih (Al-Albani).

Abu Iyaad. (2013). *Where Does the Intellect (Aql) Reside, In the Heart or the Brain?* http://www.ibntaymiyyah.com/articles/jxazygi-where-does-the-intellect-aql-reside-the-heart-or-the-brain.cfm (accessed 30 May 2022).

Abu l-Lait as-Samarqandi. (n.d.). *The Islamic concept of belief in the 4th/10th century*. Abū l-Lait as-Samarqandī's commentary on Abū Ḥanīfa (died 150/767) al-Fiqh al-absaḍ. Introduction, text and commentary by Hans Daiber. (1995). Studia Culturae Islamicae, Tokyo, Institute for the Study of

Languages and Cultures of Asia and Africa (ILCAA), Tokyo University of Foreign Studies.

Abu-Raiya, H. (2012). Towards a systematic Qura'nic theory of personality. *Mental Health, Religion & Culture*, 15(3), 217–233.

Abu Zainab. (2015). *30 Quotes of Imam Al-Ghazālī*. https://topislamic.com/30-quotes-imam-ghazali (accessed 23 May 2022).

Afesh, M. (n.d.). Qur'anic Healing: A Clinical Psychological Study, Chapter Two (The Spirit and The Soul), The Soul According to Ibn-Sina. https://quranichealing.net/the-spirit-and-the-soul/the-soul-according-to-ibn-sina (accessed 13 February 2022).

Afridi, M.A. (2013). Contribution of Muslim Scientists to the World: An Overview of Some Selected Fields. *Revelation and Science*, 3(1), 47–56.

Ahmad (a). *Hiss al-Muslim* 120. 1/391, and Al-Albani graded it authentic in al-Silsilah al-Saheehah, 199.

Ahmad, A. (1992). Qur'anic Concepts of Human Psyche. In Z.A. Ansari (Ed.) (1992). *Quranic Concepts of Human Psyche*. Islamabad, Pakistan: International Institute of Islāmic Thought and Islāmic Research Institute Press.

Ahmed, S.K. (2015). *An Introduction to the Three Types of Nafs*. https://www.ilmgate.org/an-introduction-to-the-three-types-of-Nafs (accessed 22 May 2022).

Akhmetova, E. (2021). ITKI 6001 *Methodology of Scientific Research and Concept Formation*. Georgia: Institute of Knowledge Integration Academy (IKI-IIIT).

Akhmetova, E., & Rafikov, I. (2021). *Course on Methodology of Scientific Research and Concept Formation* (ITKI 6001). Institute of Integrated Knowledge. http://ikiacademy.org.

Al-Adab Al-Mufrad (a). *991*. In-book reference: Book 42, Hadith 27. English translation: Book 42, Hadith 991. Sahih Al-Albani.

Al-Adab Al-Mufrad (b). *301*. Excellence in Character. English translation: Book 14, Hadith 301. Arabic reference: Book 1, Hadith 301. Sahih (Al-Albani).

Al-Akiti, M.A. (1997). *The Meaning of Nafs*. https://www.livingislam.org/nafs.html (accessed 22 May 2022).

Al-'Alwani, T.J. (2005). *Issues in Contemporary Islamic Thought*. Herndon, VA: International Institute of Islamic Thought.

Al-Athari, 'Abd-Allah Ibn 'Abd al Hameed. (2003). *Islamic Beliefs. A Brief Introduction to the 'Aqeedah of Ahl Assunah wal-Jama'ah*. Riyadh: International Islamic Publishing House.

Al-Attas, S.M.N. (1985). *Islam, Secularism and the Philosophy of the Future*. London: Mansell Publishing Limited.

Al-Attas, S.M.N. (1995). *Prolegomena to the Metaphysics of Islam*. Kuala Lumpur: International Institute of Islamic Thought and Civilization.

Al-Balkhī. (n.d.). *Masalih al-Abdan wa al-Anfus*. Hand-written manuscript no. 3741, Istanbul: Ayasofya Library, 273.

Al-Balkhī, A.Z., Misri, M., & al-Hayyat, M. (2005). In taḥqīq wa-dirāsat Maḥmūd al-miṣrī, taṣdīr Muḥammad Haytham al-Khayyāṭ. (Masālih al-abdān wa-al-anfus, Eds.), 1st ed. Al-Qāhirah: Maʻhad al-Makhṭūṭāt al-ʻArabīyah.

Al-Bayjūrī. (2002). Cited in Keshavarzi, H., & Ali, B. (2020). *Foundations of Traditional Islamically Integrated Psychotherapy (TIIP)* (pp. 272–273). New York: Routledge.

Al-Faruqi, I.R. (1980). *Islam and Culture*. Kuala Lumpur: Angkatan Bella Malaysia (ABIM).

Al-Ghazālī, A.H. (1980). Ihya' 'Ulum al-Din. Vol. 3. Beirut, 1982, p. 3; ibid. Vol. 1, p. 5; cf. R. J. McCarthy, *Freedom and Fulfillment; An Annotated Translation of al-Ghazali's al-Munqidh min al-Dalal and Other Relevant Works of al-Ghazali*, Boston. Appendix V, p. 365.

Al-Ghazālī, A.H. (1993). The Book of Destructive Evils. In A.H. Al-Ghazālī, *Revival of religious learnings (Ihya Ulum-Id-Din)*, Vol. 3. (Trans.Al-Haj Maulana Fazlul-Ul Karim). Karachi: Darul-Ishaa.

Al-Ghazālī, A.H. (1995). *Disciplining the soul, refining the character, and curing the sicknesses of the heart*. Cambridge: Islamic Texts Society.

Al-Ghazālī, A.H. (2005). Disciplining the Soul & Breaking The Two Desires *(Kitab Riyadat al-Nafs & Kitab Kasr al-Shahwatayn)* Books 22 and 23 of the Revival of the Religious Sciences *(Ihya ulum al-din)* (Trans.Timothy J. Winter (Shaykh Abdal Hakim Murad)). Cambridge: Islamic Texts Society.

Al-Ghazālī, A.H. (2009). *The Book of Knowledge. (The Revival of the Religious Sciences #1)*. New Delhi: Adam Publishers.

Al-Ghazālī, A.H. (2010). The Marvels of the Heart: Science of the Spirit. Book 21, in *Ihyā' 'ulūm al-dīn (The Revival of the Religious Sciences)*. Walter James Skellie (Translation). Louisville, KY: Fons Vitae.

Al-Ghazālī, A.H. (2014). *Mukhtaṣar: Ihyā' 'Ulūm al-Dīn* (Trans.M.K. Lympia), Cyprus: Spohr Publishers.

Al-Hassan, A.Y. (1996). Factors Behind the Decline of Islamic Science After the Sixteenth Century. In S.S. Al-Attas (Ed.), *Islam and the Challenge of Modernity, Proceedings of the Inaugural Symposium on Islam, and the Challenge of Modernity: Historical and Contemporary Contexts* (pp. 351–399), Kuala Lumpur, 1–5 August 1994. International Institute of Islamic Thought and Civilization (ISTAC).

Alizi, A. (2017). *How can we redefine psychology Islamically yet still acceptable by the scientific community?* https://psychologyiium.wixsite.com/website/post/2016/05/09/this-is-your-second-post-1 (accessed 19 July 2022).

Al-Jawzi, A.A. (2004). *Akhbar al-Azkiya'*. Beirut: Dar Ibn Hazm.

Al-Kanadi, Abu Bilal Mustafa. (1996). *Mysteries of the Soul Expounded*. Jeddah, Saudi Arabia: Abul-Qasim Publishing House.

Al-Karam, C.Y. (2018). *Islamically Integrated Psychotherapy: Uniting Faith and Professional Practice*. Conshohocken, PA: Templeton Press.

Al-Karam, C.Y. (2020). *A Refined Vision of Islamic Psychology: Outer, Inner, and Mainstream*. Unpublished (Personal Communication).

Al-Mehri, A.B. (2010). *The Qur'an*. With Surah Introductions and Appendices. Saheeh International Translation. Birmingham: Maktabah Booksellers and Publishers.

Al-Qarni, Ali ibn Abd Allah. (2003). *al-Fitrah: Haqiqatuha wa madhahib al-nas fiha*. Riyadh: Dar al-Muslimin li al-nashr wa al-tawzi.

Al-Qurtubi. (n.d.). Tafseer Al-Qurtubi, 9/27. *Tafseer e Qurtubi Arabic (Al Jam'e Al Ahkam Al Quran)*, 24 Vols. Ar-Risala. http://hasbunallah.com.au/tafseer-e-qurtubi-arabic-al-jame-al-ahkam-al-quran (accessed 22 March 2022).

Al-Raysuni, A. (2005). *Imam Al Shatibi's Theory of the Higher Objectives and Intents of Islamic Law*. Herndon, VA: The International Institute of Islamic Thought.

Al-Rāzī, M.Z. (1978). *Kitab al-Ṭibb al-Rūhānī (Book of Spiritual Medicine)*. Cairo: Maktabat al-Nahda al Missiriya.

Al-Tuwaijri, Muhammad Ibn 'Abdul Mohsin. (2016). *Psychology from an Islāmic perspective*. https://societysstranger.wordpress.com/category/Islāmic-psychology (accessed 26 May 2022).

Alwee, A.I. (2005, 27 August). *Ethical Dimension of Islam*. Young AMP's Focus Group Discussion Series No. 1, National University of Singapore. http://thereadinggroup.sg/Articles/Ethical%20Dimension%20of%20Islam.pdf (accessed 7 March 2022).

Amer, H. (2015). *The Psychology of al-Ghazālī*. https://issuu.com/mould2/docs/psychology_of_al_ghazali (accessed 23 March 2022).

American Psychiatric Association. (2013). *Diagnostic and Statistical Manual of Mental Disorders, Fifth Edition* (DSM-5). Washington, DC: American Psychiatric Association.

Amr, S.S., & Tbakhi, A. (2007). Abu Bakr Muhammad Ibn Zakariya Al Razi (Rhazes): Philosopher, Physician and Alchemist. *Annals of Saudi Medicine*, 27(4), 305–307.

An-Najār, F.Q. (2004). *Al-Dirāst al-Nafsiyyah 'ind al-Imām Ibn Taymīyyah*. Riyad: Fahrasah Katabat al Malik Fahd al Waṭaniyyah.

An-Nasa'i (a). *Sunan an-Nasa'i 5041*. In-book reference: Book 48, Hadith 2. English translation: Vol. 6, Book 48, Hadith 5044. Sahih (Darussalam).

An-Nasa'i (b). *Sunan an-Nasa'i 3217*. In-book reference: Book 26, Hadith 22. English translation: Vol. 4, Book 26, Hadith 3219. Sahih (Darussalam).

An-Nasa'i (c). *Sunan an-Nasa'i 5538*. In-book reference: Book 50, Hadith 111. English translation: Vol. 6, Book 50, Hadith 5540. Sahih (Darussalam).

An-Nawawi (a). *Forty Hadith of an-Nawawi*. Hadith 27, 40 Hadith an-Nawawi. Ahmed bin Hambal and Al-Darimi.

An-Nawawi (b). *Forty Hadith of an-Nawawi*. Hadith 19, 40 Hadith an-Nawawi. Tirmidhî.

Ansar, M.A.H. (2019). *Ibn Taymīyyah Expounds on Islām: Selected Writings of Shaykh Al Islām Taqi Ad Din Ibn Taymīyyah on Islāmic Faith, Life and Society*. Dar-Ul-Thaqafah.

Armour, J.A. (2007). The Little Brain on the Heart. *Cleveland Clinic Journal of Medicine*, 74(Suppl 1), S48–S51. Doi:10.3949/ccjm.74.suppl_1.s48.

Asadi, S., Gholizadeh, Z., Jamali, M., Nazirzadeh, A., & Habibi, S. (2016). VMAT2 Gene Molecular study of 2,000 peoples in the Religious Behavior and Belief in God of the citizens of the city of Tabriz in IRAN. *Symbiosis: International Journal of Genetic Science*, 3(1), 1–6.

Awaad, R., & Ali, S. (2015). Obsessional Disorders in al-Balkhi's 9th century treatise: Sustenance of the Body and Soul. *Journal of Affective Disorders*, 180, 185–189. doi:10.1016/j.jad.2015.03.003.

Awaad, R., & Ali, S. (2016). A modern conceptualization of phobia in al-Balkhi's 9th century treatise: Sustenance of the Body and Soul. *Journal of Anxiety Disorders*, 37, 89–93.

Awaad, R., Elsayed, D., Ali, S., & Abid, A. (2020). Islamic Psychology: A Portrait of its Historical Origins and Contributions. In H. Keshavarzi, F. Khan, B. Ali, & R. Awaad (Eds.), *Applying Islamic Principles to Clinical Mental Health Care: Introducing Traditional Islamically Integrated Psychotherapy* (pp. 69–95). New York: Routledge.

Awaad, R., Mohammad, A., Elzamzamy, K., Fereydooni, S., & Gamar, M. (2019). Mental health in the Islāmic golden era: The historical roots of modern psychiatry. In H. Moffic, J. Peteet, A. Hankir, & R. Awaad (Eds.), *Islamophobia and Psychiatry* (pp. 3–17). Cham: Springer.

Azar, B. (2010). A Reason to Believe. *American Psychological Association: Monitor on Psychology*, 41(11), 52. http://www.apa.org/monitor/2010/12/believe.aspx (accessed 21 May 2022).

Badawi, E.M., & Haleem, M.A. (2008). *Arabic–English Dictionary of Qur'anic Usage*. Handbook of Oriental Studies/Handbuch der Orientalistik, Section One: The Near and Middle East. Leiden and Boston, MA: Brill.

Badri, M.B. (1979). *The Dilemma of Muslim Psychologists*. London: MWH London.

Badri, M.B. (2000). *Contemplation: An Islamic Psychospiritual Study*. Herndon, VA: The International Institute of Islamic Thought.

Badri, M.B. (2013). *Sustenance of the Soul: The Cognitive Behaviour Therapy of a Ninth Century Physician*. London: International Institute of Islamic Thought.

Badri, M.B. (2021). Preface. In H. Keshavarzi, F. Khan, B. Ali, & R. Awaad (Eds.), *Applying Islamic Principles to Clinical Mental Health Care: Introducing*

Traditional Islamically Integrated Psychotherapy (pp. xxi–xxiii). New York: Routledge.

Bakhtiar, L. (2019). *Quranic Psychology of the Self: A Textbook on Islamic Moral Psychology*. Chicago, IL: Kazi Publications, Inc.

Barrett, J.L. (2012). *Born Believers: The Science of Children's Religious Belief*. New York: Free Press.

Bazzano, E.A. (2015). Ibn Taymiyya, Radical Polymath, Part I: Scholarly Perceptions. *Religion Compass*, 9(4), 100–116.

Beckford, M. (2008, 24 November). Children are born believers in God, academic claims. *The Telegraph*. http://www.telegraph.co.uk/news/religion/3512686/Children-are-born-believers-in-God-academic-claims.html (accessed 25 March 2022).

Besterfield-Sacre, M., Gerchak, J., Lyons, M., Shuman, L.J., & Wolfe, H. (2004). Scoring concept maps: An integrated rubric for assessing. *Journal of Engineering Education*, 93(2), 105–115.

Betteridge, S. (2012). *Exploring the Clinical Experiences of Muslim Psychologists in the UK when working with Religion in Therapy*. Doctoral thesis, Counselling Psychology, University of East London. https://repository.uel.ac.uk/download/52858939beb78a68bed745f29c03fe2f0479f4e203e057d3b-b651e7446abb501/1913143/Sara_Betteridge_Doctoral_Thesis%5B1%5D.pdf (accessed 22 March 2022).

Bhat, M.A. (2016). Human Psychology (fitrah) from Islamic Perspective. *International Journal of Nusantara Islam*, 3(4), 161–174.

Bloom, P. (2013). *Just Babies: The origins of good and evil*. New York: Crown.

Bone, D. (2010, 30 October). The Importance of Listening. *emel*, Issue 73. http://www.emel.com/article?id=77&a_id=2165 (accessed 15 March 2022).

Britannica, Editors of Encyclopaedia. (n.d.). "*Tawhid*." *Encyclopedia Britannica*. https://www.britannica.com/topic/tawhid (accessed 14 July 2022).

Bukhari (a). *Sahih al-Bukhari 1385*. In-book reference: Book 23, Hadith 137. USC-MSA web (English) reference: Vol. 2, Book 23, Hadith 467.

Bukhari (b). *Sahih al-Bukhari 5744*. In-book reference: Book 76, Hadith 59. USC-MSA web (English) reference: Vol. 7, Book 71, Hadith 640.

Bukhari (c). *Riyad as-Salihin 97*. Chapter: *The Struggle* (in the Cause of Allāh) (11). In-book reference: Introduction, Hadith 97.

Bukhari (d). *Sahih al-Bukhari 7307*. In-book reference: Book 96, Hadith 38. USC-MSA web (English) reference: Vol. 9, Book 92, Hadith 410.

Bukhari (e). *Sahih al-Bukhari 100*. In-book reference: Book 3, Hadith 42. USC-MSA web (English) reference: Vol. 1, Book 3, Hadith 100.

Bukhari (f). *Sahih al-Bukhari 52*. In-book reference: Book 2, Hadith 45. USC-MSA web (English) reference: Vol. 1, Book 2, Hadith 50.

Bukhari (g). *Sahih al-Bukhari 5769*. In-book reference: Book 76, Hadith 83. USC-MSA web (English) reference: Vol. 7, Book 71, Hadith 664.

Bukhari & Muslim (a). Bukhari; 11:208, Muslim; 1:539. Cited in *Blessings of Dhikr*. http://muslimmatters.org/2009/06/12/yasir-qadhi-khutbah-transcript-blessings-of-dhikr (accessed 28 March 2022).

Bukhari & Muslim (b). Bukhari, 5865; Muslim, 2735, from the hadith of Abu Hurayrah.

Bukhari & Muslim (c). Bukhari, 4728; Muslim, 2192. Cited in *The Virtues of Ruqyah and Du'ah to be Recited Therein*. http://www.missionislam.com/health/ruqyahvirtues.html (accessed 28 March 2022).

Bukhari & Muslim (d). *Mishkat al-Masabih 2762*. In-book reference: Book 11, Hadith 4.

Carlson, R., & Shield, B. (1989). *Healers on healing*. New York: Tarcher/Putnam.

Cheavens, J.S., & Guter, M.M. (2018). Hope therapy. In M.W. Gallagher & S.J. Lopez (Eds.), *The Oxford Handbook of Hope* (pp. 133–142). Oxford: Oxford University Press.

Chittick, W. (1983). *The Sufi Path of Love: The Spiritual Teachings of Rumi*. New York: State University of New York Press.

Colman, A.M. (2015). *Dictionary of Psychology*, 4th ed. Oxford: Oxford University Press.

Cowan, J.M., & Wehr, H. (Eds.). (1976). *A Dictionary of Modern Written Arabic*. 3rd ed. New York: Spoken Language Service.

Daghestani, A.N. (1997). Images in psychiatry: Al-Rāzī (Rhazes). *American Journal of Psychiatry*, 154(11), 1493–1635.

Daley, B.J. (2004). Using Concept Maps in Qualitative Research. *Concept Maps: Theory, Methodology, Technology*, Proceedings of the First International Conference on Concept Mapping, Pamplona, Spain. http://cmc.ihmc.us/Papers/cmc2004-060.pdf (accessed 21 March 2022).

Dalhat, Y. (2015). Concept of *al-Aql* (Reason) in Islam. *International Journal of Humanities and Social Science*, 5(9), 77–83.

Dar al-Iftaa Al-Missriyyah (2022). *The Research Methodology in Traditional Islamic Scholarship*. https://www.dar-alifta.org/foreign/ViewArticle.aspx?ID=113 (accessed 19 March 2022).

De Cillis, M. (2018). Muslims and Free Will. Oasis 26. Milan: Oasis International Foundation. https://www.oasiscenter.eu/en/muslims-and-free-will (accessed 8 March 2022).

Deuraseh, N., & Abu Talib, M. (2005). Mental Health in Islāmic Medical Tradition. *The International Medical Journal*, 4(2), 76–79.

Dhanani, A. (2018). *Muslim Philosophy and the Sciences*. London: The Institute of Ismaili Studies. https://www.iis.ac.uk/academic-article/muslim-philosophy-and-sciences#medicine%20-%20Muslim%20sciences (accessed 18 March 2022).

Duan, C., Knox, S., & Hill, C.E. (2018). Advice Giving in Psychotherapy. In E.L. MacGeorge & L.M. Van Swol (Eds.), *The Oxford Handbook of Advice* (online). Oxford Handbook Online. doi:10.1093/oxfordhb/97801906301 88.013.11.

Dubovsky, S.L. (1983). Psychiatry in Saudi Arabia. *American Journal of Psychiatry*, 140, 1455–1459.

Durães Campos, I., Pinto, V., Sousa, N., & Pereira, V.H. (2018). A Brain Within the Heart: A Review on the Intracardiac Nervous System. *Journal of Molecular and Cellular Cardiology*, 119, 1–9.

Effectiviology. (2022). *The Confirmation Bias: Why People See What They Want to See.* https://effectiviology.com/confirmation-bias (accessed 9 March 2022).

Egnew T.R. (2005). The meaning of healing: Transcending suffering. *Annals of family medicine*, 3(3), 255–262.

El-Hazmi, M.A.F. (Ed.). (2002). *Ethics of Genetic Counseling in Islamic Communities.* Riyadh, KSA: Al-Obeikan Bookstore.

Elqabbany, M. (2021). *On Fitrah, Morality, Nature, and Equivocation.* https://www.themuslim500.com/campaign/2021/Muslim500-2021-Published.html (accessed 21 May 2022).

El-Rouayheb, K. (2006). Opening the Gate of Verification: The Forgotten Arab-Islamic Florescence of the 17th Century. *International Journal of Middle East Studies*, 38(2), 263–281.

Eltaiba, N. (2007). *Perceptions of mental health problems in Islam: A textual and experimental analysis.* PhD Thesis, University of Western Australia. http://research-repository.uwa.edu.au/en/publications/perceptions-of-mental-health-problems-in-islam-a-textual-and-experimental-analysis(f4c538ab-00ef-4df5-8b50-a523991c796a).html?uwaCustom=thesis (accessed 17 March 2022).

Esposito, J. (2004). *The Oxford Dictionary of Islam.* Oxford: Oxford University Press.

Etymonline.com. (2020). *Online Etymology Dictionary.* https://www.etymonline.com (accessed 19 July 2022).

Fakhry, M. (2001). *Averroes (Ibn Rushd): His Life, Works and Influence.* Oxford: Oneworld Publications.

Famous Scientists. (2020). *Ibn Rushd.* Famous Scientists: The Art of Genius. https://www.famousscientists.org/ibn-rushd (accessed 23 March 2022).

Farooqi, Y.N. (2006). Understanding Islāmic perspective of mental health and psychotherapy. *Journal of Psychology in Africa*, 16(1), 101–111.

Fidanboylu, K.H. (2017). Muslim Contributions to Mental Disorders and Mental Health: Ibn-Sina and Al-Ghazali. https://www.academia.edu/8908081/Muslim_Contributions_to_Mental_Disorders_and_Mental_Health_Ibn-Sina_and_Al-Ghazali (accessed 17 March 2022).

Firth, K., Smith, K., Sakallaris, B.R., Bellanti, D.M., Crawford, C., & Avant, K.C. (2015). Healing, a Concept Analysis. *Global Advances in Health and Medicine*, 4(6), 44–50.

Frank, J.D., & Frank, J.B. (1991). *Persuasion and healing: A comparative study of psychotherapy*. Baltimore, MD: Johns Hopkins University Press.

Forshaw, D., & Rollin, H. (1990). The history of forensic psychiatry in England. In R. Bluglass, & P. Bowden (Eds.), *Principles and Practice of Forensic Psychiatry* (pp. 61–101). Edinburgh: Churchill-Livingstone.

Griffel, F. (2009). *Al-Ghazâlî's Philosophical Theology*. New York: Oxford University Press.

Gulam, H. (2018). The Intertwined Relationship Between the Nafs (Carnal Soul), Aql (Reasoning) Qalb (Heart). *Jurnal Ilmiah Islam Futura*, 17(2), 200–213.

Günther, S. (2012). *Averroes and Thomas Aquinas on Education*. Washington, DC: Georgetown University Press.

Haddad, Y. (1991). *The Muslims of America*. New York: Oxford University Press.

Haeri, F. (1989). *The Journey of the Self*. New York: Harper San Francisco.

Hamer, H.D. (2004). *The God Gene: How Faith is Hardwired Into Our Genes*. Cranleigh: Anchor Books.

Hammarberg, K., Kirkman, M., & de Lacey, S. (2016). Qualitative research methods: When to use them and how to judge them. *Human Reproduction*, 31(3), 498–501.

Haque, A. (n.d.). *Psychology from Islamic Perspective*. https://www.academia.edu/13065499/Islamic_Psychology (accessed 18 May 2022).

Haque, A. (1998). Psychology and Religion: Their Relationship and Integration from Islāmic Perspective. *The American Journal of Islāmic Social Sciences*, 15, 97–116.

Haque, A. (2004). Psychology from Islamic Perspective: Contributions of Early Muslim Scholars and Challenges to Contemporary Muslim Psychologists. *Journal of Religion and Health*, 43(4), 357–377.

Haque, A. (2018). Psychology from an Islamic Perspective. In S. Fernando & R. Moodley (Eds.), *Global Psychologies* (pp. 137–150). London: Palgrave Macmillan.

Haque, A., & Keshavarzi, H. (2014). Integrating indigenous healing methods in therapy: Muslim beliefs and practices. *International Journal of Culture and Mental Health*, 7(3), 297–314.

Hassan, A. (2022). *Hijacking of the Minbar*. Personal communication.

Hassan, K.M. (1994). The Islamic Worldview. In A.M. Yaacob & A.F.A. Rahman (Eds.), *Towards a Positive Islamic World-View: Malaysian and American Perceptions* (pp. 11–33). Kuala Lumpur: Institute of Islamic Understanding Malaysia.

Hoover, J. (2016). "Fiṭra." In K. Fleet, G. Krämer, D. Matringe, J. Nawas, & E. Rowson (Eds.), *Encyclopaedia of Islam, THREE.* 10.1163/1573-3912_ei3_COM_27155 (accessed 20 May 2022).

Husayn, M.K., & Al-'Uqbi, M.A. (1977). *Tibbal-Razi: Dirasah wa-tahlil li-kitab al-hawi.* Beirut: Dāral-Shūrūq, al-Qāhirah.

Iakhin, F. (2022). *Islāmic Psychology: Islāmic monotheism as the foundation of Islāmic psychology.* Cited in course in Islāmic psychology, IKI Academy, ITKI 6206 (accessed 8 March 2022).

Ibn al-Qayyim Al-Jawziyyah. (2011). *Ighāthat al-laḥfān fi maṣāyid al-shayṭān,* ed. Muṣṭafā ibn Sa'īd Ītīm, Muḥammad 'Azīz Shams, and Bakr ibn 'Abd Allāh Bū Zayd, vol. 1. Mecca: Dār 'Ālim al-Fawā'id.

Ibn al-Qayyim Al-Jawziyyah (a). *Zaad al-Ma'aad,* 4/352. Fatwa No. 9691. Cited in The Qur'an and medicine, Islam Q&A. http://islamqa.info/en/ref/9691/Cure%20for%20our%20hearts%20from%20all%20diseases (accessed 26 March 2022).

Ibn al-Qayyim Al-Jawziyyah (b). *Madarij as-Salikin* fi Manazili Iyyaka Na'budu wa Iyyaka Nasta'in, vol. 1. Cited in M.A. Al-Akiti. (1997). *The Meaning of Nafs.* https://www.livingislam.org/nafs.html (accessed 22 May 2022).

Ibn al-Qayyim Al-Jawziyyah (c). *Zaad al-Ma'aad* (3/9–12). Cited in Islam Q&A. (2001). *Greater and lesser jihaad.* https://islamqa.info/en/answers/10455/greater-and-lesser-jihaad (accessed 25 May 2022).

Ibn al-Qayyim Al-Jawziyyah (d). *Ighathatu'l-Lahfan fi Masayid al-Shaytan,* vol. 1, 11/11–191. Cited in Ibn al-Qayyim. *Diseases of The Hearts & Their Cures* (Trans. Abu Rumaysah) (pp. 33–42). Birmingham: Daar Us-Sunnah Publishers.

Ibn Al-Sunni, Imam Ahmad, & Al-Haakim. (n.d). Ibn al-Sunni in *'Aml al-Yawm wa'l-Laylah,* p. 168; and by al-Haakim, 4/216. Classed as Sahih by al-Albani in *al-Kalim al-Tayyib,* 243. Cited in Islam Q&A. (2000). 7190: Can a man harm his beautiful wife with the "evil eye"? https://islamqa.info/en/7190 (accessed 22 March 2022).

Ibn an-Nafees. (n.d.). Cited in Javadi., B., Ahmad, S., & Emami, A. (2012). *Al-Mujaz fi al-Tibb* (Concise in Medicine). Tehran: Institute for Study of Medical History, Islamic and Complementary Medicine, Tehran University of Medical Sciences.

Ibn Hazm al-Andalusi. (1985). *Al-Akhlaq wa'l-Siyar.* Beirut: Dar al-Kutub al-'Ilmiyyah.

Ibn Kathir. (2000). *Tafsir ibn Kathir* (Trans. J. Abualrub, N. Khitab, H. Khitab, A. Walker, M. Al-Jibali, & S. Ayoub). Saudi Arabia: Darussalam Publishers and Distributors.

Ibn Khaldun. (n.d.). Cited in Dar al-Iftaa Al-Missriyyah. (2022). *The Research Methodology in Traditional Islamic Scholarship.* https://www.dar-alifta.org/foreign/ViewArticle.aspx?ID=113 (accessed 19 March 2022).

Ibn Majah (a). *Sunan Ibn Majah 81.* In-book reference: Introduction, Hadith 81. English translation: Vol. 1, Book 1, Hadith 8. Sahih (Darussalam).

Ibn Majah (b). *Sunan Ibn Majah 3994.* In-book reference: Book 36, Hadith 69. English translation: Vol. 5, Book 36, Hadith 3994. Hasan (Darussalam).

Ibn Majah (c). *Sunan Ibn Majah 3992.* In-book reference: Book 36, Hadith 67. English translation: Vol. 5, Book 36, Hadith 3992. Hasan (Darussalam).

Ibn Majah (d). *Sunan Ibn Majah 4004.* In-book reference: Book 36, Hadith 79. English translation: Vol. 5, Book 36, Hadith 400. Hasan (Darussalam).

Ibn Majah (e). *Sunan Ibn Majah. Zuhd.* English reference: Vol. 5. Book 37, Hadith 4216. Arabic reference: Book 37, Hadith 4356. Sahih (Darussalam).

Ibn Manzûr. (1988). *Lisân al-'Arab, al-Muhît.* Vol. 4 (Ed. A. al-'Alayali). Beirut: Dâru Lisân al-'Arab.

Ibn Qutayba al-Daynuri. (1983). *Islah fi ghalat Abi Ubayd.* Beirut: Dar al-Gharb al-Islami.

Ibn Rajab (a). *Jaami' al-'Uloom wa'l-Hukam* (p. 80), cited in Islam Q&A. (2018). Etiquette of giving advice. https://islamqa.info/en/answers/225160/etiquette-of-giving-advice (accessed 14 March 2022).

Ibn Rajab (b). *Kitab al-Dhayl 'alá Tabaqat al-Hanabilah,* 2:448; cf. the translation in Ibn Qayyim al-Jawziyya on the Invocation of God, xiii.

Ibn Rajab (c). Fath al-Baari. Cited in Islam Q&A. (2013). *Does the soul come out of the body during sleep?* https://islamqa.info/en/answers/160880/does-the-soul-come-out-of-the-body-during-sleep (accessed 26 May 2022).

Ibn Sina. (1959). *An-Nafs (The Soul).* In F. Rahman (Ed.), *Avicenna's de Anima.* London: Oxford University Press.

Ibn Sirin (n.d.). *Mishkat al-Masabih 218.* In-book reference: Book 2, Hadith 20.

Ibn Sulaymaan. (n.d.). Cited in F. Iakhin. (2002). IKI Academy, ITKI 6206 Islamic Psychology. *The inner world of a human being according to Islam.* https://elearning.ikiacademy.org/pluginfile.php/6108/mod_resource/content/1/Lecture%203%20-%20presentation.pdf (accessed 26 May 2022).

Ibn Taymīyyah, Aḥmad ibn 'Abd al-Ḥalīm. (1402/1981). *Amrāḍ al-Qulūb wa Shifā'uhā,* 3rd ed. Cairo: Al-Maṭba 'ah al-Salafiyah.

Ibn Taymīyyah, T.A. (1988). *Risalah fi al-Aql wa al-Rûh.* Beirut: Darr al-Hijrah.

Ibn Taymīyyah, T.A. (1991). *Dar' ta'arud al-Aql wa'l-Naql.,* vol. 6 (pp. 67–73). Cork, Ireland: Sifatu Safwa Corporation.

Ibn Taymīyyah, T.A. (2000). *Expounds On Islam: Selected Writings of Shaykh al-Islam Taqi ad-Din Ibn Taymīyyah on Islamic Faith, Life, and Society.* Compiled and translated by Muhammad 'Abdul-Haqq Ansari. Fairfax, VA: The Institute of Islamic and Arabic Sciences in America (IIASA).

Ibn Taymīyyah, T.A. (2004). *Majmū'it al-fatāwā* (Ed.A. Al-Jazzār & A. Al-Bāz), vol. 10. Medina: King Fahd Complex for the Printing of the Holy Quran.

Ibnu Ashur, Muhammad al-Tahir. (2009). *Maqāsid al-Sharī'ah al-Islamiyyah.* Qaherah: Dar al-Salam.

Ibrahim, F.A. (1985). Effective cross-cultural counseling and psychotherapy: A frame-work. *The Counseling Psychologist*, 13, 625–638.

Ibrahim, F.A. (1999). Transcultural counseling: Existential worldview theory and cultural identity. In J. McFadden (Ed.), *Transcultural counselling*, 2nd ed. (pp. 23–58). Alexandria, VA: American Counseling Association.

Imam Abu Bakr ibn al-Arabi. (n.d.). Cited in in Dar al-Iftaa Al-Missriyyah. (2022). *The Research Methodology in Traditional Islamic Scholarship*. https://www.daralifta.org/foreign/ViewArticle.aspx?ID=113 (accessed 19 March 2022).

Imam Al-Ghazālī. (n.d.). *Al-Iqtisad Fil I'tiqad*. Arabic. Dar Al-Minhaj. Birmingham: Kitaabun.

Imam Al-Tabari. (n.d.). *Tafsir of al-Tabari: Jami' al-Bayan fi Tafsir al-Qur'an*, 30 vols., Chapter 12, V. 53. Bulaq1323.

Imam Malik. (1983). Cited in Qadi 'Iyad, *Tartib al-Mudarik*, vol. 1 (p. 144). Saudi Arabia: Wizarat al-Awqaf wa'l-Shu'un al-Islamiyyah.

Imam Nawawi. (n.d.). *Futahat ar-Rabbani cala-l-Adhkar an-Nawawiyya*, vol. 1 (pp. 106–109).

Imam Zarkashi. (n.d.). Cited in Dar al-Iftaa Al-Missriyyah. (2022). *The Research Methodology in Traditional Islamic Scholarship*. https://www.daralifta.org/foreign/ViewArticle.aspx?ID=113 (accessed 19 March 2022).

International Association of Islamic Psychology. (2018). *What is Islamic Psychology?* https://www.islamicpsychology.org/what-is-islamic-psychology (accessed 3 February 2022).

Islam Q&A. (2001). *Who are Ahl al-Sunnah wa'l-Jamaa'ah?* https://islamqa.info/en/answers/10777/who-are-ahl-al-sunnah-wal-jamaaah (accessed 11 March 2022).

Islam Q&A. (2002a). *Fataawa Islamiyyah*, 4/465, 466. http://islamqa.info/en/ref/21677 (accessed 28 March 2022).

Islam Q&A. (2002b). *The virtues of ruqyah and du'aa's to be recited therein*. http://islamqa.info/en/3476 (accessed 28 March 2022).

Islam Q&A. (2003a). *What Is Sufism?* https://islamqa.info/en/answers/47431/what-is-sufism (accessed 11 March 2022).

Islam Q&A. (2003b). 20954: *The Evil Eye and Protection Against it*. https://islamqa.info/en/20954 (accessed 22 March 2022).

Islam Q&A. (2009). *What is the fault of children born in a kaafir environment?* https://islamqa.info/en/answers/11783/what-is-the-fault-of-children-born-in-a-kaafir-environment (accessed 18 May 2022).

Islam Q&A. (2017). *The covenant taken from the sons of Adam is the fitrah*. https://islamqa.info/en/answers/248517/the-covenant-taken-from-the-sons-of-adam-is-the-fitrah (accessed 19 May 2022).

IslamWeb. (2012). *Allah's Knowledge is infinite*. https://www.islamweb.net/en/article/137164/allahs-knowledge-is-infinite (accessed 21 May 2022).

Jamal al-Din, N. (1994). *Miskawayh* (AH 320–421/AD 932–1030). *PROSP-ECTS*, 24(1–2), 131–152.

James, W. (1890). *The principles of psychology*. New York: Holt.

Kaplick, P.M., & Skinner, R. (2017). The evolving Islam and psychology movement. *European Psychologist*, 22(3), 198–204.

Karzoon. A. (1997). *Manhaj al-Islaam fi Tazkiyah al-Nafs*, Vol. 1. Jeddah: Daar Noor al-Maktabaat.

Kasule, O.H. (2008). *The Concepts of Health: An Islamic Perspective*. Paper presented at The Annual Training for Better Organization and Islamic Health Conference organized by the Islamic Medical Faculties of Indonesia, Universitas Islam Sultan Agung Semarang, 20 December 2008. https://omarkasuletib.blogspot.com/2011/04/081220p-concepts-of-health-islamic.html (accessed 25 March 2022).

Kasule, O.H. (2015). Integration of Knowledge (IOK) and Textbook Writing for Islāmic Universities. *International Journal of Islāmic Thoughts* 4 (1), 123–126.

Kasule, O.H. (2021). *Tauhid as the Basis for Integration of Knowledge*. Presented at the Orientation of the Institute for Integration of Knowledge (IKI) on 29 May 2021.

Katouzian-Safadi, M., & Bonmatin, J.M. (2003). The use of honey in the simple and composed drugs at Rhazés. *Revue D'Histoire De La Pharmacie* (Paris), 51(337), 29–36.

Keshavarzi, H., & Ali, B. (2021). Foundations of Traditionally Islamically Integrated Psychotherapy (TIIP). In H. Keshavarzi, F. Khan, B. Ali, & R. Awaad (Eds.), *Applying Islamic Principles to Clinical Mental Health Care: Introducing Traditional Islamically Integrated Psychotherapy* (pp. 13–37). New York: Routledge.

Keshavarzi, H., & Haque, A. (2013). Outlining a psychotherapy model for enhancing Muslim mental health within an Islāmic context. *International Journal for the Psychology of Religion*, 23(3), 230–249. doi:10.1080/10508619.2012.712000.

Keshavarzi, H., Khan, F., Ali, B., & Awaad, R. (Eds.). (2021). *Applying Islamic Principles to Clinical Mental Health Care: Introducing Traditional Islamically Integrated Psychotherapy*. New York: Routledge.

Khan, F. (2020). Quantitative and Qualitative Assessment of the Ontological Domains of the Psyche of TIIP. In H. Keshavarzi, F. Khan, B. Ali, & R. Awaad (Eds.), *Applying Islāmic Principles to Clinical Mental Health Care: Traditional Islamically Integrated Psychotherapy* (pp. 117–140). New York: Routledge.

Khan, F., Keshavarzi, H., & Rothman, A. (2021). The Role of the TIIP Therapist Scope of Practice and Proposed Competencies. In H. Keshavarzi, F. Khan, B. Ali, & R. Awaad (Eds.), *Applying Islamic Principles to Clinical Mental Health Care: Introducing Traditional Islamically Integrated Psychotherapy* (pp. 38–66). New York: Routledge.

Krstic, K. (1964). Marko Marulic – The Author of the Term "Psychology." *Acta Instituti Psychologici Universitatis Zagrabiensis*, 36, 7–13.

Kukanova, B., & Mravec, B. (2006). Complex Intracardiac Nervous System. *Bratislavske lekarskelisty*, 107(3), 45–51.

Kulju, K., Stolt, M., Suhonen, R., & Leino-Kilpi, H. (2016). Ethical competence: A concept analysis. *Nursing Ethics*, 23(4), 401–412.

Lakhtakia, R. (2014). A Trio of Exemplars of Medieval Islamic Medicine. *Sultan Qaboos Univ Med J*, 14(4), e455–e459.

Laoust, H. (2012). Ibn Taymiyya. In P. Bearman, Th. Bianquis, C.E. Bosworth, E. van Donzel, & W.P. Heinrichs (Eds.), *Encyclopaedia of Islām*, 2nd ed (online). 10.1163/1573-3912_Islām_SIM_3388 (accessed 23 March 2022).

Leaman, O. (1998). *Ibn Rushd, Abu'l Walid Muhammad (1126–98)*. Routledge Encyclopedia of Philosophy, Taylor and Francis. https://www.rep.routledge.com/articles/biographical/ibn-rushd-abul-walid-muhammad-1126-98/v-1 (accessed 23 March 2022).

Leaman, O. (Ed.) (2006). *The Qur'an: An Encyclopedia*. Abingdon, Oxon: Routledge.

Levin, J. (2018). Scientists and healers: Toward collaborative research partnerships. *Explore*, 4(5), 302–310.

Long, W. (2014). Critical reflections on the Islamicisation of Psychology. *Revelation and Science*, 4, 14–19.

Majeed, A., & Jabir, K.P. (2017). The Contribution of Muslims and Islāmic Concepts: Rethinking and Establishing the Actual Origin of Concepts and Thought in Psychology. *The International Journal of Indian Psychology*, 4(2), 68–77.

Malkawi, F.H. (2014). *Epistemological Integration: Essentials of an Islamic methodology*. Herndon, VA: The International Institute of Islamic Thought.

McElliott, D. (2010). Healing: The journey from concept to nursing practice. *Journal of Holistic Nursing*, 28(4), 251–259.

McLeish. K. (1995). *Key Ideas in Human Thought*. Rocklin, CA: Prima Lifestyles.

Merriam-Webster. (n.d.). *Heal*. Merriam-Webster Dictionary. https://www.merriam-webster.com/dictionary/heal (accessed on 25 March 2022).

Metcalfe, J., & Shimamura, A.P. (1994). *Metacognition: Knowing about knowing*. Cambridge, MA: MIT Press.

Modanlou, H. D. (2008). A tribute to Zakariya Razi (865–925 AD), an Iranian pioneer scholar. *Archives of Iranian Medicine*, 11(6), 673–677.

Mohamed, W.M. (2012). *IBRO history of neuroscience* [Scholarly project]. In IRBO. http://ibro.org/wp-content/uploads/2018/07/Arab-and-MuslimContributions-to-Modern-Neuroscience.pdf (accessed 23 March 2022).

Mohamed, Y. (1996). *Fitrah: The Islamic Concept of Human Nature*. London: TA-HA Publishers Ltd.

Mohamed, Y. (2009). Human Natural Disposition (Fitrah). In A. Haque & Y. Mohamed (Eds.), *Psychology of Personality: Islamic Perspectives* (pp. 3–18). Singapore: Cengage Learning Asia.

Mohamed, Y. (2020). *Perspectives on Islamic Psychology: al-Raghib al-Isfahani on the Healing of Emotions in the Qur'an*. Irving, TX: Yaqeen Institute for Islamic Research. https://app.yaqeen.io/read/paper/perspectives-on-islamic-psychology-healing-of-emotions-in-the-quran (accessed 27 March 2022).

Muslim (a). Hadith #7. Zarabozo, J.M. (2008). *Commentary on the Forty Hadith of Al-Nawawi*, Vol 1 (p. 397). Denver, CO: Al-Basheer Company for Publications and Translations.

Muslim (b). *Sahih Muslim 388a*. In-book reference: Book 4, Hadith 17. USC-MSA web (English) reference: Book 4, Hadith 751.

Muslim (c). Cited in *Ajwa* the king of dates. http://saudiarabiadates.com/benefits.htm (accessed 22 March 2022).

Muslim (d). *Sahih Muslim 2710d*. *The Book Pertaining to the Remembrance of Allāh, Supplication, Repentance, and Seeking Forgiveness*. In-book reference: Book 48, Hadith 78. USC-MSA web (English) reference: Book 35, Hadith 6547.

Muslim (e). *Sahih Muslim 2999*. In-book reference: Book 55, Hadith 82. USC-MSA web (English) reference: Book 42, Hadith 7138.

Muslim (f) & Qurtubi's at-Tadhkirah. Cited from Abu Bilal Mustafa al-Kanadi (1996). *Mysteries of the Soul Expounded*. Jeddah, Saudi Arabia: Abul-Qasim Publishing House.

Muslim (g). *Sahih Muslim 144a*. *The Book of Faith*. In-book reference: Book 1, Hadith 276USC-MSA web (English) reference: Book 1, Hadith 267.

Muslim (h). *Mishkat al-Masabih 1628*. In-book reference: Book 5, Hadith 104.

Muslim (i). *Sahih Muslim 144a*. *The Book of Faith*. In-book reference: Book 1, Hadith 276USC-MSA web (English) reference: Book 1, Hadith 267.

N., Sam M.S. (2013, April 7). PARADIGM, PsychologyDictionary.org. https://psychologydictionary.org/paradigm (accessed March 8, 2022).

Najātī, M.U. (1993). *al-Dirāsāt al-nafsānīyah 'inda al-'ulamā' al-Muslimīn*. Cairo: Dār al-Shurūq.

Nasr, S.H. (1975). Life Sciences, Alchemy and Medicine [in 7th–11th-century Iran]. In R.N. Frye (Ed.), *The Cambridge History of Iran* (pp. 396–418). Cambridge: Cambridge University Press.

newworldencyclopedia.org. (n.d.). *Ijtihad*. New World Encyclopedia. https://www.newworldencyclopedia.org/entry/Ijtihad (accessed 16 March 2022).

Nofal, N. (1993). AL-GHAZALI (A.D. 1058–1111; A.H. 450–505) *Prospects: The Quarterly Review of Comparative Education*, 23(3–4), 519–542. http://www.ibe.unesco.org/sites/default/files/ghazalie.pdf (accessed 16 March 2022).

Norager, T. (1998). Metapsychology and Discourse: A Note on some Neglected Issues in the Psychology of Religion. *The International Journal for the Psychology of Religion*, 6, 139–149.

Novak, J.D., & Gowin, D.B. (1984). *Learning how to learn*. New York: Cambridge University Press.

Nursi, B.Z. (2011). *The Flashes*. 5th ed. *Risale-i Nur* Collection, vol. 3. Istanbul, Turkey: Sozler Publications.

Oziev, G. (2022). IKI Academy Course on Objectives of the Shari'ah, ITKI 6101. Topic 4 (Part 1) *The objectives of the Lawgiver in legislation*. https:// ikiacademy.org (accessed 22 July 2022).

Philips, A.A.B. (2005). *The Fundamentals of Tawheed (Islāmic Monotheism)*. Riyadh: International Islamic Publishing House.

Qadhi, Y. (2009). Transcript: *Blessings of Dhikr*. http://muslimmatters.org/ 2009/06/12/yasir-qadhi-khutbah-transcript-blessings-of-dhikr (accessed 28 March 2022).

Qadi 'Iyad. (n.d.). *The Research Methodology in Traditional Islamic Scholarship*. Dar al-Iftaa Al-Missriyyah. https://www.dar-alifta.org/foreign/ViewArticle. aspx?ID=113 (accessed 19 March 2022).

Qamar, A.H. (2013). The Concept of the 'Evil' and the 'Evil Eye' in Islam and Islamic Faith-Healing Traditions, *Journal of Islamic Thought and Civilization*, 3(2), 44–53.

Qutb, S. (1983). Khashaish Al-Tashawwur Al-Islamiy Wa Muqawwimatuhu. Beirut: Daar al-Masyriq.

Rafikov, I., & Akhmetova, E. (2020). Methodology of integrated knowledge in Islamic economics and finance: Collective ijtihad. *ISRA International Journal of Islamic Finance*, 12(1), 115–129.

Ragab, A. (1999). On the Methodology of Islamizing the Social Sciences. *Intellectual Discourse*, 7, (1), 27–52.

Rahmaa Institute. (n.d.). *Islamic Etiquette to Effective Listening*. http://www. rahmaa.org/resources/effective-listening (accessed 15 March 2022).

Rahman. S.Z. (2003). Indian Studies on Ibn Sina's Works. *Avicenna Scientific and Practical International Journal of Ibn Sino International Foundation* (Tashkent/ Uzbekistan), 1–2, 40–42.

Rassool, G. Hussein. (2000). The Crescent and Islām: Healing, nursing and the spiritual dimension. Some considerations towards an understanding of the Islāmic perspectives on caring. *Journal of Advanced Nursing*, 32(6), 1476–1484.

Rassool, G. Hussein. (2016). *Islāmic Counselling: An introduction to theory and practice*. Hove, East Sussex: Routledge.

Rassool, G. Hussein. (2019). *Evil Eye, Jinn Possession and Mental Health Issues: An Islāmic Perspective*. Oxford: Routledge.

Rassool, G. Hussein. (2020). *Health and Psychology: An Islamic Perspective*. Vol. 1. London: Islamic Psychology Publication (IPP). Amazon/Kindle.

Rassool, G. Hussein, Baig, K.B., Iqbal J., Ahmad, S.M., Asad, S., Luqman M., Majeed, S., Rabbani, A., Jameel, R., Latif, S., Asad, M., Khalid, S., Jamil, F., Tanvir, M., Hafsa, S.Z.N., Kanwal, R., Saeed, W., Adeeb, M., Nawaz, K., Mudassar, U., Fatima, M., & Arooje, K. (2020). *Conceptual Definition of Islāmic Psychology*. Workshop on "Islāmic Psychology Curriculum Development," 10 February to 13 February 2020, Riphah Institute of Clinical and Professional Psychology/Centre for Islāmic Psychology. Riphah International University, QIE Campus, Lahore, Pakistan.

Rassool, G. Hussein. (2021a). *Islamic Psychology: Human Behaviour and Experience from an Islamic Perspective*. Oxford: Routledge.

Rassool, G. Hussein. (2021b). Decolonising psychology and its (dis)contents. In G. Hussein Rassool, *Islāmic Psychology: Human Behaviour and Experiences from an Islāmic Perspective* (pp. 583–601). Oxford: Routledge.

Rassool, G. Hussein. (2021c). *Ilm An-Nafs–Science of the Soul: Themes in Islamic Psychology*. London: Islamic Psychology Publishing (IPP) & Institute Of Islamic Psychology Research. Amazon/Kindle.

Rassool, G. Hussein. (2021d). Islamic Psychology: Context, Definitions, and Perspectives. In G. Hussein Rassool, *Islāmic Psychology: Human Behaviour and Experience from an Islamic Perspective* (Chapter 1). Oxford: Routledge.

Rassool, G. Hussein. (2022). Foundation of Islāmic Psychology: The 'Dodo Bird' Revival. In G. Hussein Rassool & M. Luqman (Eds.), *Foundations of Islāmic Psychology: From Classical Scholars to Contemporary Thinkers* (pp. 3–15). Oxford: Routledge.

Rassool, G. Hussein, & Luqman, M.M. (2022). *Foundation of Islāmic Psychology: From Classical Scholars to Contemporary Thinkers*. Oxford: Routledge.

Renima, A., Tiliouine, H., & Estes R.J. (2016). The Islāmic Golden Age: A Story of the Triumph of the Islāmic Civilization. In H. Tiliouine & R. Estes (Eds.), *The State of Social Progress of Islāmic Societies: Social, Economic, Political, and Ideological Changes* (pp. 25–52). Cham: Springer.

Rodolfa, E., Bent, R., Eisman, E., Nelson, P., Rehm, L., & Ritchie, P.L. (2005). A Cube Model for Competency Development: Implications for Psychology Educators and Regulators. *Professional Psychology: Research and Practice*, 36(4), 347–354.

Rodriguez, D., Patel, R., Bright, A., Gregory, D., & Gowing, M. (2002). Developing competency models to promote integrated human resource practices. *Human Resource Management*, 41(3), 309–324.

Rønnestad, M.H., & Skovholt, T.M. (2003). The journey of the counselor and therapist: Research findings and perspectives on professional development. *Journal of Career Development*, 30(1), 5–44.

Rothman, A., & Coyle, A. (2018). Toward a Framework for Islamic Psychology and Psychotherapy: An Islamic Model of the Soul. *Journal of Religion and Health*, 57(5), 1731–1744. 10.1007/s10943-018-0651-x.

Rottman, J., & Kelemen, D. (2012). Is There Such a Thing as a Christian Child? Evidence of Religious Beliefs in Early Childhood. In P. McNamara & W.J. Wildman, (Eds.), *Science and the World's Religions, Vol. 2, Persons and Groups* (pp. 205–238). Santa Barbara, CA: Praeger.

Roudgari, H. (2018). Ibn Sina or Abu Ali Sina (c. 980–1037) is often known by his Latin name of Avicenna (ævɪˈsɛnə/). *Journal of Iranian Medical Council*, 1(2).

Saʻdi. (n.d.). *Tafseer as-Saʻdi.* Cited in Islam Q&A (2018). Etiquette of giving advice. https://islamqa.info/en/answers/225160/etiquette-of-giving-advice (accessed 14 March 2022).

Safi, L. (2014). *The Foundation of Knowledge: A Comparative Study in Islamic and Western Methods of Inquiry.* Herndon, VA: The International Institute of Islamic Thought.

Saheeh International. (n.d.). *English Translation of the Meaning of the Holy Qur'ān.* Alexandria, Egypt: Conveying Islamic Message Society.

Saleem, T., & Kahlily, M.T. (2021). A journey from Muslim psychology to Islamic psychology in Pakistan. In A. Haque & A. Rothman (Eds.), *Islamic Psychology around the Globe* (pp. 213–227). Seattle, WA: International Association of Islamic Psychology Publishing.

Seedat, M. (2020). Signifying Islamic Psychology as a Paradigm: A Decolonial Move. *European Psychologist*, 26(2), 131–141. 10.1027/1016-9040/a000408 (accessed 17 June 2022).

Şentürk, R. (2021). Foreword. In H. Keshavarzi, et al. (Eds.), *Applying Islamic Principles to Clinical Mental Health Care: Introducing Traditional Islamically Integrated Psychotherapy* (pp. xvi–xix). New York: Routledge.

Shafi, Shaikh Abu Rumaysah Refi. (2011). *The Types of Hearts.* https://www.islam21c.com/spirituality/3333-three-types-of-hearts (accessed 28 May 2022).

Shafii, M. (1985). *Freedom from the self: Sufism, meditation, and psychotherapy.* New York: Human Sciences Press.

Sham, F.M. (2015). Islamic Psychotherapy Approach in Managing Adolescent Hysteria in Malaysia. *Journal of Psychological Abnormalities in Children*, 4(3), 142. 10.4172/2329-9525.1000142.

Sharfuddin, S. (2021). *The Concept of Rûh in Islam.* http://rahbar.co.uk/the-concept-of-rûh-in-islam (accessed 26 May 2022).

Shaykh ʿAbdul-ʿAziz ibn ʿAbdullah ibn ʿAbdul-Rahman ibn Muhammad ibn ʿAbdullah Al Baz. (n.d.). *The Sufi ʿAqidah (creed) which stipulates that Allah (Exalted be He) is everywhere.* (Part No. 9, p. 457). https://www.alifta.gov.sa/En/IftaContents/IbnBaz/Pages/FatawaSubjects.aspx?cultStr=en&View=Page&HajjEntryID=0&HajjEntryName=&RamadanEntryID=0&RamadanEntryName=&NodeID=4631&PageID=1365&SectionID=14&SubjectPageTitlesID=23402&MarkIndex=3&0#TheSuficreedholdsthat-Allahiseverywhere (accessed 11 March 2022).

Shaykh al-Islaam Ibn Taymiyah. (n.d.). *Majmoo' al-Fataawa*, vol. 2. Cork, Ireland: Sifatu Safwa Corporation.

Shaykh Assim Al-Hakeem. (n.d.). *What is Ruqyah and how one should do it?* http://www.assimalhakeem.net/what-is-ruqyah-and-how-one-should-do-it (accessed 17 March 2022).

Shaykh Ibn al-Qayyim al-Jawziyya. (n.d.). Translated from Bada'i` al-Fawa'id, vol. 2, 764–776. Egyptian Edition. Cork, Ireland: Sifatu Safwa Corporation.

Shaykh Ibn 'Uthaymeen. (n.d.). *Majmoo' Fatawa*. Cited in Islamqa (2008) 10513: Protection From the Jinn. https://islamqa.info/en/10513 (accessed 22 March 2022).

Shaykh Ibn 'Uthaymeen. (2001). *Fataawa Islamiyyah*, 4/465, 466. Cited in Islamqa. 3839: Are physical medicines better, or ruqyah and spiritual medicine? https://islamqa.info/en/3839 (accessed 17 March 2022).

Shaykh Saalih bin Fawzaan bin Abdillaah al-Fawzaan. (2013). *Kitaabut Tawheed*. Cited in Corruption of Mankind. https://knowingallah.com/en/articles/corruption-of-mankind (accessed 22 July 2022).

Sherwood, H. (2018). *Religion: why faith is becoming more and more popular.* https://www.theguardian.com/news/2018/aug/27/religion-why-is-faith-growing-and-what-happens-next (accessed 19 May 2022).

Skinner, R. (1989). *Traditions, paradigms, and basic concepts in Islamic psychology.* Paper vorgestellt auf Theory and Practice of Islamic Psychology, London.

Skinner, R. (2019). A Beginner's Guide to the Concept of Islāmic Psychology. *Journal of the British Islāmic Medical Association*, 3(1), 22–26.

Skovholt, T.M., & Jennings, L. (2016). *Master therapists: exploring expertise in therapy and counseling*, 10th anniversary ed. New York: Oxford University Press.

Solihin, M. (2012). Ghazali's Tazkiyat Al-Nafs & Its Relation with Individual's Development & Mental Health. *Psychology and Islam*. http://spychology-of-islam.blogspot.sg/2012/03/ghazali-tazkiyat-al-nafs-its-relation.html (accessed 31 May 2022).

Sonn, T., & Williamsburg, M. (2004). *A brief history of Islām*. Oxford: Wiley-Blackwell.

Soueif, M.I., & Ahmed, R.A. (2001). Psychology in the Arab world: Past, present, and future. *International Journal of Group Tensions*, 30(3), 211–240.

sunnahonline.com. *Jihad an-Nafs* (Striving against the Soul). In The Soldiers of the Heart. rom Ihya 'Ulum ad-Din (The Revival of the Religious Sciences). Cited in https://sunnahonline.com/library/purification-of-the-soul/224-jihad-an-nafs-striving-against-the-soul (accessed 25 May 2022).

Syed. I.B. (2002). Islāmic medicine: 1000 years ahead of its times. *Journal of Islāmic Medical Association*, 2, 2–9.

Tahir, M.A. (2009). *Islāmic Psychology*. https://Islāmandpsychology.blogspot.com/2009/02/muslims-in-psychology.html (accessed 21 March 2022).

Tamir, C., Connaughton, A., & Salazar, A.M. (2020). *The Global God Divide People's thoughts on whether belief in God is necessary to be moral vary by economic development, education, and age.* Pew Research Center. https://www.pewresearch.org/global/wpcontent/uploads/sites/2/2020/07/PG_2020.07.20_Global-Religion_FINAL.pdf (accessed 19 May 2022).

Taqiyuddin, M. (2020). In Search of Islamic Definition of Worldview: Elements, and Its Characters. *Zawiyah: Jurnal Pemikiran Islam*, 6(2), 206–222.

Tibi, S. (2006). Al-Razi and Islāmic medicine in the 9th century. *Journal of the Royal Society of Medicine*, 99(4), 206–207.

Tie, Y.C., Birks, M., & Francis, K. (2019). Grounded theory research: A design framework for novice researchers. *SAGE open medicine*, 7, 2050312118822927. 10.1177/2050312118822927.

Tiliouine, H. (2014). Islāmic education and youth well-being in Muslim countries, with a specific reference to Algeria. In A. Ben-Arieh, F. Casas, I. Frønes, & J.E. Korbin (Eds.), *Handbook of Child Well-Being* (pp. 1209–1226). Netherlands: Springer.

Tirmidhî (a). *Sunan at-Tirmidhî.* Saheeh al-Albaani.

Tirmidhî (b). *Jami` at-Tirmidhî 2515.* In-book reference: Book 37, Hadith 101. English translation: Vol. 4, Book 11, Hadith 2515. Sahih (Darussalam).

Tirmidhî (c). *Riyad as-Salihin 510.* Chapter: Excellence of Simple Living and being Content with Little (56). In-book reference: Introduction, Hadith 510. Hadith Hasan.

Tirmidhî (d). *Mishkat al-Masabih 2489.* In-book reference: Book 9, Hadith 25.

Tirmidhî (e). *Jami` at-Tirmidhî 3358.* In-book reference: Book 47, Hadith 410. English translation: Vol. 5, Book 44, Hadith 3358. Sahih (Darussalam).

Tirmidhî (f). *Jami` at-Tirmidhî:* Vol. 5, Book 42, Hadith 2863. Arabic reference: Book 44, Hadith 3102.

Tirmidhî (g). *Jami` at-Tirmidhî 2068.* Sahih and it was authenticated by Shaikh al-Albani.

Tirmidhî (h). *Jami` at-Tirmidhî 3859;* classed as Sahih by al-Albani in Sahih al-Tirmidhî, 852.

Tirmidhî (i). *Riyad as-Salihin. The Book of Miscellany.* Arabic/English book reference: Book 1, Hadith 442. Tirmidhî, who classified it as Hadith Hasan.

Understanding Islam. (2000). *Principles of Islamic Ethics-An Introduction.* https://www.understanding-islam.com/principles-of-islamic-ethics-an-introduction (accessed 16 March 2022).

University of Oxford. (2011). Humans 'predisposed' to believe in gods and the afterlife. *ScienceDaily.* www.sciencedaily.com/releases/2011/07/110714103828.htm (accessed 17 May 2022).

Utz, A. (2011). *Psychology from an Islamic Perspective.* Riyadh: International Islamic Publishing House.

Watson, J.B. (1913). Psychology as the behaviorist views it. *Psychological Review*, 20, 158–178.

Wheeldon, J., & Åhlberg, M.K. (2012). Concept maps and mind maps: Theory, definitions, and approaches. In *Visualizing social science research: Maps, methods, & meaning* (pp. 21–38). Thousand Oaks, CA: Sage Publications, Inc.

Wilcox. L. (1995). *Sufism and psychology*. Chicago: Abjad.

Wolpe, J. (1968). Psychotherapy by reciprocal inhibition. *Conditional Reflex: A Pavlovian Journal of Research & Therapy*, 3(4), 234–240.

www.islamreligion.com. Islāmic-monotheism. https://www.islamreligion.com/articles/10334/Islāmic-monotheism (accessed 28 February 2022).

www.missionislam.com. *Maintaining the Characteristics of the Fitrah*. http://www.missionislam.com/knowledge/Fitrahmaintain.htm (accessed 19 May 2022).

Yalom, I.D. (2005). *The theory and practice of group psychotherapy*. 5th ed. New York: Basic Books.

Younos, Y.M. (2017). *Principles of Islamic Psychology*. Bloomington, IN: Institute of Objective Studies.

Zarabozo, J. (2002). *Purification of the Soul: Process, Concept, and Means*. Denver, CO: Al-Basheer Company for Publications and Translations.

INDEX